These essays address the subject-matter of theology: is it
the mystery of God, and everything there is considered in
relation to that mystery as source, and life, and destiny?
Or is it what we call 'religion' and 'religious belief'; a
district of experience and language and behaviour which
individuals may inhabit if they feel so inclined, a region of
diminishing plausibility and cognitive significance, a
territory quite distinct from those we know as 'politics',
and 'art', as 'science' and 'law' and 'economics'? The
adoption of the latter view, beginning in the seventeenth
century, became, with far-reaching consequences, a
defining feature of the modern Western imagination.

But the 'modern' world is ending, and the consequent
confusion also contains the possibility of discovering new
forms of ancient wisdom which the 'modern' world
obscured from view. These essays explore this suggestion
in four directions: in regard to relations between
Christianity and Hinduism (Part One contains the 1994
Teape Lectures); relations between theology and
science; the secularity of Western culture, and questions
of Christian hope.

THE BEGINNING AND THE END
OF 'RELIGION'

THE BEGINNING AND THE
END OF 'RELIGION'

NICHOLAS LASH

Norris-Hulse Professor of Divinity,
University of Cambridge

CAMBRIDGE
UNIVERSITY PRESS

Published by the Press Syndicate of the University of Cambridge
The Pitt Building, Trumpington Street, Cambridge CB2 1RP
40 West 20th Street, New York, NY 10011-4211, USA
10 Stamford Road, Oakleigh, Melbourne 3166, Australia

© Cambridge University Press 1996

First published 1996

Printed in Great Britain at the University Press, Cambridge

A catalogue record for this book is available from the British Library

Library of Congress cataloguing in publication data
Lash, Nicholas.
The beginning and the end of 'religion' / Nicholas Lash.
p.   cm.
Some of the lectures were originally delivered as the
1994 Teape lectures.
Includes bibliographical references (p.   ) and index.
ISBN 0 521 56232 5 (hc.) – ISBN 0 521 56635 5 (pbk.)
1. Theology. 2. Religion. 3. Christianity and other religions –
Hinduism. 4. Hinduism – Relations – Christianity. 5. Theology –
Methodology. 1. Teape lectures. 11. Title.
BR50.L345   1996
200–dc20   95–46553   CIP

ISBN 0 521 56232 5 hardback
ISBN 0 521 56635 5 paperback

Contents

vii

viii
Contents

Preface

Not the beginning or the end of faith, or hope, or charity. Not the beginning or the end of prayer or proclamation, of the duty laid upon all humankind to work for peace, and justice, and the integrity of God's creation. But the view that 'religion' is the name of one particular district which we may inhabit if we feel so inclined, a region of diminishing plausibility and significance, a territory quite distinct from those we know as 'politics' and 'art', as 'science' and 'law' and 'economics'; *this* view of things, peculiar to modern Western culture, had a beginning, in the seventeenth century, and (if *'post*-modern' means anything at all) is now coming to an end.

The essays and lectures collected here explore this suggestion and its implications in four main directions. Whereas, however, the chapters in Part Two consider, in broad and general terms, questions concerning the relations between theology and the sciences (Chapters 4, 5, 6), the secularity of modern Western culture (Chapters 7, 8, 9, 10) and issues of hope or eschatology (Chapters 11, 12, 13, 14), Part One, consisting of the Teape Lectures that I gave in India in 1994, has a somewhat more specific focus, arising from the conditions of that lectureship.

That modern Western concepts of 'religion' are ill fitted to describe the traditions of the 'East' – of India, China, and Japan – is something of a commonplace by now. That these concepts distort the so-called traditions of the 'West' ('so-called' because neither Judaism, Christianity nor Islam took their rise in Europe) no less disastrously is a lesson that is proving more difficult to learn. Hence my suggestion that we try to understand the great traditions, not as 'religions' in the modern sense, but as *schools* whose pedagogy has, albeit differently in each case, the common twofold purpose of weaning us from our idolatry and purifying our desire.

The Teape Lectures, which have now been in existence for some fifty years, were endowed by the Reverend W. M. Teape in memory of B. F. Westcott, his teacher in Cambridge and, later, his bishop, to promote dialogue between Christians and Hindus. According to Teape's will, the subject of the lectures is to be 'The Upanishads in the Catholic Church' (I rather think he had the Church of England primarily in mind!). In view of my family's long associations with India and, especially, in recognition of my uncle W. Q. Lash's lifelong dedication to Hindu–Christian relations, it was with particular pleasure that I accepted the invitation from the Teape Trustees to give the 1994 lectures.

The lectures were given in Calcutta, Delhi, Bangalore and Pune, and my wife and I owe an immeasurable debt of gratitude for all the kindness shown to us by so many people, especially the Principal of Bishop's College, Calcutta, and the Principal of St Stephen's College, Delhi; by the President and faculty of Dharma Vidya Kshetram in Bangalore, and by the Sisters and Friends of the Christa Prema Seva Ashram in Pune.

Amongst many other people who have helped to make these essays less imperfect than they would otherwise have been, I am particularly grateful to Janette Gray, RSM, for her painstaking work on the bibliography and index, and to Jennifer O'Dell, Anna Marino and Ann West for preparation of the typescript. Finally, my thanks to Alex Wright of the Cambridge University Press for his encouragement and patience.

Acknowledgements

The author and publisher are grateful to the publishers of the following items which have previously appeared in print:

'Observation, revelation and the posterity of Noah' in *Physics, Philosophy and Theology. A Common Quest for Understanding*, (ed.) Robert John Russell, William R. Stoeger, SJ, and George V. Coyne, SJ (Vatican City: The Vatican Observatory, 1988).

'When did the theologians lose interest in theology?' in *Theology and Dialogue. Essays in Conversation with George Lindbeck*, (ed.) Bruce D. Marshall (Notre Dame: University of Notre Dame Press, 1990).

'Hoping against hope, or Abraham's dilemma' in *Modern Theology*, 10, 3 (1994), pp. 233–46.

'Eagles and sheep. Christianity and the public order beyond modernity', in German as 'Adler und Schafe. Christentum und Öffentliche Ordnung jenseits der Moderne', in *Kirche und Theologie im Kulturellen Dialog*, (ed.) Bernhard Fraling, Helmut Hoping and Juan-Carlos Scannone (Freiburg: Herder, 1994), pp. 61–75.

'Incarnation and determinate freedom' in *On Freedom. Boston University Studies in Philosophy and Religion, Vol. 10*, (ed.) Leroy S. Rouner (Notre Dame: University of Notre Dame Press, 1989), pp. 15–29.

'Beyond the end of history?' in *Why Theology?*, (ed.) Claude Geffré and Werner Jeanrond, *Concilium*, 1994/6, pp. 47–56.

PART I

A meeting-place for truth

CHAPTER I

The beginning and the end of 'religion'?

THE FIELD OF GOD'S WHISPERING

Every Teape Lecturer is invited to reflect upon 'The Upanishads in the Catholic Church', but the field, or context of reflection, varies, as do the individual lecturers who seek, upon that field, to find their way, to gain some knowledge (to take the thirteenth chapter of the Gita as an allegory).[1]

I shall, in these three lectures, have something to say about religion at the ending of the 'modern' world; about prophecy, and peace, and justice; and about the mystery of God, the mystery that is reality, and wisdom, and delight. Before setting out upon the journey, however, I want briefly to identify the speaker and the background against which he speaks.

First, the background, which (in my judgement) is the need to keep continually in mind the way in which this world of ours, however it arose,[2] has now become, to an extent that was unimaginable even a few decades ago, one single complex fact, one seamless web of cause and consequence. This oneness of our world is, moreover, increasingly the oneness of an *artefact*: an expression of human energy, and ingenuity, and greed. Pollution of the air and sea, deforestation, annihilation of innumerable species, exhaustion of non-renewable resources: all these are things that human beings do. It is increasingly the

---

[1] The chapter in which Krishna teaches Arjuna to discriminate between *prakrti* and *purusa*, between the field and the knower of the field.
[2] See *Rig Veda*, 10.129.6, 7. All references to the Veda are to Wendy Doniger O'Flaherty, *The Rig Veda. An Anthology* (London: Penguin Books, 1981).

case that famine and disease and destitution are disasters no more 'natural' than is the collapse of a dwelling which the landlord had neglected to repair.[3]

Hence, in no small measure, the crisis of our time: the extent to which our ingenuity has outstripped our wisdom. We have made the world a single, swift and dangerous chariot, but there is little wisdom in the charioteer.[4] Nor is there much time left. It is 'evening in the forest' and, when we think we hear the sound of someone crying, we are right to be afraid, but it is ourselves we have to fear.[5]

This is the background. What about the speaker? On what grounds did I accept, with gratitude, the invitation from the Teape Committee to give these lectures? I certainly cannot claim to be an expert in the field. I know little of Indian history and culture and, in spite of the best efforts of an excellent teacher forty years ago, I do not read Sanskrit. (That teacher was Father Hubert Olympius Mascarenhas, Principal of St Sebastian Goan High School in Bombay, whose remarkable little book, *The Quintessence of Hinduism*, was published in the spring of 1951, while I was living for a few months with my uncle, Bill Lash, who then was Bishop of Bombay.)[6]

But all my roots were grown in Indian soil. I was born in Lansdowne, in what was then the United Provinces. My father, a soldier, was born in Calcutta, where his father was port chaplain for the Missions to Seamen. My grandfather, incidentally (who himself was born in what is now Palayankottai in Tamil Nadu, where his father was a CMS priest),[7] published, in 1923,

---

[3] See Nicholas Lash, *Believing Three Ways in One God. A Reading of the Apostles' Creed* (London: SCM Press, 1992), pp. 114–15.

[4] See *Katha Upanishad*, 3.3. Unless otherwise indicated, references to the Upanishads are to Juan Mascaro, *The Upanishads* (London: Penguin Books, 1965).

[5] See *Rig Veda*, 10.146.4.

[6] See H. O. Mascarenhas, *The Quintessence of Hinduism. The Key to Indian Culture and Philosophy* (Bombay: St Sebastian Goan High School, 1951). William Quinlan Lash was Bishop of Bombay from 1947 until 1962.

[7] In 1858 'the training school for women teachers opened on a permanent basis at Palamcottah, and was called the Sarah Tucker Institution after the sister of John Tucker. The work of this institution took a great step forward from the beginning of 1867, when A. H. Lash arrived with his wife to take charge' (M. E. Gibbs, *The Anglican Church in India, 1600–1970* (Delhi: SPCK, 1972), p. 251).

an excellent small guide to the caves at Elephanta for the use
of English merchant seamen visiting Bombay.[8] My mother was
born in Bangalore, where her father was serving in the ICS.
Her mother's grandfather, Thomas Lumisden Strange, was a
High Court judge in Madras, of which city his father, Sir
Thomas Andrew Strange, had been appointed first Chief
Justice in December 1800. (You will hear more from some of
these characters as we go along.)

It is, therefore, as a kind of traveller, a pilgrim, that I give
these lectures. Every Christian, and hence every Christian
theologian, is called to journey in the direction of deeper
knowledge of the things of God, and the journey is a home-
coming, for God is our end as well as our beginning. These
lectures have, for me, the poignancy of being a home-coming
not only in parable but in fact (though which the fact and
which the parable I leave to the philosophers to decide!).

In 1947 Bill the bishop published a little book entitled: *To
High Kailas*.[9] Seven men – a professor, a political activist, a
clerk, a singer, a *sadhu*, a schoolmaster and the narrator (the
last two being English, the others Indians) – meet in a rest-
house in the foothills of the Himalayas. When six of them have
told their stories, they turn to the *sadhu* and enquire: '"What
are we seeking, swamiji?" "You are seeking to escape from
men", came the answer. "What are you doing, swamiji?" "I am
on my way to God".' The *sadhu* then turns to the narrator:
'"What do you do, brother?" "I return to men", I answered.'
The reader is, I think, invited to understand that the narrator
and the *sadhu* are going in the same direction.

There is one more preliminary remark that I would like to
make. Of the many different ways in which theology has been
distinguished from philosophy, I know none more fruitful
than that proposed, more than nine hundred years ago, by
Anselm of Canterbury. Philosophical discourse is soliloquy; in

---

[8] It was entitled: *Elephanta. Written mostly for and dedicated entirely to, The Rovers under the
Red Duster*. It was priced at four annas and published discreetly, the only indication
of authorship being my grandfather's initials, N[icholas] A[lleyne] L[ash], at the
end.

[9] Will Quinlan, *To High Kailas* (Hind Kitabs, 1947).

philosophical reflection, the only voice heard is that of the philosopher. The theologian, in contrast, is trying to say something sensible in the presence of God. Theological discourse is rooted in worship, in address to God. It is, says Anselm, not 'soliloquy' but 'allocution'.[10] The theologian's speech is, therefore, uttered in response to the prior utterance of God's eternal Word. But it can only be so, and remain so, on condition that the theologian stays attentive to the stillness of God's speech. As Elijah learned, listening to the still small voice on Horeb; as Arjuna discovered from a conversation whispered against the battle's tumult: God does not shout.[11] Sometimes, as in Gethsemane, the stillness of God's speaking seems unbearable. God's utterance is everlasting but he does not shout and, if we shout, we shall neither hear each other nor the mystery which calls us and commands the way we are to go.

THOMAS LUMISDEN STRANGE

The path I want to travel in this first lecture will, at one point, take us as far afield as England in the seventeenth century. However, the best place to begin will be Madras, in 1827. In that year, my great-great-grandfather, Thomas Lumisden Strange, became a Writer in the East India Company's civil service. He rose through the ranks of the judiciary until, after a period on the bench of the High Court, he retired in 1863, at the age of fifty-five, and returned to England.

Having spent his youth, like 'most young men, in heedlessness and self-indulgence', he was a stranger to 'personal exercises in Bible reading' and to prayer until, in 1838, a German missionary 'lent [him] a pamphlet on the Destinies of the British Empire, by a Mr Thorpe, a well-known dissenting

---

[10] Anselm draws the distinction at the end of the Preface to the *Proslogion*. See *St Anselm's Proslogion. With a Reply on Behalf of the Fool by Gaunilo and the Author's Reply to Gaunilo*, translated, with an introduction and philosophical commentary, by M. J. Charlesworth (Oxford: Clarendon Press, 1965), p. 104.

[11] See 1 Kings 19.12; *Bhagavad Gita*, 18.75. Unless otherwise indicated, references to the Gita are to Juan Mascaró (trans.), *The Bhagavad Gita* (London: Penguin Books, 1962).

minister of Bristol'. Converted by Thorpe's prophecies of
impending judgement on the Raj, Judge Strange became, for
twenty years, a member of the Plymouth Brethren.[12] At the
end of this period, his Christian faith, already eroded by
consideration of the historical evidence, finally crumbled
before the heroism with which a condemned man, a convert to
Christianity, confessed on the gallows his faith in Rama. On
the strength of this experience, Strange became convinced
that 'the Christ idea' and 'the God idea' not only could, but
should, be firmly separated[13] and, in collaboration with the
freethinker Thomas Scott (an exact contemporary who had
cast off his Catholicism in 1856), he wrote, in retirement, a
stream of pamphlets with titles such as: *How I Became and
Ceased to be a Christian*, *What is Christianity?*, *The Supreme Power in
the Universe*, and so on.

The theme of these writings is that 'the primitive faith
imparted by the Most High to those in a condition to receive
it', a faith 'of the simplest order',[14] requiring 'no study, and . . .
no passage of time, for its attainment', and consisting in the
belief 'that the almighty being standing as the author and the
ruler of all is our ever-present and unalterable friend',[15] has, in
every culture, been corrupted and obscured from view by
human pride and curiosity.

The primitive faith held 'by all the enlightened races with
whom we stand allied in community of thought . . . is best
expressed by the most ancient of these stocks in the most
ancient of their records, namely the Hindus in their Vedas.
The Vedic people . . . had no temples, no priesthood, no
ceremonials, but each felt that he had open access to his
Maker.' In time, however, there emerged 'an astute and
interested priesthood' which, feeding the people 'with fresh

[12] Thomas Lumisden Strange, *How I Became and Ceased to be a Christian* (London:
Trübner and Co., 1881), pp. 11, 12.
[13] See Strange, *How I Became*, pp. 8, 15.
[14] Thomas Lumisden Strange, *What is Christianity? An Historical Sketch; Illustrated with a
Chart* (London: Trübner and Co., 1880), p. 6.
[15] Thomas Lumisden Strange, *How I Became*, p. 5; *The Supreme Power in the Universe*
(London: Thomas Scott, 1877), p. 23.

delusions', led Hinduism, as it led Judaism and Christianity, into 'idolatry' and superstition.[16] Fortunately, the 'deep truth of the primitive faith' still lurks 'in the bosoms of the better instructed, as it will be always avowed by educated Hindus when the appeal is made to them'. And, since the same is now true of educated Christians, there are grounds for hope in 'the recovery of the primitive faith as implanted in the human breast before man came in with his "inventions"'.[17]

Thomas Strange was not a particularly learned man, nor was he an original thinker. But it is precisely the extent to which he represents a widespread, influential, nineteenth-century mood, or view of things, that makes him interesting. How familiar he was with the work of Ram Mohan Roy, and whether directly or indirectly, I do not know. But there are evident affinities. And just as Ram Mohan, 'for all his avowed susceptibility to Muslim and Christian teaching ... regarded himself as a Hindu seeking to reform Hinduism from within',[18] so Thomas Strange, although awakened by India from the Christianity which he had previously espoused, had his heart set on what he himself called 'a further reformation of the Christian faith'.[19]

In illo tempore, in the 'beginning-time' of myth, a daylight time of simple speech and common goals and clear ideas, everyone had 'equal access to the One True God'.[20] And the dread disease which, blocking the sunlight of God's truth from view, disrupted social harmony and common understanding, was 'the canker of priestcraft'. Ram Mohan's account of Hinduism's decline is more or less identical to Thomas Strange's description of the fall of Christianity: 'Hinduism had become degenerate ... because it had fallen into the grip

[16] Strange, *What is Christianity?*, pp. 6–8, 64; cf. *How I Became*, p. 19.
[17] Strange, *What is Christianity?*, pp. 8, 68.
[18] Julius Lipner, *Hindus. Their Religious Beliefs and Practices* (London: Routledge, 1994), p. 66.
[19] Strange, *What is Christianity?*, p. 68.
[20] The phrase is Lipner's, describing Ram Mohan's reforming vision. But, of course, what we hope for 'in the end' is close cousin to what we believe to have been the case 'in the beginning'. See Lipner, *Hindus*, p. 119.

of self-seeking priests who played on the fears and superstitions of a people largely ignorant of their religion's original
high standards of belief and practice.'[21]

That diversity and change, time and discord and exhaustion, difference and decay, belong to the surface or appearance
of reality, and not to its still heart and centre, is a conviction
which finds endlessly various expression, from Advaitic
Vedanta to Neoplatonism. Thus, for example, whatever the
influence of an English education on Vivekananda, his vision
of the inner unity of humankind beneath the 'outer differences
of race, religion, sex and condition of life'[22] had rich resources
within Indian culture upon which to draw.

Nevertheless, two central features of the nineteenth-
century reformers' vision have their roots not in India, but in
seventeenth-century Europe. These are, on the one hand, the
recasting of the distinction between outer appearance and
inner reality into a narrative of primal purity corrupted
and complicated in the course of time, and, on the other, the
combination of a passion for plain speech and clear ideas with
antipathy to ritual and 'priestcraft'. It is in early modern
England, and especially in the University of Cambridge, that
we shall find the workshop in which these elements of what
was to become the dominant account of 'religion' and 'the
religions' were first forged.

Before turning there, however, consider this nice nest of
paradoxes. In 1902, a Roman Catholic Bengali brahmin,
Brahmabandhab Upadhyay, lecturing in England, announced
that, because Indians have 'been taught in various ways by
English teachers that there is no life of God apart from nature'
and that 'God and the world make up one organism', therefore
'English education stands as the first and foremost stumbling
block' in the way of Christianity's reception in India.[23] Thus,
while the Indian Catholic brahmin upbraids the English for
their monism, the English ex-Christian Thomas Strange is
provoked, by the devotion of a dying Indian, affectionately to

[21] Lipner, *Hindus*, pp. 65, 64.   [22] Lipner, *Hindus*, p. 67.
[23] Brahmabandhab Upadhyay, 'Christianity in India', *The Tablet*, 3 January 1903, 8.

interpret Indian culture through spectacles originally designed (though this he did not know) in England.

(Incidentally, while lecturing in Cambridge, Upadhyay won the university's approval 'to establish a teaching post in Hindu philosophy provided a suitable Indian incumbent and Indian money could be found. Eventually, the proposal foundered on the Indian side.'[24] I am delighted to report that, ninety years later, thanks to generous Indian benefaction and through the good offices of Upadhyay's editor, Julius Lipner, this vision has recently been realised with the establishment, in Cambridge, of the Dharam Hinduja Institute of Indic Research.)

A SIMPLE STRATEGY FOR A COMPLEX WORLD

In modern parlance, it is customary to speak of many religions and therefore also of the 'Hindu religion'. Actually, according to Hindu doctrine, there is only one religion for all men, that, namely, which is constituted and defined by man's relation to the Infinite . . . each person is free to choose and adopt whatever style or manner of approach to the Infinite he finds is best suited to his temperament and natural disposition.[25]

On this account, it makes no more sense to speak of 'the religions', in the plural, than it would (for instance) to speak about 'the humankinds', though no two human beings are the same.

The view that Mascarenhas is contesting, according to which there are a number of different religions, related to each other as species of a common genus, was first invented in seventeenth-century England. It appears, at the beginning of the century, in Richard Hooker, and the distinction drawn by Edward Brerewood, in 1614, between 'four sorts of Sects of Religion' – Christianity, Mahometanism, Judaism and paganism – soon became standard.[26] Drawn in these terms,

---

[24] Julius Lipner and George Gispert-Sauch (eds.), *The Writings of Brahmabandhab Upadhyay*, 1 (Bangalore: United Theological College, 1992), p. xli.

[25] Mascarenhas, *Quintessence*, pp. 33–4.

[26] See Peter Harrison, *'Religion' and the Religions in the English Enlightenment* (Cambridge: Cambridge University Press, 1990), p. 39. Harrison quotes the fifth

this distinction would have puzzled Cardinal Nicholas of Cusa who spoke, in the fifteenth century, of that one religion, *una religio*, the 'unattainable truth about God . . . of which all existing belief systems are but shadowy reflections'.[27] And yet Cusa's Platonism does contain the seeds of subsequent developments. (The cardinal, incidentally, might have had quite an interesting conversation with Father Mascarenhas.)

The construction of the 'genus and species' model of relationships between 'the religions' was but one component in the project of 'enlightenment'. This project, suspecting all 'local' reasoning, all particular custom and convention, as arbitrary, divisive, insecure, sought, in its stead, 'to place reason upon a secure and universal foundation'.[28] To say that the modern world is ending is to acknowledge that this universalising project can now, in turn, be seen to be little more than the expression of one particular set of 'local' circumstances: the circumstances of seventeenth-century Europe.

It follows, however, that if the ending of the modern world is to be negotiated fruitfully – towards our common peace and truth and flourishing, and not towards our deepening destruction – we need to re-examine the circumstances which brought that world to birth. The two aspects on which I shall now briefly comment are: first, the way in which knowledge was then newly organised and, secondly, the impact of the quest for social harmony on the understanding of religion.

---

edition of Brerewood's *Enquiries Touching the Diversity of Language and Religion through the Chief Parts of the World* (London, 1674). In an essay published since these lectures were delivered, William T. Cavanaugh has summarised, with admirable lucidity and due reference made to Wilfred Cantwell Smith's seminal *The Meaning and End of Religion* (New York: Macmillan, 1962), the story of what he calls 'the creation of religion' in early modern Europe: see William T. Cavanaugh, '"A fire strong enough to consume the house": the Wars of Religion and the rise of the State', *Modern Theology* (October 1995), 397–420.

27 Harrison, *'Religion' and the Religions*, p. 12. Harrison is paraphrasing passages from Nicholas Cusanus, *De pace fidei*, (ed.) Raymund Klibansky (London: Warburg Institute, 1956).

28 John Milbank, 'The end of dialogue' in Gavin D'Costa (ed.), *Christian Uniqueness Reconsidered. The Myth of a Pluralistic Theology of Religions* (New York: Orbis Books, 1990), p. 174.

In the first place, then, the 'brave new world'[29] now opened up through the invention of printing and the voyages of discovery was so vast, so complex, so diverse, as to require new instruments for its conceptual mapping and control. Thus it was that the fusion of the late medieval passion for plain speech and single meanings with the Renaissance rediscovery of Stoicism's 'nature' – a world seen as homogeneous through and through, made of one kind of stuff and driven by one set of forces – gave birth to a new ideal for the working of the mind, namely: 'a science that has an unequivocal language with which it speaks and uniform objects of which it speaks'.[30] No time nor patience now for narrative, or poetry, or paradox. Theologians, philosophers and scientists alike developed a single-minded passion for pure prose. All knowledge is of objects, and objects are to be measured and described, as objectively and simply and straightforwardly as possible.

This development had a dramatic impact on the way in which 'divine revelation' was understood. The traditional view had been that, 'in the process of revelation, God reveals himself. Now God reveals saving knowledge, similar in kind [to] (if different in content)'[31] from such knowledge as might be gained from the study of the natural world.

We might not immediately notice this when we hear Francis Bacon saying, in 1605, that 'sacred theology must be drawn from the word and oracles of God; not from the light of nature, or the dictates of reason'.[32] But all this amounts to is the claim that the knowledge of God and knowledge of the natural world come about through studying different objects, reading different books: the Scriptures and the 'book of nature'. In Bacon's own words: 'though revelation and sense may differ both in matter and manner, yet the spirit of man and its

[29] William Shakespeare, *The Tempest*, Act v, Scene 1.
[30] Amos Funkenstein, *Theology and the Scientific Imagination from the Middle Ages to the Seventeenth Century* (Princeton: Princeton University Press, 1986), p. 41.
[31] Harrison, *'Religion' and the Religions*, pp. 24–5.
[32] Francis Bacon, *First Part of the Great Instauration. The Dignity and Advancement of Learning*, Book IX, in Joseph Devey, *The Physical and Metaphysical Works of Lord Bacon* (London: Henry G. Bohn, 1864), p. 369.

cells are the same; and . . . receive different liquors through different conduits'.[33]

Within this scheme of things, the relation of human beings to the Holy One, once understood as creaturely dependence relearned as friendship, is now reduced to knowledge of an object known as 'God'. All objects of enquiry are shaped by the methods used for their investigation. The invention of 'religion' carried with it the reduction of faith's attentive wonder to the entertaining of particular beliefs.

But, if coming to the knowledge of God *is* a process of the same kind as that by means of which we come to knowledge of the natural world, then how are we to account for the diversity of religious practices and beliefs? The answer, it may surprise you to learn, is to be discovered in the story of the Tower of Babel, for difference is a consequence of sin.

BABEL AND CATHOLICISM: THE DANGER OF DIVERSITY

'This', said Samuel Purchas in 1613, 'is the effect of sinne and irreligion, that the name and practise of Religion is thus diversified, else had there bin, as one God, so one religion and one language, wherein to give it with just reason, a proper name.'[34] And, in case his readers were in doubt as to the chief cause of religious corruption and complexity, he told the Archbishop of Canterbury, in his dedicatory Preface, that he wrote the book so that others might learn 'two lessons fitting the times, the unnaturalnesse of faction and atheism . . . And if I live to finish the rest, I hope to show the paganism of anti-christian popery.'[35]

For seventeenth-century Englishmen, it was axiomatic that 'any change was necessarily for the worse, any novelty in thought, decadent'. As Matthew Hale put it in 1677: 'truth is more ancient than error'. Religious diversity, in this scheme of

---

[33] Bacon, *Advancement of Learning*, Book II, p. 78.
[34] Samuel Purchas, *Purchas His Pilgrimage, Or: Relations of the World and the Religions Observed in all Ages and Places Discovered, from the Creation unto this Present* (London: 1613), Book I, Chapter 4.
[35] Purchas, *His Pilgrimage*, Preface.

things, was but one unfortunate result of a process of universal degeneration.[36]

During the seventeenth century, the terms 'theism' and 'deism' found their way from France to England and were used, interchangeably for a while, to denote the beliefs of those who affirmed the existence of a Supreme Being, source and author of the world, while rejecting revelation and Christian doctrine. The general deist view was that 'pluralism was unnatural, and combined with intolerance, gave rise to untold human misery. The cure was to be a return to the unsullied religion of the *illud tempus* which would result in a universal worship of the one God, and bring an end to religious strife.'[37]

No group of deists were more influential than the so-called Cambridge Platonists, amongst whom Ralph Cudworth is credited with the first recorded use of the term 'theism' (1678), while his colleague Henry More came up a few years earlier (1660) with 'monotheism'. More was fairly typical of these English Protestants in the extent to which his 'understanding of the role of idolatry in the history of religion' was 'conditioned by his attitude towards Catholicism'. In 1695 Charles Blount formulated the thesis of an original natural religion corrupted as a result of the introduction 'by the priest-hood' of 'polytheism and sacrifice'[38] (which, as we have seen, was almost exactly the view expressed a century and a half later by Ram Mohan and Thomas Strange).

Samuel Purchas, whom we have met already, seems to have been the first to use the term 'polytheism' in English (like all these words, it was first thought up, a little earlier, in France). The context in which he does so is, for the time, almost ecumenical in its generosity: 'Who knoweth, whether in the secret dispensation of divine providence, which is a co-worker in everie worke, able even out of evill to bring good, the donations, the navigations of papists, the preaching of friars and jesuits may be fore-runners of a further and truer

---

[36] See Harrison, *'Religion' and the Religions*, pp. 103, 132, 104.
[37] Harrison, ibid., p. 74.   [38] See Harrison, ibid., pp. 135, 73; cf. pp. 143–4.

manifestation of the gospell, to the new-found nations?' For men like 'Fr[ancis] Xavier, and the rest of them . . . doe beat down infidelitie with diligent catechisings; although upon that golden foundation they build afterwards their own haye and stubble, with their rack of confession, and rabble of ceremonies, and (the most dangerous to new converts) an exchanged polytheism in worshipping of saints, images, and the host.'[39]

The 'fundamental theological question of the age of reason was how revealed religion was related to natural religion'. One of the later deists, John Toland,

like many of his contemporaries, came to the conclusion that revealed religion in its uncorrupted state was identical to natural religion – that original and rational form of human piety which any reasonable individual could arrive at . . . With the passing of time, Christianity had come to suffer the fate of the primitive natural religion, and through human proneness to superstition, and with the encouragement of the priests, had degenerated into its present condition.[40]

For the seventeenth-century deists, as for Ram Mohan Roy and Thomas Strange in the nineteenth century, most people have got religion disastrously wrong, the forms of its degeneracy varying from Catholicism to popular Hinduism. But the story can, of course, be told another way. It is now generally agreed that 'the religions of the East' were invented by the European imagination in the early nineteenth century, and that the conceptual framework used for this invention was most ill suited to its contents. That framework was, as we have seen, fashioned in the seventeenth century. In our own day, as we emerge from the culture of modernity, it becomes easier to see that this modern framework of 'religion' distorts the so-called 'religions of the West' – Judaism, Christianity and Islam – no less disastrously than it does the traditions of prayer and practice, thought and discipline and devotion, now known as Hinduism, Buddhism, or Confucianism.

[39] Purchas, *His Pilgrimage*, Book I, Chapter 9.
[40] Harrison, *'Religion' and the Religions*, p. 164.

FROM PUBLIC ORDER TO PRIVATE PLEASURE

Before considering what *other* framework than that of 'religion' might now serve the purposes of Christians, Hindus, Buddhists, Jews and Muslims in search of common action and deeper mutual understanding, we need briefly to follow the modern theories through to their exhaustion.

During the eighteenth century, the distinction between natural and revealed religion was redescribed as lying between natural and 'positive' religion: between, on the one hand, the recognition – accessible to all rational beings – that the workings of the marvellous machinery of the world show the hand of the machine's designer, and, on the other, the arbitrary inventions and divisive positings of particular sects and interest groups. And in due time, of course, natural religion, in turn, was understood to be a kind of fiction: the projection onto some divinity of human fears and dreams and aspirations.[41] Thus ends the story of 'religion' and 'the religions', as conceived from the standpoint of 'enlightenment'; a story which had its beginning in the seventeenth century. Amongst the ways in which this ending has been understood, however, there are two which seem to me misleading.

In the first place, it is often said, as Harvey Cox said thirty years ago, that 'secularisation simply bypasses and undercuts religion and goes on to other things . . . Religion has been privatised.'[42] It would, however, be more accurate to say that it is the role of religion as a medium of truth that has been privatised. Religion, in societies that imagine themselves secular, is, like art and music, allowed to be about the Beautiful. Sometimes, it is allowed to be about the Good. What is excluded, by the dominant ideologies, is any suggestion that the business of religion is, no less than that of science, with public truth.

---

[41] See Michael J. Buckley, SJ, *At the Origins of Modern Atheism* (New Haven: Yale University Press, 1987).

[42] Harvey Cox, *The Secular City. Secularization and Urbanization in Theological Perspective* (London: SCM Press, 1965), p. 2.

It is also often said that the more secularised a society, the more irreligious it becomes. Yet, in Britain, usually regarded as among the more comprehensively secularised societies in Western Europe, not only does there seem to be more vitality of worship and devotion – Christian, Jewish, Muslim, Sikh and Hindu – than the discourse of 'high society' would lead one to suppose, but the bookshops are awash with literature on astrology and yoga, on spirituality and mysticism, on para-psychology and science fiction, on cults and quackery of every kind. This dissociation between disaffected public order – the territory of what counts as 'rational' behaviour – and anarchic private fantasy has seldom, if ever, been so thorough or, perhaps, so dangerous.

THE RECOVERY OF NARRATIVE

'History, poetry, and philosophy', said Francis Bacon, 'flow from the three distinct fountains of the mind, viz. the memory, the imagination, and the reason.' Moreover, he went on, 'history and experience' (which he allocated to memory) 'are one and the same thing ... so are philosophy and the sciences' (which he made the realm of 'reason'). On the basis of this structural dissociation of memory from argument, of narrative from reason, Bacon arranged all disciplines and discourses in a pattern which was taken up by Diderot, in 1750, virtually unchanged, in his Prospectus for that bible of French 'enlightenment', the *Encyclopédie*.[43]

According to this pattern, history, memory and experience are of little interest except as conveyors of the raw material for reason (and Bacon does not waste much time upon imagination). The place of reason was to be the central space, the universal forum owned and governed, not by wayward human agents or competing particular interests and

---

[43] Bacon, *Advancement of Learning*, Book II, p. 78; see P. N. Furbank, *Diderot. A Critical Biography* (London: Secker and Warburg, 1992), pp. 32–3. The similarity between the two schemes can be seen at a glance from Nicholas Lash, 'Reason, fools and Rameau's nephew', *New Blackfriars*, 76 (1995), 368–77.

prejudices, but by impersonal and calculable forces which it is our human task to understand and, so far as possible, to control.

The tragedy of modern Western culture – which is no longer 'Western' but, in its pervasiveness and, increasingly, in its independence of political control, is in danger of becoming simply the system of the world – is that its breathtaking achievements, in science and technology, in medicine and agriculture, education and communication, and in the increasing sophistication of its acknowledgement of universal human rights, have to be set against the dark and bloodstained background of the cost, in human suffering and the devastation of the planet, of the length of time that it has taken us to learn that there is no neutral vantage-point, no universal standpoint, no 'nowhere in particular', from which truth may be discerned and the pattern of right action estimated. (It is no disparagement of modern science to insist that, while numbers may indeed be neutral, the uses of numbers never are.)

It is always on the field of battle, in the midst of action, that we are challenged to consider and to clarify, to cleanse the mind and heart and purify the springs of action. The 'ditch' which, in the eighteenth century, Lessing saw, and feared to be unbridgeable, between the accidental truths of history and necessary truths of reason, simply does not exist: the truths of reason are never quite as necessary as those who formulate them may suppose, and historical contingency may bear the truth of God.

I am not arguing that human beings are incapable of metaphysics, or that they 'only' tell stories (a formulation which betrays the rationalist's mistrust of narrative as a vehicle of truth). It would be more accurate to say that narrative comes first, and that the formal systems we construct – whether in philosophy or science – are coloured, shaped, determined, by the story-telling soil from which they spring.[44] (But this is, I

---

[44] See Nicholas Lash, 'Ideology, metaphor and analogy', *Theology on the Way to Emmaus* (London: SCM Press, 1986), pp. 95–119.

think, a lesson which Indian philosophers learned many years ago.)

The European and North American thinkers of the seventeenth and eighteenth centuries were not wrong to be suspicious of 'tradition-specific or "sectarian" religious discourse'.[45] Nor was it dishonourable to seek, beyond the obscenity of violence perpetrated in the name of God, for reasoned peace. Their mistake lay in the expectation that the human grasp of truth could ever be other than tradition-constituted. We are not incapable, as human beings, of making sense of things, of speaking truth and acting with integrity. But all these things we do from somewhere, shaped by some set of memories and expectations, bearing some sense of duty borne and gifts that have been given. All sense, and truth, and goodness, are carried and constituted by some story, some pattern of experience, some tradition.

Nor are the traditions of narrative and devotion, of proclamation and repentance, of celebration and compassion, of speech and silence, of structure and slavery and liberation, that we call 'religions', an exception to this general rule. From which it follows that it is mistaken to suppose that religions may be confidently claimed to be 'just different ways of worshipping or contemplating the same Ultimate Reality. What is experienced as "Ultimate" is specific to the tradition concerned . . . Nor are religions just different paths to a same goal; they are different paths to different goals. The goal aimed at is as tradition-specific as the path taken. The goal is constituted as goal by the path chosen.'[46]

EDUCATION FROM IDOLATRY, AND THE PURIFICATION OF DESIRE

Am I, with this emphasis on difference, suggesting that we pull up the drawbridge on 'dialogue', and cease to work for deeper

---

[45] John Clayton, 'Thomas Jefferson and the Study of Religion.' An Inaugural Lecture Delivered at the University of Lancaster, 18 November 1992, p. 12.
[46] Clayton, pp. 22–3.

mutual understanding and more effective common action between different traditions? By no means. But we need no longer to suppose, as Samuel Purchas did, that difference is a consequence of sin and that, in order to do our duty and be obedient to truth, we must reduce all languages to one. Shaped by different stories, following different paths towards our destinies, we may still learn, from time to time, to our surprised delight, that we walk together towards the distant snows.

I have been suggesting that an episode in the history of religion is now ending as the world of which it formed a part, the 'modern' world of European 'enlightenment', draws – not without darkness, danger and confusion – to a close. In these circumstances, perhaps the best thing we can do is, so far as possible, to come at the questions from a different angle.

Emile Durkheim once defined religion as 'the system of symbols by means of which society becomes conscious of itself'. On this account, religious ritual is to be construed as the 'totality of [social] practices concerned with sacred things';[47] concerned, that is to say, with dreams, ideas, beliefs and institutions, times and places which prove too hot to handle, too dangerous to touch. The list of religious rituals might, therefore, include: beliefs and practices protective of 'the market', or of national identity, or of the superiority of male gender; of a sense of how things hang together, of treasured places, memories and stories; of things we are too terrified to mention, or of instincts, prejudices and convictions lying at the very heart of who and how we take ourselves and other things to be.

(Notice, incidentally, that, on this account, the narratives of secularisation may serve, in fact, to render ideologically invisible the sacral or religious character of many of our most powerful institutions and foundationally entrenched

---

[47] Emile Durkheim, *Suicide: A Study in Sociology*, trans. John A. Spaulding and George Simpson (London: Routledge and Kegan Paul, 1970), p. 312; 'Concerning the definition of religious phenomena', in W. S. F. Pickering, ed., *Durkheim on Religion; A Selection of Readings and Bibliographies* (London: Routledge and Kegan Paul, 1975), p. 88.

beliefs.[48] Banks, bureaucracies and stock exchanges might turn out to be temples, in which all power and honour, all agency and possibility, is ascribed 'not to us, Lord, not to us', but to the market or the system of the world. In which case, once we had done a little demythologising, the destitution of the poor might turn out to be attributable, not to cosmic fate, but to the sacrificial system of which they are the victims and which the rest of us sustain. Such possibilities should not, at least, be deemed beyond consideration.)

The modern dissociation of memory from argument, of narrative from reason, made us forget how deeply all understanding and imagination is shaped by memory, coloured by circumstance, constituted by tradition. With this forgetfulness we lost sight of the extent to which the ancient traditions of devotion and reflection, of worship and enquiry, have seen themselves as *schools*. Christianity and Vedantic Hinduism, Judaism and Buddhism and Islam are schools (or so, at least, I hope to argue in the following two lectures) whose pedagogy has the twofold purpose – however differently conceived and executed in the different traditions – of weaning us from our idolatry and purifying our desire.

All human beings have their hearts set somewhere, hold something sacred, worship at some shrine. We are spontaneously idolatrous – where, by 'idolatry', I mean the worship of some creature, the setting of the heart on some particular thing (usually oneself). For most of us there is no single creature that is the object of our faith. Our hearts are torn, dispersed, distracted. We are (to use the seventeenth-century term) polytheists. And none of us is so self-transparent as to know quite where, in fact, our hearts are set.

Against this background, the great religious traditions can be seen as contexts in which human beings may learn, however slowly, partially, imperfectly, some freedom from the

---

[48] This case has been powerfully argued by John Milbank, *Theology and Social Theory: Beyond Secular Reason* (Oxford: Basil Blackwell, 1990); for extensive discussion of which, see the special issues devoted to it of *Modern Theology* (October 1992) and *New Blackfriars* (June 1992).

destructive bondage which the worship of the creature brings.[49] There I will leave the matter because, as I have indicated, I shall have something to say about both purification of desire and education from idolatry in the next two lectures. I turn instead to the more mundane matter of making sense of other people's stories and ideas.

CONTAINERS, COMPANIES AND CONTEXTS

Theories of meaning (I simplify outrageously) come largely in two kinds. On the one hand, there are those who see each word as the container of its meaning, as the skin contains the mango or the can the Coke. We put words side by side and build up meaning, as a builder might construct a wall. When listening to a stranger or translating from a language not our own, we expect each word in the stranger's discourse more or less to correspond to some one word in our own.

On the other hand, there are those who understand that words take their meaning from the company they keep. Words have no particular meaning outside a context – whether that context is a larger text or a performance in which the speaker is engaged. (Even a cry of 'Help!' is uninformative unless I have some sense of the predicament from which it springs!)

The more rationalist the temper of a culture, the more (it seems) it will be drawn towards the trap of 'container' thinking. Thus, for example, scholars in the nineteenth century, oblivious to the fact that 'neither Indian languages nor Chinese have anything corresponding to the Western term and concept of *"religion"*',[50] hunted for some one word which would best translate 'religion' and, unfortunately, '*dharma* ... came readily to mind'.[51] Quite apart, however, from the fact that the 'fit' between *dharma* and 'religion' is very poor indeed, the assumption that these two terms mean more or less the same overlooks the extent to which the meaning

---

[49] See Nicholas Lash, *Believing Three Ways*, p. 21.
[50] Felix Wilfred, *From the Dusty Soil* (Madras: University of Madras, 1995), p. 185.
[51] Lipner, *Hindus*, p. 217.

of *each* of them has varied according to the contexts and the circumstances of its use.

We can end, as we began, upon the field – 'the field of truth' that is 'the battle-field of life':[52] the field, or ground, or context,[53] which shapes the pattern of our actions; the 'natural law',[54] the order and the ordering of things, the way things go, the way we go with the grain of things; the responsibility we bear, the duty we discern, upon *this* field, in these particular circumstances. If these hints and glosses and suggestions go any way toward capturing something of the grammar of so protean a word as *dharma*, then it seems evident that there is no single word in English whose map of usage closely corresponds, and certainly not 'religion' in either of the two different traditions of its use that I have touched on.[55]

If 'container' theories are congenial to rationalism's propensity for abstract definition, then the recovery of narrative, of the primacy of practice, and the rediscovery of the tradition-constituted character of truth, may generate renewed appreciation of the fact that it is from the company

---

[52] *Bhagavad Gita*, I.I. Winthrop Sargeant prefers 'field of virtue' (*The Bhagavad Gita*, translated Winthrop Sargeant, revised edition edited by Christopher Chapple (New York: State University of New York Press, 1994), p. 39), whereas Antonio de Nicolas, surrendering the inequal struggle, settles for 'field of *dharma*' (*The Bhagavad Gita*, (trans.) Antonio de Nicolas (York Beach, Maine: Nicolas-Hays, 1990), p. 25).

[53] In helpful glossary entries on *dharma* and *kuruksetra*, de Nicolas says that 'dharma is the particular context within which a series of actions are determined'; 'dharma stands for the conditions or contextual situation within which certain actions must necessarily occur', *Bhagavad Gita*, (trans.) de Nicolas, pp. 138, 139.

[54] See Mascarenhas, *Quintessence*, p. 106; we are, however, sternly warned by Julius Lipner that '"Law" is a very inadequate translation for *dharma*' (*Hindus*, p. 84).

[55] The only word I know whose range of sense – from shape and measure and proportion, cause and order (with all the rich ambivalence that these last two terms carry) to context and reason, necessity and reasons given – covers anything like the same territory that *dharma* seems to do is the Latin word *ratio*, as used by Aquinas. And it is interesting to observe that both terms can carry connotations of 'field' or 'ground' or 'background'. But I do not think that *ratio* has ever meant 'religion'!

For a thorough and careful discussion of the ways that *dharma* has been treated in the encounter between Indian and European thought, see Wilhelm Halbfass, *India and Europe: An Essay in Understanding* (Albany, New York: State University of New York Press, 1988), pp. 310–48.

it keeps that the meaning of a word is best ascertained. It follows, of course, that there are no short cuts, through the definition of key terms and concepts, past the courteous and exacting labour of attending, as carefully and with as much imaginative sympathy as possible, to the detail of each other's practices and stories, to the different ways in which, in fact, we make our way upon the field.

A MEETING-PLACE FOR TRUTH

The 'public square' of European and North American 'enlightenment' sought to be a neutral space in which human beings might meet, their business governed by rationality alone. The recognition that no such space exists, nor can it be constructed, raises (as Nietzsche knew) the nightmare possibility that, if not reason, then violence alone is ruler of the world. And if the last word, like the first, is not with violence but with peace, then the primacy of peacefulness must, even now, be *shown*.[56]

Where the conversation, or dialogue, between different traditions is concerned, this requires some method of procedure which combines 'public contestability and respect for particularity and difference'.[57] John Clayton has suggested that the *vada*-tradition in Indian philosophy, admitting as it does tradition-specific reasons in public rationality and aiming not at consensus, but at clarification, might serve as a model.[58]

I am not sufficiently familiar with these traditions of debate to assess this suggestion, let alone to develop it, but, as Clayton presents it, it seems in most suggestive harmony with the debating traditions of the medieval European universities, on the one hand, and, on the other, with the proposals for the

---

[56] Milbank's *Theology and Social Theory* is an impressively wide-ranging attempt, against the Nietzschean narrative of the primacy of violence, to interpret our understanding of the modern world in relation to Augustine's story, in the *City of God*, of the constitutive and promised peacefulness of God.

[57] Clayton, 'Jefferson and the Study of Religion', p. 26.

[58] See 'Jefferson and the Study of Religion', pp. 27, 32.

future of the university 'beyond modernity' worked out by Alasdair MacIntyre in his Gifford Lectures.[59]

There may be no neutral ground on which to meet, but that is no reason why different traditions should not establish mutual territory. In 1933, according to Bill Lash's papers, Mahatma Gandhi visited the Christa Prema Seva ashram in Pune. 'He had', says Bishop Lash, 'no eye for the lay out, or the garden, and only a caustic comment for the Chapel, in Indian style, and adorned with paintings by a Christian Indian artist. He was chiefly interested in the materials in which it was built – too luxurious – and the latrines – scarcely up to his standards.'[60] But Ghandi came, and took an interest, and the interest gave great encouragement.

Elsewhere in his papers, the bishop records that

It has long been the custom to have public lectures in the reading hall of our ashram at Poona. They are on a variety of subjects, gener- ally topical, literary, philosophic, religious, or political. It has been the custom also to allow expression to as wide a variety of points of view as possible. The basic principles of such an ashram should be so profound that the several sides of truth should find a common meeting place upon its premises. Free discussion appears a more fruitful method of reconciling seeming opposites, and correcting vagaries, than any other.[61]

It was that note of Bishop Lash's which suggested to me the title for these lectures.

---

[59] See Alasdair MacIntyre, *Three Rival Versions of Moral Enquiry* (London: Duckworth, 1990).

[60] The paper, dated August 1969, and consisting of seven pages of typescript and a (not always identical) manuscript version of sixteen pages, is entitled 'Challenging a Mahatma'. Eighteen years later, in 1951, I was best man at that artist's wedding and when, in January 1995, these lectures were delivered in Pune under the auspices of the ashram, his widow, Ivy da Fonseca, arranged for a number of his pictures to be on display.

[61] From fourteen typed pages of autobiographical material entitled 'Indian Table Talk'. A slip attached reads: '?Eve of War. 1939'.

CHAPTER 2

Prophecy and peace

AN UNSPECIFIC ACHE

The Ardnamurchan peninsula, in the western highlands of Scotland, is beautiful but bleak; remote, austere, easily romanticised by those who briefly visit it. The poet Alasdair Maclean, born and raised in a croft at its extremity, describes autumn on the Ardnamurchan: 'Everything seems drenched in a gentle melancholy, that unspecific ache that is the heritage of man.'[1]

The *Chandogya Upanishad* speaks of 'the real city of Brahman', wherein 'all desires are contained', as the place where we are 'free from sin, free from old age, free from death, free from sorrow, free from hunger, free from thirst'.[2]

Is the ache for ever unspecific, or might its pain be stilled, its yearning satisfied? Does the journey beyond thirst lie by way of its suppression or of its assuagement? Is that 'peace' to which both Hindu and Christian literature make frequent reference to be understood as the fulfilment of desire or as the consequence of its suppression?[3] These are among the questions on which I propose to offer some reflections.

In Chapter One, I told the story of that episode in the history of religion which is now ending with the superseding of

---

[1] Alasdair Maclean, *Night Falls on Ardnamurchan. The Twilight of a Crofting Family* (London: Penguin, 1986), p. 84.

[2] *Chandogya Upanishad*, 8.1.5 (quoted from S. Radhakrishnan, *The Principal Upanisads* (London: George Allen and Unwin, 1953), p. 689).

[3] See, for example, the contrast (to which I shall return) between *Bhagavad Gita* 2.70 and 2.71.

the culture of 'enlightenment' of which it formed a part; an episode whose assumptions set the framework and agenda for nineteenth-century exchanges between the cultures of India and European (especially British) culture. I suggested that, instead of envisaging the cultural traditions that we call 'religions' primarily as associations of subscription to particular beliefs, it would be more fruitful to consider them as schools whose pedagogy has the twofold purpose of weaning us from our idolatry and purifying our desire. It is with the second of these purposes that I am now concerned.

Desire, and hope, and expectation, are shaped by need and memory. I shall, accordingly, first say something about differences of memory, then about differences of hope. This will enable me to move the discussion on to three further topics: the desire of God, harmony and healing, and the appearance of the holy.

In both Christianity and Hinduism, peace, true peace, that 'final peace' in which, like birds returning to the tree, all things find rest, is *promised*.[4] And we know this, not as a hypothesis or speculation, but as something that we *learn* in our remembrance of an uttered Word. The focus of this lecture, therefore, is – in the classic terminology of Christian doctrine – the redemptive incarnation or appearance of God's eternal Word. (Whereas the focus in Chapter Three will be on the Christian doctrine of God as holy trinity.)

God's word made manifest

DIFFERENCES OF MEMORY

Father Mascarenhas put the problem bluntly: 'For the presentation of the Christian doctrine of the Incarnation, we are on terribly boggy ground in Hinduism.'[5] One thing, at least, is clear: if we *start* with the assertion of Jesus Christ's 'uniqueness' we shall soon sink into a morass of mutual misunderstanding. What is less clear, however, is the extent to which

---

[4] See *Prasna Upanishad*, fourth question (which concerns 'that Spirit on whom all the others find rest'), 4.7.
[5] Mascarenhas, *Quintessence*, p. 26.

the grounds of this incomprehension are to be sought in faith or in philosophy; in a constitutive feature of the Gospel without which Christianity would simply cease to be itself, or in different imaginative structures of time and space, of memory and meaning.

In an illuminating essay, 'The Jordan, the Tiber, and the Ganges', Raimundo Panikkar reacted with asperity to those who charged him with evading the 'scandal of particularity'. 'I insist', he said, 'that with such a view of Christ I am not escaping the scandal of the incarnation and the process of redemption. I am not ignoring these historical facts. It is simply that I do not worship history, nor do I limit reality – not even human reality – to history, nor history to the Abrahamic history.'[6]

In a most appreciative study of this essay, Bishop Rowan Williams, while applauding Panikkar's insistence on the *ambiguity* of what he called 'the Christian preoccupation with history' (which has too often helped to generate destructive and imperial ideologies of linear progress), nevertheless wondered whether he does not take too much for granted the finished form of Christian distinctions between uttered Word and outpoured Spirit, thereby underestimating the need continually to be attentive to 'the historically distinct focus of the events of Jesus' story'[7] and the subsequent interpretative processes which clarified these distinctions. Without such sustained attention, Williams suggests, the balance between unity and plurality which Panikkar so brilliantly constructs would collapse either into yet another 'imperialistic Christian claim to *theoretical* finality', or into the kind of 'merely tolerant pluralism' which both he and Panikkar deplore.[8]

In the Introduction to his edition of the Gita, Juan Mascaro claimed that there are 'two great branches of literature not

---

[6] Raimundo Panikkar, 'The Jordan, the Tiber, and the Ganges. Three kairological moments of christic self-consciousness' in John Hick and Paul F. Knitter (eds.), *The Myth of Christian Uniqueness* (London: SCM Press, 1988), p. 114.

[7] Rowan Williams, 'Trinity and pluralism', in Gavin D'Costa (ed.), *Christian Uniqueness Reconsidered*, pp. 6, 8.

[8] See Williams, 'Trinity and pluralism', p. 8.

found in Sanskrit. There is no history and there is no tragedy .
. . Sanskrit literature is, on the whole, a romantic literature
interwoven with idealism and practical wisdom and with a
passionate longing for spiritual vision . . . the mind of India has
never tired in the search for Light'.[9] The style of Mascaro's
translations bears witness to his belief in the romantic
character of the writings he so deeply loved. But what of his
assertion that, in this literature, there is no history and no
tragedy?

The related claim that 'traditional Hinduism' lacks 'the
groundwork for a concept of history in the modern sense'
irritates Julius Lipner, who describes it as a 'gross over-
simplification'. However, the chapter he devotes to 'Modes of
reckoning time and "progress"', while it demonstrates that 'in
traditional religious Hindu consciousness time is not simply
some cyclic or repetitive process but a framework for real
development and growth',[10] nevertheless does little to suggest
that past particularity – the single culture-shaping, history-
defining deed, with all its consequences, which, once enacted,
can never be undone – plays the same part in Hindu thought
and devotion that it has done in Judaism, Christianity and
Islam.[11]

The suggestion is not that memory plays a lesser part in
Indian than in Western and Middle Eastern cultures, but that
'remembering' means different things in different places,
carries a different kind of freight, and generates different
kinds of expectation. Both Christianity and Hinduism give a
central place to myth or epic, to that 'once upon a time' whose
purport rests precisely on the fact that no time in particular
is thereby mentioned! But there is not, I think, in Indian

[9] Mascaro, *Bhagavad Gita*, pp. 9–10.
[10] Lipner, *Hindus*, pp. 251, 251–74, 273.
[11] I note with interest Wilhelm Halbfass' cautious judgement that 'the non-historical
mode of self-presentation is still significant in modern Hindu thought and self-
awareness' (*India and Europe*, p. 367). Halbfass connects this with the extent to
which 'traditional Hindu thought and literature' has shown 'virtually no interest in
foreign countries, societies, cultures or religions' (p. 253). It is as if diachronic and
synchronic self-sufficiency go hand in hand.

sacred literature, a sentence bearing the weight borne, in Christianity, by 'suffered under Pontius Pilate'.[12]

In his Lowell Lectures of 1926, Alfred North Whitehead described Buddhism as 'the most colossal example in history of applied metaphysics. Christianity', he went on, 'took the opposite road. It has always been a religion seeking a metaphysic, in contrast to Buddhism which is a metaphysic generating a religion.'[13] To which my Cambridge predecessor, Donald MacKinnon, added this gloss: 'If Whitehead is right in speaking of Christianity as a religion perennially in search of a metaphysic, but never able to rest in one, we must also say that faith must ever seek to fulfil itself in vision, yet know that its quest must always ultimately fail, and require to be begun anew.'[14]

Slogans such as Whitehead's are, I know, extremely dangerous, because they so easily become substitutes for, rather than stimulants to, hard thought and disciplined reflection. I would, nevertheless, like to risk a slogan of my own. Physics speaks of structures, of atemporal arrangements. But temporality has structures, too, as all musicians know. If we take metaphysics to mean our general sense and understanding of the structure of the world, beyond particular categories and things and instances, then we might describe as 'metachronics' our attempts to understand the whence and whither of the world, its 'metatemporal' structure beyond particular episodes, epochs, stories and occasions.[15] It is, we

[12] See Lipner's discussion of the translation of *itihasa* by 'epic' (*Hindus*, p. 125). It is not without significance that when, in his discussion of 'remembering', Lipner says that '*smrti* recalls exemplary figures and events of "the past"' (p. 75) the last two words should be in inverted commas.

[13] Alfred North Whitehead, *Religion in the Making* (Cambridge: Cambridge University Press, 1927), pp. 39–40. Whitehead graduated at Cambridge in 1883, the year in which his elder brother, Henry, was appointed Principal of Bishop's College, Calcutta, from which post he went on to become, in 1899, Bishop of Madras (see Gibbs, *Anglican Church in India*, pp. 309–10).

[14] Donald M. MacKinnon, *Themes in Theology. The Three-fold Cord: Essays in Philosophy, Politics and Theology* (Edinburgh: T. & T. Clark, 1987), p. 194.

[15] The proposal is not original. In his 1966 Sarum Lectures, Bishop Christopher Butler spoke of the 'gradual realisation' in ancient Israel 'that the ultimate explanation of history must be found beyond history. This I suggest is analogous

might say, attentiveness to the possibility that world history is <
music and not merely noise.

beware
the
Gods

Christian faith seeks metachronic understanding as the
Hindu quest for wisdom and integrity, I rather think, does not.
But MacKinnon's gloss on Whitehead, with its warning that to
rest in present understanding – ever to suppose that now, at
last, we really 'see' – is fatally to fall victim to illusion, would
nevertheless serve as a reminder of what close cousins
Christianity and Vedantic Hinduism may be in their
insistence on the ambiguity, the provisionality, in some sense
at least the unreality, of all the things we think we know and
are. The difference between them, I am suggesting, lies not
in this but in the different structures of remembrance and
expectation within which this insistence finds expression.

Let me now return to that Upanishad from which I set out:
to the reference to 'the real city of Brahman' as lying beyond
sin, old age and death; a city where we might be free from
sorrow, hunger, thirst.[16] My suggestion is that, at least as
a matter of emphasis where the shaping frameworks of
imagination are concerned, Hindu wisdom has its heart set
deeper down, beyond the surface of the world, whereas the
Christian heart is set beyond this time, beyond the edge of
time, towards the dawning of eternity.

And yet, that unsurpassable particularity of memory which
furnishes Christian faith with its defining centre – the
datability of God's Word's death on Calvary – requires of
Christian hope that it takes time quite seriously, deadly
seriously, for no future is God's future that does not contain all
past and present time, not only held but healed. It follows (as
MacKinnon's gloss on Whitehead reminds us) that God's
future is not a future we can dream of or imagine; it is, rather,
the God-given agenda for our redemptive work.

It is the emphasis, in Christianity, on the ineradicability of

to the internal pressure that drove Aristotle on from the Physics to the Metaphysics
... what metaphysics is to physics, that metachronics is to history' (Christopher
Butler, *The Theology of Vatican II* (London: Darton, Longman and Todd, 1967),
pp. 148–9).

[16] *Chandogya Upanishad*, 8.1.5.

the fact and memory of suffering which generates that sense of
tragedy which (Mascaro suggests) is not found in Sanskrit
literature. And if the stress should now be placed, initially, on
suffering, this is because it is the price paid in pain and bloodshed by the victims which Western myths of 'progress' have
been structured to forget. Nevertheless, that quite specific
and particular memory of suffering which generates and
shapes the Christian understanding is a memory not only of
agony undergone but, even more deeply, beyond that agony, of
the love which brought it and brought through it pain's
promised transformation: Calvary's darkness remembered,
even now, as the Easter daybreak of eternal light.

In a much earlier work than that from which I quoted
previously, Donald MacKinnon wrote: 'Man is brought face to
face with God, not through his effort, but through his failure.
That is the paradox that lies at the very heart of the New
Testament.' Later in the same essay, he spoke of 'the supreme
insight of the distinctively Christian doctrine of God' as being
'the primacy of the divine initiative'.[17] Distinctively Christian,
yes, but not, I think, exclusively so. Although I have been
trying to put my finger on a difference between characteristically Christian and Hindu structures of remembering,
amongst the things these structures have in common is a
recognition that remembrance is of what we have received.
Gift, in both traditions, lies deeper than achievement.

In saying this, I have in mind a passage such as the following,
from the *Katha* and *Mundaka* Upanishads: 'Not by instruction
may this Supreme-Self be gained, nor by intellect, nor by much
scripture-learning. Whomsoever He chooses, by such may He
be gained, to such an one this Supreme-Self reveals His own
reality.' Mascarenhas (whose translation I have used here)
says of this verse: 'Quite certainly, then, these Upanisads
teach a doctrine of divine grace.'[18] It is, surely, the grounded-
ness of truth in gift which, for Christian and Hindu alike,
renders the purification of understanding from the illusory

[17] D. M. MacKinnon, *God the Living and the True* (London: Dacre Press, 1940), pp. 76, 81.
[18] *Katha Upanishad*, 1.2.23; *Mundaka Upanishad*, 3.2.3; Mascarenhas, *Quintessence*, p. 75.

forms with which egotism invests it so peremptory and permanent a task?

DIFFERENCES OF HOPE

The character of remembrance shapes the character of expectation and desire. Differences of memory engender differences of hope. These differences are, of course, not absolute. In Hinduism, as in Christianity, peace and harmony are held out as the hoped-for goal and destiny of all things. And, in some texts, that *moksa* in which our peace and freedom from the travails of this world consists is characterised in terms that come quite close to Christian accounts of 'beatific vision', of knowing even as we are known.[19] Or, at least, this seems to be the case if, for example, it is permissible to interpret the 'I am *Brahman*' of *Brihad-aranyaka Upanishad* 1.4.10 as Mascarenhas does and not (with Julius Lipner) as a statement of '*absolute* identity'.[20]

Such passages, thus read, would then point forward, as it were, to the verse which Zaehner called 'the turning-point and ... watershed' of the Gita: 'And when he sees me in all and he sees all in me, then I never leave him and he never leaves me.'[21] But these waters are too deep for someone with my slight acquaintance with the texts to swim in. What I want to emphasise is the extent to which the construal of passages that speak of peace and harmony as the promised end of human

[19] See 1 Corinthians 13.12 (AV).
[20] See Mascarenhas, *Quintessence*, p. 76: 'This when correctly interpreted in the context of orthodox Hindu tradition according to our exegesis means: "I have realised my principial unity and identity with the Infinite by His divine grace ... My corresponding responsibility is that I must cherish and love all beings even as the Infinite does, since by cognition I am supremely one with the Infinite"'; Lipner, *Hindus*, p. 322, my stress. (I understand that Lipner here stays close to Sankara, whereas Mascarenhas sits near Ramanuja's feet.)
[21] R. C. Zaehner, *The Bhagavad-Gita. With a Commentary based on the Original Sources* (Oxford: Clarendon Press, 1969), p. 27; *Bhagavad Gita*, 6.30. For reasons that I shall indicate in Chapter Three, his later comment, on the same verse, that 'The importance of this stanza can hardly be exaggerated ... it is the great divide between the "pantheistic" and "theistic" portions of the poem' (pp. 234, 235), seems to me too casually to distinguish between the two.

remember the future?

longing is made more difficult by the ambivalence which attends the treatment of desire.

'Desire', says the creation hymn in the *Rig Veda*, 'came upon that one in the beginning; that was the first seed of mind.'[22] According to Panikkar (who translates *kama*, in that passage, as 'love' rather than 'desire'), 'Primordial love is neither a transitive nor an intransitive act . . . it is the constitutive act by which existence came into being. Without love there is no being.'[23] And de Nicolas says that 'Desire is the fountain of creation in Indian philosophy from the Rg Veda through the Upanisads to the Gita.'[24]

Against this, however, we have to set such passages as these:

When all desires that cling to the heart are surrendered, then a mortal becomes immortal . . . When all the ties that bind the heart are unloosened, then a mortal becomes immortal

The wise who, free from desires, adore the Spirit pass beyond the seed of life in death. A man whose mind wanders among desires, and is longing for objects of desire, goes again to life and death according to his desires. But he who possesses the End of all longing, and whose self has found fulfilment, even in this life his desires will fade away.[25]

The ambivalence is, moreover, heightened if we take this with the previous stanza (which I give in Radhakrishnan's translation, the cool tone of which contrasts with Mascaro's lyricism):

Whatever world a man of purified nature thinks of in his mind and whatever desires he desires, all these worlds and all these desires he attains. Therefore, let him who desires prosperity worship the knower of the self.[26]

---

[22] *Rig Veda*, 10.129.4.
[23] Raimundo Panikkar, *The Vedic Experience. Mantramanjari. An Anthology of the Vedas for Modern Man and Contemporary Celebration* (London: Darton, Longman and Todd, 1977), p. 57; cf. p. 58.
[24] De Nicolas, *Gita*, p. 145. It is, admittedly, not *kama* that he is glossing here, but the *yatha icchasi tatha kuru* of *Gita*, 18.63.
[25] *Katha Upanishad*, 2.3.14, 15; *Mundaka Upanishad*, 3.2.1, 2.
[26] *Mundaka Upanishad*, 3.1.10, quoted from Radhakrishnan, *Principal Upanisads*, p. 689. W. B. Yeats and Purohit Swami gave the last phrase cited as: 'but the Self attained, one desire satisfied, all are satisfied' (Bede Griffiths, *Universal Wisdom* (London: Fount, 1994), p. 67).

And if, when we come to the Gita, some passages seem to offer an interpretative thread, by distinguishing appropriate from inappropriate desire, others afford no such easy escape route from the dilemma. Thus, on the one hand, we have Krishna's announcement: 'I am desire when this is pure, when this desire is not against *dharma*.' Elsewhere, however, having told Arjuna that 'All is clouded by desire: as fire by smoke, as a mirror by dust', and that 'Wisdom is clouded by desire, the everpresent enemy of the wise', Krishna commands him: 'Be a warrior and kill desire, the powerful enemy of the soul.'[27]

That love is both the fountain of creation and the enemy of the soul; that all things are created by desire and, by desire, destroyed: these fundamental facts about the world have been familiar, from the beginning, to all the great traditions. And thus it is that to be a Christian or a Hindu, a Muslim or a Buddhist, is to know oneself apprenticed to a school the purpose of whose pedagogy is the purification of desire.

Moreover, notwithstanding the diversity of language and belief, of devotion and philosophy, of spirituality and social ethics, not only among all these traditions but within each one of them, it would be generally agreed that egotism lies at the root of love's destructive power. 'Can that be Love', asked the poet William Blake, 'that drinks another as a sponge drinks water?'[28] Egotism is the inability or refusal to relate, to find one's place, to make one's contribution to the whole. The unquiet self, driven either to dominance or to self-destruction, knows no house, can find no resting-place, no peace. Egotism, in the last resort, is the denial, by the creature, of its created-ness.

When, therefore, I speak of the ambivalence of the treatment of desire in some of the Upanishads and in the Gita, I am not referring to the fact that, in these texts, love works for

---

[27] *Gita*, 7.11; 3.38, 39, 43. It is, however, worth noting that, in 3.38, Winthrop Sargeant has 'As fire is obscured by smoke, And a mirror by dust . . . So the intellect is obscured by *passion*' (my stress).

[28] William Blake, 'Visions of the Daughters of Albion.(7.17)' in *Blake. Complete Writings*, (ed.) Geoffrey Keynes (Oxford: Oxford University Press, 1972), p. 194. I am grateful to Michael Kirwan, SJ, for drawing my attention to this line.

good and ill, for both the wounding and the healing of the world. The ambivalence that I have in mind concerns the outcome rather than the process; attends the question as to whether peace fulfils desire or springs from its suppression.

Consider the contrast between two consecutive verses of the Gita. 'He attains peace into whom all desires flow like water entering the sea' (2.70) – according to Zaehner, this is an image of fulfilment, of desire 'sublimated into tranquillity'. 'The man who abandons all desires, and acts without yearning, without possessiveness, without ego (not making himself to be the doer), he finds peace' (2.71) – this verse Zaehner sees as expressing the 'Buddhistic ideal of the total severance of the temporal (*samsara*) from the eternal (*nirvana*), which in practice means the total *suppression* of desire'.[29]

Does the contrast between these verses need to be drawn *quite* as sharply as Zaehner does, and in quite that manner? I once had the good fortune to visit Borobudur, in Java. To climb those great terraces, moving from the energetic complexity of the reliefs at the lower levels to the still simplicity of the *stupas* at the top, with an ever-broadening vista of the surrounding countryside as one does so, is to wonder whether at least the Buddhism that built *that* place, that seven-storied mountain, was not dedicated rather to the purification and fulfilment than to the 'suppression' of desire. I am now, however, getting out of my depth again, and will step back onto safer ground by saying a word about the way in which, in Christianity, the purification of desire is patterned to discipleship, to the following of Christ.

It is customary to refer to Judaism, Christianity and Islam as 'prophetic' traditions. As such, they are traditions grounded in, directed by, an uttered word. And the prophetic word is heard, in remembrance, for the purification of desire. Its office is, not to predict the future, but to announce God's judgement on the present – although, in that announcement, a promise is

---

[29] *Gita*, 2.70 (de Nicolas); R. C. Zaehner, *The Bhagavad-Gita*, p. 157; *Gita*, 2.71 (de Nicolas; for the penultimate phrase, Zaehner has 'who does not think, "This I am", or "This is mine"'; Zaehner, *Bhagavad-Gita*, p. 158 (his stress)).

declared. Thus, when the one confessed in Christianity as the full flesh and final focus of God's utterance takes up his task, he gathers up the voice of prophecy:

He opened the book and found the place where it was written, 'The Spirit of the Lord is upon me, because he has anointed me to preach the good news to the poor. He has sent me to proclaim release to the captives and recovery of sight to the blind, to set at liberty those who are oppressed . . . ' And he closed the book, and gave it back to the attendant, and sat down; and the eyes of all in the synagogue were fixed on him. And he began to say to them, 'Today this scripture has been fulfilled in your hearing.'[30]

Christian discipleship, understood as obedience to the Word made flesh, as the following of Christ, seeks not to stifle or suppress desire, but to release it from the chains which bind it in egotism's nervous and oppressive grasp. And if the more prudent strands in Christian tradition have been as reluctant as Vedantic Hinduism to attempt the contradictory task of depicting unimaginable bliss,[31] there is no doubt that the specificity of Christian memory finds its counterpart in the assurance that all desire will find fulfilment in the life of one remembered as crucified and risen; that he is 'the first fruits of those who have fallen asleep'.[32]

THE DESIRE OF GOD

To speak of 'the desire of God' is to speak ambiguously, because the phrase may mean either our desire of God or God's desire of us. We might say that the Christian project of discipleship, conceived as lifelong schooling in the purification of desire, is a matter of discovering that, whatever we desire, our desiring of it is only the desire of God in the measure that it is conformed to and transformed by God's previous desire of us. Our yearning, purified, shares in that yearning from which the world is made.

But surely, according to Christian tradition, the world is

---

[30] Luke 4.17–21.
[31] See Lipner, *Hindus*, p. 323.   [32] 1 Corinthians 15.20.

made *ex nihilo*, out of nothing? Yes, indeed, but this does not make the world a barren woman's son but, rather, the child of absolutely pure desire.[33] To acknowledge primordial love to be the 'act by which existence came into being' is thereby to recognise that it is out of pure desire, disinterested love, that everything is made. Moreover, in discovering that this is what the world is made of, we thereby learn the way we have to go, the path our ethics and our politics are required to follow, for all things must be made to be the way that they are made to be: in love.

My aim, in thus introducing the topic of the love of God, is to undercut accounts of love which, antithetically contrasting the love which constitutes and heals the world, on the one hand, with the creature's sinful striving, on the other, have ruled out as inappropriate all talk of divine 'desire'. Thus, for example, Christians have sometimes spoken as if the love of creatures were a distraction from the love of God; as if the discipline of growing in the love of God were a matter of learning to love creatures less – even (in some versions) of learning to hold them in contempt. And yet, it is not for us to love the creature less than the Creator does who cherishes all things into being with infinite expenditure of interest and care.

Rather than speak of two contrasting loves, it would seem better simply to speak of love in all its different forms, each one requiring, in its own way, the purification which conforms the giving of the gift to the requirement of the person, time, and place, expecting nothing in return.[34]

Dichotomies of divine and human love are usually dependent on some version of the spirit–matter dualisms that have so deeply marked the modern mind. This may, therefore, be an appropriate point at which to register my regret at some of the ways in which these dualisms appear to influence the uses of 'spirit' by translators into English of, and commentators on, the Upanishads and the Gita. This influence is traceable in the

---

[33] On 'the barren woman's son' as the epitome of 'absolute nothing' (*atyantabhava*), see Mascarenhas, *Quintessence*, p. 52.

[34] See *Bhagavad Gita*, 17.20.

range of different notions that 'spirit' is made to represent. This is especially true in Mascaro's translations, in which the term is sometimes a suggestive rendering to which no one word in the Sanskrit corresponds;[35] sometimes directly characterises that which the text austerely indicates by indirection;[36] sometimes translates *atman* or *purusa*.[37] Sometimes 'spirit' translates *prana*, the breath of living things;[38] at other times – as with Zaehner's rendering of *Yogi* as 'athletes of the spirit' – it is doing very different duty.[39]

The fact that one word, 'spirit', is used to translate several different Sanskrit terms is not, in itself, the problem. After all, 'spirit', in English, has a range of sense which takes it all the way from whisky to the ethos of a nation, from liveliness to the holy mystery that creates the world. The difficulty arises, rather, from the tendency to take the term as categorical description of (to put it crudely) a kind of stuff. Fine stuff, to be sure, thin, conscious stuff; stuff most unlike the lumps of stuff that we call 'matter'. Thus Zaehner describes the philosophy of *Samkhya* as a 'dualism of spirit and matter'; Mascaro speaks

---

[35] See, for example, his translation of *Maitri Upanishad*, 2.3–5, and *Gita*, 2.1. The latter, which Mascaro gives as 'Then arose the Spirit of Krishna and spoke to Arjuna, his friend, who with eyes filled with tears, thus had sunk into despair and grief', Sargeant renders: 'To him thus overcome by pity, despairing, Whose eyes were filled with tears and downcast, Krishna spoke these words.'

[36] Compare Mascaro's translation of *Gita*, 2.17, with Zaehner's. Where Mascaro has: 'Interwoven in his creation, the Spirit is beyond destruction. No one can bring to an end the Spirit which is everlasting', Zaehner has: 'Yes, indestructible [alone] is that [*tad*], – know this, – by which this whole universe was spun [*tatam*]: no one can bring destruction on that which does not pass away.' Similarly, where Radhakrishnan has: 'That [*tad*] which is hidden in the Upanisads which are hidden in the Vedas...', in *Svetasvatara Upanishad*, 5.6 (*Principal Upanisads*, p. 739), Mascaro prefers 'There is a Spirit hidden in the mystery of the *Upanishads* and the *Vedas*.'

[37] See *Gita*, 3.17, 6.5. The latter example is especially unfortunate: 'Arise therefore! And with the help of thy Spirit lift up thy soul: allow not thy soul to fall. For thy soul can be thy friend, and thy soul can be thine enemy.' Compare Kees W. Bolle's version: 'Man should discover his own reality and not thwart himself. For he has the self as his only friend, or as his only enemy' (quoted from Griffiths, *Universal Wisdom*, p. 122), or, with less reductive emphasis, that of Winthrop Sargeant: 'One should uplift oneself by the Self; One should not degrade oneself; For the Self alone can be a friend to oneself, And the Self alone can be an enemy of oneself.'

[38] In *Maitri Upanishad*, 6.19, Mascaro has 'spirit of life' where Radhakrishnan had 'breathing spirit'.

[39] See *Gita*, 6.27, 28. This time, Mascaro is more reticent, and has simply 'Yogi'.

lost in translation

of 'the chains that bind us to matter', and Lipner speaks of the
familiar world of space and time, the world of *prakrti*, as 'non-
spiritual', in contrast to the still, timeless, blissful world of 'the
spiritual (usually called *purusa* or *atman*)'.[40]

My difficulty is that such accounts of what does and does not
count as 'matter', or as 'spirit' – and I am speaking not of the
texts that are being interpreted, but of the tools used for their
interpretation – owe more to the thought-world of seventeenth-century Europe than they do to either Aristotle or the
Bible. Whereas the Bible knows the difference between
the spirit (which is not in our control) by which all things are
made to breathe and live and be, and the spirit's absence,
which is desert, deadness and decay; and Aristotle knows the
difference between the possibility of things and the different
ways in which these possibilities are given form and actuality;
the seventeenth-century imagination knew only things of two
different kinds: the kind you measure – which John Locke
called 'bare incogitative matter'[41] – and the kind (called
'mind' or 'spirit') that does the measuring.

My point is simply that the Teape Lecturer's task of
entering into conversation with the ancient Indian texts is
made more difficult by the extent to which the ghosts of a
long-dead epistemology still shroud the translations in a kind
of mist. Upadhyay may have deplored the influence on Indian
education of nineteenth-century British Hegelianism, but I
have the impression that, notwithstanding the fact that
Hegel's own view of all things Indian 'epitomizes the
European claims to "understand" and supercede India and
the Orient',[42] his non-dualistic treatment of *Geist*, or spirit,
and of spirit's appearance in the world, might well serve as a

---

[40] Zaehner, *Bhagavad-Gita*, p. 171; Mascaro, *Upanishads*, p. 18; Lipner, 'On woman and
salvation in Hinduism: paradoxes of ambivalence' in Ninian Smart and Shivesh
Thakur (eds.), *Ethical and Political Dilemmas of Modern India* (London: Macmillan,
1993), p. 166.

[41] John Locke, *An Essay Concerning Human Understanding*, Bk. IV, Ch. 10 para.10, quoted
from Edward Craig, *The Mind of God and the Works of Man* (Oxford: Clarendon Press,
1987), p. 41.

[42] Halbfass, *India and Europe*, p. 434. For an excellent survey of Hegel's reading of
India, and of the Indian reception of Hegel, see Halbfass, pp. 84–99.

more helpful philosophical interlocutor in conversations between students of the Hindu and the Christian Scriptures than some of the other European systems used have proved to be.

Hegel did, after all, not only attempt to restore 'the sense of the continuity of living things which [had been] damaged by Cartesianism', but he did so in the course of striving for an account of God, or Spirit, as never existing 'separately from the universe which he sustains and in which he manifests himself', and he offered an account of the universe which required it both to be grasped as something like 'a life-form' and to 'be read as something analogous to a text in which God says what he is'.[43] Before we sink into the quicksands of Hegelian metaphysics, however, let me return to the main thread of my reflections, on the love of God.

That, as our end and destiny, we are promised peace – the gathering into one circle of the scattered rays of light, the stillness of the ocean's depth[44] – is, as we saw earlier, something that we learn; in learning it, we discover that we are desired by God. This quite extraordinary insight which, from Deuteronomy to the Fourth Gospel, is central to the message of the Jewish and the Christian Scriptures, does not seem far from the lesson that Arjuna learns in hearing Krishna's whispered word, 'I love you well'; learning it, he is enabled in tranquillity to declare, 'I shall act according to your word.'[45]

Two questions immediately arise: how might this discovery be made, and what form does God's desiring take? The urgency of the first question arises from the deepening deterioration of the planet's plight. As a thickening web of economic power – largely exercised beyond accountability to

---

[43] Charles Taylor, *Hegel* (Cambridge: Cambridge University Press, 1975), pp. 83, 87, 88.

[44] See *Prasna Upanishad*, 4.2, 6.5. A detailed comparison of upanishadic and New Testament eschatology would have to consider whether the rivers' loss of 'name' and 'form', as they flow into the ocean, amounts to fulfilment or to extinction of identity. In which context, it might be useful to keep in mind Felix Wilfred's observation that 'In the Indian approach to the universal, what is common to all rivers would be not so much riverness as the ocean' (*Dusty Soil*, p. 25).

[45] *Gita*, 18.64 (Zaehner), 18.73 (Bolle).

nation-states – tightens its grip upon the world, exhausting non-renewable resources and driving millions further into destitution and towards despair, how might the victims of the system learn themselves desired by God, find in Gethsemane their agony's compassion? In such thick darkness, how might God's stillness radiate as joy?

In 1945, Bill Lash visited England for the first time in ten years. From conversations there, he was encouraged by a sense of dawning recognition that nothing less than the whole of humankind must be acknowledged as 'the unit . . . in looking forward to the future'.[46] That this post-war recognition has faded again, in England, during the intervening fifty years does not diminish its validity. The heart of the relationship between the human world and God, according to the Gospel, can find expression in the simple formula: 'we have been made capable of friendship' (where the passive form announces this capacity as grace, as given in the fact of God's desiring, and the range of reference of 'we' is unrestricted; it refers to everyone).[47] Of course, we can only *learn* this in particular places, as particular communities of generosity arise. It is only in particulars that universals live. In that note from 1945, Bishop Lash observed that 'people cannot be organised in groups larger than those of which they are conscious of being a part'.

Let me remind you that the question I am considering is: how might the discovery be made that we are desired by God? Technically, this is a question about the intelligibility of the doctrine of the incarnation; of God's self-presence in the Crucified. And what I am trying to indicate is that the question is answered, the intelligibility is given, in the form of friendship. Friendship – and this word can bear so much more weight than we usually seem prepared to put upon it – is the human form that God's love takes.[48] This, I think, is what the Sri Lankan theologian Aloysius Pieris means when he says that, in

---

[46] In Bishop Lash's papers, there is a sixteen-page typescript note, entitled 'England revisited'.
[47] See below, Chapter Eleven, pp. 212–14.
[48] See Lash, *Believing Three Ways*, pp. 74–5.

Asia, 'The first meaningful christological formula – one that would . . . make sense to Christians and non-Christians alike . . . is an authentically Asian church.' It is through the birth of particular communities of friendship, of what he calls 'little laboratories of hope', that 'christologies will be born in Asia'.[49]

I am reminded of an undated sermon of Bill Lash's, on the incarnation, entitled 'The divine condescension':

Returning at the beginning of November from Calcutta I stopped for twenty-four hours at Wardha. There I was taken to visit the extremely simple Ashram made in the quarters of the depressed classes. I asked my conductor what the Ashramites were doing for the Harijans among whom they were living. 'At present', he answered, 'we are giving them their neighbourhood.'

HARMONY AND HEALING

A little earlier I asked two questions: how might the discovery of God's desire be made, and what form does God's desiring take? My characterisation of friendship as the human form that God's love takes might seem to answer both of them. And yet, the failure to distinguish between them has too often led to their being considered in ways that at best ignore and at worst reinforce the conditions which perpetuate the destitution of the dispossessed, for it is one thing to know that we have been made capable of the friendship that is God's love's human form, and quite another to know how best to move to friendship from the exploitation and neglect that characterise our present situation.

One has only to make the obvious remark that those whom Gandhi called 'Harijans', or 'begotten of God', are now known as 'Dalit', the oppressed, to be reminded of the importance and the delicacy of the issues. Despised or chosen? God's elect or victims of oppression? In one form or another, such

---

[49] Aloysius Pieris, SJ, *An Asian Theology of Liberation* (Edinburgh: T. & T. Clark, 1988), pp. 63–4. See Sebastian Painadath's description of the 'ashrams of the future' as 'sacramental communities of the spiritual unity of humanity' ('Ashrams: a movement of spiritual integration' in Christian Duquoc and Gustavo Gutiérrez (eds.), *Mysticism and the Institutional Crisis. Concilium*, 1994/4, 45).

questions silence easy speech and self-indulgent piety in every culture and tradition.

Consider the difference between Luke's version of the Sermon on the Mount, and Matthew's. 'Blessed are you poor', says Luke, 'for yours is the kingdom of God.' In contrast, Matthew's version reads, 'Blessed are the poor in spirit, for theirs is the kingdom of heaven.'[50] Are these two groups the same? Does Matthew blunt the edge of Luke's clear 'preferential option'? Is poverty 'in spirit' an attitude of mind, or faith's acknowledgement of God's presence in the poor?

My business, now, is not the exegesis of these texts, which I mention for two reasons. First, the history of their interpretation serves as a reminder of how ancient the tradition is, in Christianity as in Hinduism, of acknowledging the close connection between holiness and dispossession; from which, in both traditions, arises the high value set on voluntary poverty. In the second place, however, both traditions have proved skilful at evading, in practice and in theory, the social and political implications of what Christians call God's preference for the poor.

At the beginning of the Gita, Arjuna's heart is troubled; by the end, he has discovered peace. It is not, then, perhaps surprising that de Nicolas, in his commentary, should speak of truth as '*quiet*[*ing*] our anxiety', and of the importance of disciplined commitment to a programme of '*soothing* radical needs'.[51] Nevertheless, the language is embarrassing in its implied individualism: it is my duty, surely, to meet my neighbour's needs, not merely 'soothe' them?

Our peace is God's desire. In thus acknowledging God's promised peace to be our destiny, are we to set our hearts on harmony, or on the healing of our present ills? On acceptance of the circumstance in which we find ourselves, or on resistance to injustice? Thus abstractly formulated, the questions are, of course, unreal. Discernment of the different ways in which the stern and simultaneous requirements of peace and justice are configured requires – in each new set

---

[50] Luke 6.20; Matthew 5.3.   [51] De Nicolas, *Gita*, p. 21 (my emphases).

of circumstances – fresh consideration, fresh decision, different enactment. And yet this recognition that, as Thomas Aquinas put it, generalisations in matters of ethics are of minimal utility, because actions are particular, is hardly the end of the matter.[52]

Thus, for example, what George Soares-Prabhu describes as the 'religious basis for social justice' established in Judaism and Christianity, according to which the poor are to be seen not as 'the passive victims of history but [as] those through whom God shapes his history',[53] as the instruments and privileged bearers of God's healing peace, does, admittedly, have no obvious counterpart in the Gita. There, in Chapter Five, we read that 'Men who can hold their thought in such balance have overcome the world of birth right here. God is flawless and in balance, so they live in God.' Here, holiness is, perhaps, not stoic resignation, but a matter of having succeeded in so purifying desire of egotism as to be in harmony unshaken either by pleasure or by pain.[54] And Bolle's translation of Gita 2.70 (which I quoted earlier in de Nicolas' version) runs: 'The sea gathers the waters; it fills and fills itself . . . Its equilibrium is undisturbed. So also the man into whom all desires enter – not he who goes after desires – finds peace'.

At first sight, this is so different a world of thought from that of the Sermon on the Mount – let alone from that of Amos or Isaiah! – that comparison would be quite pointless. And yet, if we keep in mind not only the distinction between voluntary poverty, dispossession undertaken in discipleship, and the poverty created and imposed by the avarice and power of others, but also the central place which something not unlike the former occupies in the spirituality of the Gita, then we can, I think, begin to see why Aloysius Pieris should argue that the 'religiousness of the poor' may be 'the locus for a theology of liberation in Asia'.[55] In other words, in poverty appropriated as

---

[52] See Prologue to Thomas Aquinas, *Summa theologiae*, IIa.IIae.

[53] George M. Soares-Prabhu, 'Class in the Bible: the biblical poor, a social class?', *Vidyajyoti*, 49 (1985), 327, 345 (quoted from Pieris, *Asian Theology*, pp. 122, 123).

[54] *Gita* (Bolle), 5.19; see 5.20.   [55] Pieris, *Asian Theology*, p. 124; see p. 88.

prophetic utterance, as the holy form and presence of God's desire for all creation's justifying harmony, the biblical and upanishadic streams may flow together towards the ocean of God's peace.

THE APPEARANCE OF THE HOLY

Bearing in mind John Clayton's warning that our goals are constituted by the paths we choose towards them,[56] I do not want to exaggerate the similarities between, for example, biblical accounts of promised peace and that presented in the Gita. The differences between them may be indicated by the different stories that they tell of God's appearance in the world.

'Only by love can men see me, and know me, and come unto me', says Krishna to Arjuna.[57] There are echoes here (which Mascaro's translation is, I rather think, designed to highlight) of that God-given love which, according to the Fourth Gospel, opens human eyes, enabling us to see the glory of the Son.[58]

Krishna's statement comes at the end of that remarkable eleventh chapter, the 'manifestation of the world form', which Zaehner calls 'the climax of the Gita'.[59] What Arjuna sees is a theophany and, seeing it, he sees the Holy One as he really is, 'in all his terrifying majesty'.[60] There are, indeed, in the Bible, disclosures of God's beauty, power and might, though none, perhaps, that match the detailed awe-inspiring majesty of Arjuna's vision. For the most part, however, theophany in the Bible develops in a different direction. Whereas Krishna's whispering masks his glory's form, the whisper which Elijah hears signals God's presence – which was absent from the storm and wind and fire, the elements of traditional theophany.

There is, we might say, a straight line from the whisper

---

[56] See Clayton, 'Jefferson and the Study of Religion', p. 23, quoted above, p. 19.
[57] *Gita*, 11.54. [58] See (e.g.) John 17.
[59] Zaehner, *Gita*, p. 303; the title of the chapter is from de Nicolas.
[60] Zaehner, *Gita*, p. 303.

which Elijah hears to the silence in Gethsemane and Jesus' dying cry on Calvary. These are theophanies, disclosures of God as he really is, unveilings of a most surprising kind of majesty and power, whose form we count as weakness. Krishna's human form is shown to be a temporary disguise whereas what is seen on Calvary discloses the true nature of divinity – though it is only in the light of Easter that we can see that this is so. Bill Lash did not, I think, exaggerate when, in his sermon on divine condescension, he described the incarnation as revealing 'Divine Glory in a way which is exactly opposite to the way in which Lord Krishna is fabled to have revealed Divine Glory in the *Bhagavad-Gita*'.

This is, I think, correct. Yet, once again, it is not the whole story, nor is it the only thing that needs to be said. To move the conversation on, we would need rather more directly to address the most difficult and important question in the world: namely, where may our human hearts alone be set for all things' peace and freedom, friendship and fulfilment? In the next lecture, therefore, I shall offer some reflections on the doctrine of God.

What form does God's desire for our fulfilment take? The answer I have so far given is: friendship. To which, in conclusion, we must now add that friendship, reconciliation, springs - according to the Christian story – from what we count as failure, for it is through blood spilt in rejection of love's invitation that, and in spite of which, love's promised peace is made.[61]

Beyond illusion, and the noise of war, we (like Arjuna) need to see God as he is. But, 'When we so see him, we are at first shocked that his face is marred above the sons of men. But as he confronts us, we are enabled to see of what stuff we ourselves are. Then no longer does it surprise us that there is no beauty that *we* should *desire him*.'[62] Remembrance of the

---

[61] See Colossians 1.20.

[62] MacKinnon, *God the Living and the True*, pp. 88–9 (his emphases); cf. Isaiah 53.2: God's servant 'had no form or comeliness that we should look at him, and no beauty that we should desire him'. At the end of the table of contents, in my copy of MacKinnon's little book, a slip of paper has been pasted. Holding the page up to the

Crucified is, indeed, distinctively Christian. But the insight
that the road to the knowledge of God lies through endless and
often painful revision of self-estimation, through the ceaseless
correction and purification of desire, is, I think, also well
known to students of the Gita.

light, we read: 'Suggestions for further study'. Turning to the end, however, we find
a handful of blank pages. I do not know what last-minute editorial or authorial
change of mind brought this about, but it provides us with a kind of parable. In
place of footnotes, apparatus, conventional display of erudition: white paper, a
space, containing something that is not said and is, perhaps, unstatable. Those who
knew the author will appreciate the poignancy of the suggestion.

CHAPTER 3

Reality, wisdom and delight

LEARNING NOT TO WORSHIP THINGS

In a paper written in December 1863, but unpublished in his lifetime, John Henry Newman reflected on what we are doing when we try to speak of God. We know, of course, that all our words and thoughts and images are quite inadequate to the task but, says Newman,

We can only remedy their insufficiency by confessing it. We can do no more than put ourselves on the guard as to our own proceeding, and protest against it, while we do adhere to it. We can only set right one error of expression by another. By this method of antagonism we steady our minds, not so as to reach their object, but to point them in the right direction; as in an algebraical process we might add and subtract in series, approximating little by little, by saying and unsaying, to a positive result.[1]

It is taken for granted, in sophisticated circles, that no one worships God these days except the reactionary and the simple-minded. This innocent self-satisfaction tells us little more, however, than that those exhibiting it do not name as 'God' the gods they worship.

In fact, whatever names we give to things, we worship things (especially ourselves) as naturally and as spontaneously as we

---

[1] John Henry Newman, *The Theological Papers of John Henry Newman. On Faith and Certainty,* partly prepared for publication by Hugo M. de Achaval; selected and edited by J. Derek Holmes (Oxford: Clarendon Press, 1976), p. 102. John Coulson took the phrase 'We can only set . . . positive result' as the motto for his study of *Religion and Imagination* (Oxford: Clarendon Press, 1981), where, for a discussion of the passage, see p. 64.

breathe and speak.[2] We have no option but to have our hearts set somewhere, to hold something sacred. The question is not *whether* we shall worship but in what direction our hearts might be set – for destruction, or for all things' peace and freedom, friendship and fulfilment? Some god or gods will hold our hearts, serve as the centre of our sacrifice – but what?

We worship things as naturally as we breathe and speak. But that is the problem – untutored, we set our hearts on *things*: on forces, elements, ideas; on people, dreams and institutions; on the world or on some item of its furnishing. We are spontaneously idolatrous. And so it is that, in their different ways, the great traditions that we call 'religions' have served as schools in which we seek some education from idolatry.

In taking the question of the ways we speak of God as the focus for this lecture, I hope not only to display affinities between what Newman called a 'method of antagonism' and the tradition of the Upanishads, but also to show how the dialectic of 'saying and unsaying' towards 'a positive result' is, in its Christian versions, grounded in the doctrine of God's Trinity. It is, I hope, hardly necessary to add that, in Christian as in Hindu thought, consideration of how God might be named, far from being a merely academic exercise, is at the heart of the religious quest. As an integral component of our education from idolatry, it is one face of the coin whose other side we have already considered under the rubric of the purification of desire. To set our minds and hearts upon that which 'cannot be spoken with words . . . whereby words are spoken' is, after all, to set out upon the 'path of wisdom'.[3]

Perhaps the best place to begin is with the elementary observation that the word 'god' is not a proper name.[4] It is the

---

[2] See the reference, in *Kaushitaki Upanishad*, 2.5, to the 'two never-ending immortal offerings of man'.

[3] *Kena Upanishad*, 2.4; *Katha Upanishad*, 2.4.

[4] Notwithstanding the fact that Jews, Christians and Muslims do also confess the name 'God' to be proper to One alone. For an excellent guide through the minefield, see David B. Burrell's discussion of 'the nature of divinity' in his *Knowing the Unknowable God: Ibn-Sina, Maimonides, Aquinas* (Notre Dame: University of Notre Dame Press, 1986), pp. 35–50.

common name for whatever people worship, whatever people take to be divine. And 'being divine' is not like being fat or thin, being British or being short-sighted. It is more like being heard or seen. Something is heard or seen if someone hears or sees it. Something is divine if someone worships it. As Raimundo Panikkar once put it, 'The idea of worship is inherent within the concept of God ... [and in that sense] God is not God by himself; he is so only for and hence *through* the creature.'[5] Not that our worship gives anything to God: it exhibits, it does not constitute, God's glory.

In contemporary uses of the word 'god', there is a common carelessness which takes two forms. On the one hand, we find it far too easy to label as 'gods' whatever *other* people worship and, on the strength of this ascription, to judge such people to be 'polytheists'. Whereas, of course, although 'we' reverence, cherish, hold in high respect and worthy of devotion a great diversity of people, values, things, ideas and dreams, we suppose ourselves to worship only that which *we* call 'god'. Thus, for example, we have already seen that the term 'polytheism' was coined, in the seventeenth century, to indicate that Indian ritual practices were really no better than the superstitions of Catholicism![6]

What, then, shall we call 'divine', identify as 'gods'? The choice lies along a spectrum at one end of which all kinds of courtesy and reverence, awe, respect and veneration are collapsed together, indiscriminately: all estimable things are 'gods' and all of us are polytheists. Although much European writing on Indian culture has tended in this direction, I can see little to be said in favour of it – except in so far as it may serve polemically to indicate that it is not so easy as modern secularism complacently supposes to worship no god whatsoever. One could go further. Whereas the notion of idolatry, of worshipping false gods, of taking some creature to be God,

---

[5] Raimundo Panikkar, *The Trinity and the Religious Experience of Man: Icon – Person – Mystery* (New York and London: Orbis Books and Darton, Longman and Todd, 1973), p. 26; he quotes, with approval, the fifth-century formulary, the *Fides Damasi*, to the effect that 'Deus' is 'nomen potestatis non proprietatis' (p. xiii).

[6] See above, Chapter One, pp. 14–15.

at least makes sense, the idea of worshipping many gods at once is less obviously intelligible. Our hearts may well be scattered and confused, but can they really be set in adoration absolutely, 'wholeheartedly', on more than one object at a time? The question is intended to be philosophical rather than anthropological, but I notice with interest that Julius Lipner does not believe that 'the Sanskritic tradition has ever advocated polytheism proper'.[7]

At the other end, Christians and Hindus, though approaching the matter in very different ways, and from different directions, might agree to keep the word 'God' holy by using it only for that unfathomable mystery with which no individual, no image, person, power, fact or thing, neither the world nor all the wonders of the world, may simply be identified. Thus, Mascarenhas' reading of the *Chandogya Upanishad* encourages me to suppose that even the resonant, reiterated 'Thou art that' need not be taken to deny that 'the Infinite . . . inasmuch as it is the Infinite, absolutely transcends my individuality'.[8]

I shall shortly say something about dualisms and non-dualisms. My present purpose is simply to urge that it is good manners, as well as good theology, to use the word 'God' – with or without an initial capital – as carefully, and sparingly, as possible. (As a small parable of courtesy, I would mention the little guide to Elephanta which my grandfather published in 1923. Whereas so many of the guidebooks speak, quite casually, of 'gods' and 'goddesses', my grandfather more prudently refers to: 'the imposing figure of the "Trimurti" or three *powers*'.[9] A small point but not, I think, quite insignificant.)

I spoke earlier of *two* common forms of carelessness, where uses of the word 'god' are concerned. People who find it easy to

[7] Lipner, *Hindus*, pp. 304–5.
[8] See *Chandogya Upanishad*, 6.8.7; 9.4; 10.3; 11.3; 12.3; 13.3; 14.3; 15.3; 16.3; Mascarenhas, *Quintessence*, p. 75. Radhakrishnan glosses *tat tvam asi*: 'This famous text emphasises the divine nature of the human soul' which, while neatly sidestepping some of the exegetical difficulties, seems to offer a philosophical account of what Christian tradition would speak of, theologically, as the indwelling of God's Spirit.
[9] N. A. Lash, *Elephanta*, p. 2 (my stress).

be certain that foreigners and strangers worship *many* gods also too often take for granted that it would be a simple matter not to worship any god at all. They suppose atheism to be as easy an option for the cultured in our world as religious belief is (they imagine) for the simple-minded. This view might be plausible if being an atheist were simply a matter of not believing there to be, outside the world we know, a large or powerful thing or being falling under some appropriate category of description (in other words, a creature of an unusual and impressive kind). But if, by 'God', we do not mean a thing of any kind, but only the holy mystery that we may mention but may never fix within the categories of our understanding, the mystery of all things breathing out of nothing into peace; if, in other words, we follow the 'methods of antagonism' with which (for instance) the classic forms of Judaism, Christianity and Islam have tried to forge their different grammars for good uses of the word, then things are not so simple. If God creates the world, then all things, all the world's constituents, have to do with God, in every move and fragment of their being, whether they notice this and suppose it to be so or not. Atheism, if it means not having anything to do with God, is thus self-contradictory and, if successful, would be absolutely self-destructive.

DUALISMS AND DIFFERENCES

In the confused condition of contemporary European culture, generalisation is a risky business. Nevertheless, it seems fairly safe to say that 'dualism' has more enemies these days than friends. But what does 'dualism' mean? The question is difficult to answer in the abstract because antipathy to dualism has become so ingrained a habit as to hide from view, beneath a mist of imprecision, its many different forms.

Let us suppose that, as a working definition, we were to settle for: an insistence on the irreducibility of some distinction or another. Would this make dualists of all those who insist that it is truth, not untruth, that obtains the victory, or that we must choose between 'two paths ... the path of wisdom and the path of ignorance', a way of freedom and a way of slavery?[10] This is not, I think, as the term 'dualism' is usually taken and yet, as I indicated in the previous chapter, biblical distinctions between 'flesh' and 'spirit' (which *are* quite often referred to nowadays as dualistic) are, for the most part, of this kind.[11]

Perhaps we might describe as dualists people who suppose that the distinction between the human body and the human mind is a distinction between two 'things' of different kinds. Some such view undoubtedly distinguishes Cartesians (as we might call them) from Aristotelians, for whom one body and one soul add up, not to two things of any kind, but to one living organism.

There is, however, one distinction the irreducibility of which is – quite simply – of *absolute* importance, and that is the distinction between, on the one hand, all the differences and distinctions in the world and, on the other, the distinction between the world and God. (Does my insistence on the irreducibility of this distinction make me, then, a dualist? On my initial definition, yes; but that just shows how important it is to be attentive to the different kinds of dualism that there are.)

All other distinctions, except that between the world and God, arise within the world and may be mapped by language and imagination. This one, alone, may not. And that is why it is so difficult to speak appropriately of God. The modern label 'negative theology' is surely most misleading.[12] It fails to indicate that (to put the point in Christian terminology) it is positive recognition of God's *holiness* which generates the

---

[10] See *Mundaka Upanishad*, 3.1.6 ('satyam eva jayate', 'truth obtains victory', the Indian national motto); *Katha Upanishad*, 1.2.4; cf. Deuteronomy 11.26–8.

[11] See above, Chapter Two, p. 40.

[12] So far as I can make out, none of the distinguished contributors to a conference held in the University of Sydney, in 1981, on 'the history and significance of negative theology' *noticed* the newness of the phrase, because they seem simply to have taken for granted that it was identical, in sense and connotation, to notions such as 'apophatic theology' and *via negativa* or 'way of negation'. See D. W. Dockrill and Raoul Mortley (eds.), *The Via Negativa*, supplementary number of *Prudentia* (Auckland: University of Auckland, 1981).

insistent habits of denial, the different 'methods of antagonism', that are at the heart of the developed discourses of not
only Judaism and Platonism, Christianity and Islam, but also
(it would seem) at least some currents of Buddhism and the
Vedanta.[13]

Draw a distinction, any distinction, within the world, and its
terms will add up either to one thing or to two. But, as
Panikkar succinctly puts it: 'God *and* the world are neither one
nor two.' I therefore sympathise with Mascarenhas' irritation
at 'Western scholars' who 'translate *advaita* by "monism"'.[14]
'Absolute non-twoness', which he seems to favour, may not
be stylistically felicitous but is, I think, somewhat less misleading.

How does the distinction between the world and God, not
itself being a distinction that lies within the world, nevertheless make its appearance in the world?[15] There is a well-known
and reputable case to be made for the view that it is different
answers to this question which differentiate the prophetic
traditions, of Judaism, Christianity and Islam, on the one
hand, from, on the other, Buddhism and Vedantic Hinduism.
Although this view does undoubtedly have something to be
said for it, I would like – very tentatively – to make a slightly
different suggestion.

In her Teape Lectures for 1989, Sister Sara Grant said that
both Sankara and Aquinas 'were non-dualists, understanding
the relation of the universe, including individual selves, to
uncreated Being in terms of a non-reciprocal relation of
dependence'. With that I have no quarrel. Later on, however,
she said that coming to terms with 'the advaita of
Sankaracarya' had left her with problems regarding some
'traditional formulations of Christian faith', amongst which
she listed: 'our dualistic way of thinking and speaking about

---

[13] See Sister Sara Grant's comments on Sankara in her discussion of 'The source of
theology' in her 1989 Teape Lectures, *Towards an Alternative Theology. Confessions of a
Non-dualist Christian* (Bangalore: Asian Trading Corporation, 1991), pp. 42–3.

[14] Panikkar, *The Trinity*, p. 36, his stress; Mascarenhas, *Quintessence*, p. 89.

[15] This question forms the focus of David Burrell's brilliant study, *Knowing the
Unknowable God*.

God as somehow "over against us", as an ultimate Object *or even Thou*'.[16]

How does the distinction between the world and God make its appearance in the world? The classic Christian answer to this question, an answer which follows the contours of the creeds, would be some version of: in life lived in justice, harmony and obedient attentiveness.

'Thou' may be uttered in many different ways, some of them as silent as God's utterance on Calvary. But a form of life which lacked all sense of responding utterance – of attentiveness, in wonder, to constitutive address – would not, I think, be Christian at all. I would be surprised, in fact, if Sara Grant were seriously to disagree with this: it seems clear, from the context, that what she had in mind were crudely literal construals of the 'conversation' between the mystery of God and humankind.

In explaining my decision to give to the opening chapter of a little book on the Apostles' Creed the perhaps surprising title of 'Amen', I said: ' "Amen" comes after, even when . . . we set it at the start, because our utterance of it is acknowledgement of God's "Amen", which always goes before.' To which I added that 'The recognition of God's integrity or truthfulness, unswerving faithfulness in execution of his promises, is so central to Judaism's faith that "Amen" may almost be taken as a name for God.'[17]

'Amen' means 'Yes'. According to Mascaro, 'One of the meanings of OM is YES. Brahman, Atman, OM, is the positive truth, the Yes, of all.'[18] I am not competent to evaluate this reading, which seems designed to bring the sense of 'OM' as close as possible to that of 'Amen'.[19] It is, however, my impression that, as expounded in the *Mandukya Upanishad*, the sense of 'OM' is suspended – as that of 'Amen', in Jewish and

---

[16] Grant, *Alternative Theology*, pp. 47–8, 55, 56 (my stress). To which last passage she added a note: 'This obviously is not to deny the existence of God as a reality independent of the thinking mind' (p. 89).

[17] Lash, *Believing Three Ways*, p. 3.   [18] Mascaro, *Gita*, p. 14.

[19] An association which Radhakrishnan makes explicitly: see his *Principal Upanisads*, p. 615.

Christian usage, is not – between a reading which would
require it to be taken as address, as 'Thou', and a sense which
would discourage and, perhaps, prevent this.[20]

In Chapter One, I suggested that Anselm's distinction
between soliloquy and allocution, monologue and address,
captured the heart of the distinction between philosophical
investigation and even the most intellectually strenuous and
conceptually rigorous instances of theological reflection.[21] In
the present context, might we not say that it is the business
of theology, rather than philosophy, to say 'Thou'? My
suggestion, then, would be that, in terms of Anselm's
distinction, texts such as the *Mandukya Upanishad* are open to,
but do not require, theological construal. How, then, does the
distinction between the world and God appear within
the world? As 'Amen', when this is well said, and, perhaps, in
some traditions of its utterance, as 'OM'.

Before moving on, there is one final point to be made.
Lipner speaks of the 'all-powerful hold' which, before the rise
of the *bhakti* movement, Indian religious ritual exercised over
the deities to whom it was directed.[22] To understand the great
traditions as schools in which we educate each other from
idolatry is thereby to understand them as places in which
ritual enactment ceases to be a matter of control – even,
perhaps especially, of controlling our renunciation of control,
our 'self-sacrifice' and our searching for the 'holy life'.[23] At its
best, I think, Protestant suspicion of the ascetical and ritual
practices associated with Catholicism springs from an
alertness to the absolutely exceptionless priority of God's
grace, God's sovereign utterance, God's 'Amen', to any human
thought or word or deed.

---

[20] If Radhakrishnan's construal of the distinction between *prajna* and *turiya*, in the
fifth and seventh verses of this Upanishad, by analogy with the distinction drawn,
in Colossians 1.15, between God's image and invisibility, lies at one end of this
spectrum (see Radhakrishnan, *Principal Upanisads*, p. 697; cf. p. 693), Lipner's gloss
of the final verse to mean that the utterance of 'OM' has the '*innate* capacity' to
bring the utterer to 'ultimate fulfilment' (Lipner, *Hindus*, p. 53, my stress) lies
clearly at the other.

[21] See above, pp. 5–6.

[22] Lipner, *Hindus*, p. 305.   [23] See *Katha Upanishad*, 1.2.15.

WATCHING ONE'S LANGUAGE

As the God of modern deism fades from view like Lewis Carroll's Cheshire Cat,[24] his only trace a smile of vague and indeterminate benignity, some people construe ineffability to mean that we may say, concerning God, more or less whatever takes our fancy. Thus, there are now American theologians who write 'G–d', instead of 'God', as a way of indicating that God, belonging to the 'realm of the ineffable', is 'in a religious sense unnameable'.[25]

What cannot be named, however, cannot be mentioned either, nor even indicated hieroglyphically. Our words and thoughts concerning God are, indeed, inadequate but, as Newman knew, their inadequacy is acknowledged, their 'insufficiency' confessed, not by talking nonsense, but by talking carefully, by taking great care what we say. A friend of mine some years ago defined the theologian as someone who watches their language in the presence of God.

In a world (such as that of seventeenth-century Europe as briefly described in Chapter One) in which direct and literal description became the paradigm of knowledge, any sense not clearly shown upon the surface of a text was imagined in some way to lie *behind* it. In such a world, whose cognitive ideal is plain speaking that has nothing up its sleeve, myth and metaphor are the stuff of fiction, and fiction is presumed 'to mask or to have mislaid the meaning it contains'.[26] But all such imagery of masks and veils, of objects lost and sought and found, supposes truth to be *inert*. The only *voices* in the modern

---

[24] 'This time it vanished quite slowly, beginning with the end of the tail, and ending with the grin, which remained some time after the rest of it had gone' (Lewis Carroll, *Alice in Wonderland* (London: New Orchard Editions, 1990), Ch. 6).

[25] Rebecca S. Chopp, *The Power to Speak: Feminism, Language, God* (New York: Crossroad, 1989), p. 32; quoted from Elisabeth Schüssler Fiorenza, *But She Said: Feminist Practices of Biblical Interpretation* (Boston: Beacon Press, 1992), p. 220. There are, I am told, some Jewish scholars who now write the name of God this way, vocalising it as 'the Holy One' or 'the Lord'. But these, of course, are names of God.

[26] Michel de Certeau, *The Mystic Fable*, 1, *The Sixteenth and Seventeenth Centuries,* trans. Michael B. Smith (Chicago: University of Chicago Press, 1992), p. 12. (First published in France in 1982, four years before de Certeau's death.)

world are those of human beings, crying inconsolably in the
wilderness, weeping in the darkness that so terrified
Pascal.[27]

I have been arguing, however, that, at least where Christian
religious and theological discourse is concerned, it is the
allocutory character of its unknowing which differentiates it
from such philosophical agnosticism. We *address* the dark,
respond in wonder to the silence which surrounds us as the
voice of God.

That, at least, is the ideal. In fact, of course, we do not easily
give up the search for idols, the quest for some more manageable word, idea or image on which to set our hearts. And so it is
that, even though we know that 'God' is not a proper name,
and that the Holy One is not a thing, a being of some particular kind, we do not easily give up the search to find some single
word, some privileged category, that would 'fix' the mystery
beneath our gaze and make it manageable.

And, whereas simple folk may fasten on 'the shining
daughter of the sky', the earth, or fire, 'the heavenly bird that
flies', or some or all of these,[28] well-educated persons like
ourselves prefer abstractions, such as 'infinity', 'transcendence', 'being'. *Esse*, in Latin, is the verb's infinitive: it means
'to be'. We might do well to say that to be God is, indeed, to be,
but when we shift the grammar of the word and talk of 'being'
(with or without a capital initial!) we are drawn back nearer
the illusion that God may now be *placed* upon the map of things,
located in the category of 'being'.

'The to-be-known I will declare, knowing which one attains
the Immortal – the beginningless, highest Brahman. It is said
to be neither existent nor non-existent',[29] neither *sat* nor *asat*.
In his discussion of this passage, Mascarenhas interprets
asat as 'not-being' or 'unmanifest'– like emptiness or silence –

[27] 'Le silence éternel de ces espaces infinis m'effraie' (Blaise Pascal, *Pensées*, (ed.)
Francis Kaplan (Paris: Editions du Cerf, 1992), 3.206).

[28] See *Rig Veda*, 1.92.7, 1.164.46.

[29] *Bhagavad Gita*, 13.12, in the translation provided by Julius Lipner in: 'Samkara on
metaphor with reference to Gita 13.12–18' in R. W. Perrett (ed.), *Indian Philosophy of
Religion* (Dordrecht: Kluwer Academic Publishers, 1989), p. 177.

rather than as 'non-being', or contradiction.[30] The Christian reader will remember the respect with which Aquinas handled the Dionysian claim that God is 'not [an] existent but is above existence': 'non est existens sed supra existentia'.[31]

'We can only set right one error of expression by another.'[32] It is my impression that Newman would have found friends amongst the great commentators on the Upanishads. If, however, we were to leave the matter there, it might seem as though the patterns of our speech, in trying to say something sensible of God, were simply dialectical, oscillating like a pendulum between 'this' and 'not-this', 'that' and 'not-that'.

Formally, this may be so, and yet, in Christianity, there are deeper rhythms that give life to the dialectic as we are drawn to speak, in turn, of Father, Son, and Spirit. For the remainder of this lecture, therefore, I want to address, more directly than I have done thus far, the specifically Christian doctrine of God, and I shall do so in conversation with others who have found analogies between this doctrine and what is spoken of in the *Svetasvatara Upanishad* as 'the threefold Brahman' or 'supreme triune reality'.[33]

THE REALITY OF WISDOM AND DELIGHT

In these lectures, I have been suggesting that we should understand the great traditions as schools whose pedagogy serves to wean us from idolatry. In his little book on the doctrine of God's Trinity, Raimundo Panikkar defined idolatry as 'the

---

[30] See Mascarenhas, *Quintessence*, p. 67.

[31] Thomas Aquinas, *Summa theologiae*, 1a, 12. 1. ad 3. See Thomas Gilby's helpful comment on this passage in his Introduction to the Blackfriars edition (p. xxxii). Amongst the innumerable studies of Aquinas on God and *esse*, I would recommend the section on the 'grammar of *esse*' in David B. Burrell, *Aquinas: God and Action* (London: Routledge and Kegan Paul, 1979), pp. 42–54, and John F. Wippel's essay on 'Metaphysics' in Norman Kretzmann and Eleonore Stump (eds.), *The Cambridge Companion to Aquinas* (Cambridge: Cambridge University Press, 1993), pp. 85–127.

[32] Newman, *Theological Papers*, p. 102.

[33] *Svetasvatara Upanishad*, 1.12, in the translations of, respectively, Radhakrishnan (*Principal Upanisads*, p. 717) and Mascarenhas (*Quintessence*, p. 22).

transference to a creature of the adoration due to God alone, i.e. an adoration which stops short at . . . some object upon which has descended the glory of the Lord'.[34]

Alerted to God's presence by some person, some occurrence, fact or thing; some dream or project, institution or idea, we take off our shoes, bow down and offer sacrifice. Here, we recognise, is God. At once, however, our first lesson has to be: where God is, is not God; this sanctuary of God's presence is, however holy, not divine. In Christianity, as in Judaism, the enigma of God's revelation of his name to Moses, at the burning bush, has served as paradigm of this discovery.[35]

How, I asked earlier, does the distinction between the world and God make its appearance in the world? The answer that we might now give is: as acknowledgement of holiness, of that which lies beyond our comprehension and control.[36]

Panikkar translates *karmamarga* as 'iconolatry', which he defines as that tradition of worship, of veneration of the images, which takes an object of idolatry as 'point of departure for a slow and arduous ascent towards God'. For Panikkar, however, iconolatry requires to be, not merely supplemented but in some measure surpassed by two other modes of spirituality: first, 'personalism' or *bhaktimarga*, and then *advaita* or *jnanamarga*. And, he asks, has 'the christian conception of the Absolute . . . passed beyond the iconolatrous stage inherited from Israel, an iconolatry merely purified and corrected by the personalism to which the evolution of the western world has given rise?'[37]

The difficulties he is hinting at are real and fundamental. Nevertheless, the way he puts the question is misleading, because it overlooks two things. First, it overlooks the depth of Israel's dedication to transcending iconolatry, a dedication

---

[34] Panikkar, *The Trinity*, pp. 15–16.
[35] See Exodus 3.1–15.
[36] De Certeau, in the course of a fascinating discussion of the 'identity between Christ's "yes" and the "I am" (the Other) of the burning bush' (*Mystic Fable*, p. 175) quotes Angelius Silesius: ' "*Gott spricht nur immer Ja.*" "God always says only Yes [or: I am]" ' (*Cherubinischer Wandersmann* 2.4).
[37] Panikkar, *The Trinity*, pp. 16, 25.

which found expression in the peremptory prohibition of
graven images. Secondly, Panikkar's formulation underestimates the abiding strength and influence, in Christianity,
of the conviction, born of the confluence of its Jewish elements
with currents flowing from Neoplatonism, that – as Aquinas
laconically expressed it – we come to the knowledge of God
through learning that we do not know what God is.[38]

In some recent theology, there is a tendency for Aquinas'
insistent nescience to be treated as a stroke of genius (or an
aberration, depending on your taste!) more or less peculiar to
him, and in some way untypical of Christianity as a whole. But
this is simply an illusion generated by that forgetfulness of
patristic and medieval Christianity which was fostered by the
self-assurance of early modern rationalism. I forget who first
spoke of 'the licence of affirmation in Western theology', but
would plead that this disease is more accurately seen as having
briefly interrupted the tradition, during the seventeenth and
eighteenth centuries, rather than as being generally represen-
tative of it.[39]

My immediate concern, however, is not with the historical
issues, fascinating and important though these are. I simply
want to emphasise the centrality, in Christianity, of the recognition that the reality of God is beyond our understanding.
Even within the world of God's creation, our minds are stopped
by sheer contingency and seemingly inexorable fate; there is
too much that makes no sense, fashion it or fancy as we will.

---

[38] The prologue to the First Part of the *Summa theologiae* summarises its project (which
Aquinas has just expounded in the prefatory first Question) as that of making God
known: 'principalis intentio hujus sacrae doctrinae est Dei cognitionem tradere'.
Then, having considered, in Question 2, the question whether God is to be said to
'exist': 'utrum Deus sit', he announces, in his prologue to Questions 3 to 13, that 'we
cannot know what God is, but only what he is not': 'de Deo scire non possumus quid
sit sed quid non sit'.

[39] 'The Greek silence still runs through the Logos of Christian antiquity. It fascinates
patristic theology' (de Certeau, *Mystic Fable*, p. 115). De Certeau documents the
extraordinary fascination exercised by Dionysius, the '*apex theologorum*' (p. 103),
the hero of those whose theology 'signifies by what it takes away' (p. 137), during the
first half of the seventeenth century: i.e, at precisely the period when a new and
very different framework of discourse and imagination was breaking through (see
p. 77).

Acknowledging the limits of our actions' scope, and the fragility of all our understanding, confessing all existence set in 'absolute dependence',[40] we confront the 'void of vastness',[41] confess the darkness, beyond all things' existence, of ultimate reality.

To stay, frozen, in this recognition, however, our hearts set absolutely on this night's inscrutability, would be to make an idol of the dark. Idolatry's seductive power may find expression in many forms of worship of the void, of gnosticism, nihilism and despair.[42]

The darkness is not God, but only points to God, and we may not make of the dark an 'object' at which, in Panikkar's expression, adoration 'stops'. In the school of Christianity, the darkness' silence is interrupted by a voice: a Word once uttered, life once lived and death once undergone. Moreover, hearing, in *that* Word's utterance, the word that speaks the *world* into existence, we are made attentive to the messages, the meaning, sense and harmony, that all things made and uttered embody and display.

However, to stay, frozen, in this attentive reverence to given meaning, our hearts set absolutely on remembrance, would be to make an idol of the word once uttered. Idolatry's seductive power may find expression in all kinds of fundamentalism, traditionalism and nostalgia.

All meaning speaks of God, but we may not make of any meaning, text, or message, not even the very flesh of God's own Word, God's broken speech on Calvary, an object at which adoration *stops*.[43] God is what God says, but what God says, in Jesus' life poured out, gives life, breathes Easter freedom into

---

[40] See the famous fourth thesis of Schleiermacher's *Glaubenslehre*, which announces 'the self-identical essence of piety' to be 'the consciousness of being absolutely dependent, or, which is the same thing, of being in relation to God' (Friedrich Schleiermacher, *The Christian Faith* (Edinburgh: T. & T. Clark, 1928), p. 12).

[41] *Maitri Upanishad*, 2.4.

[42] See Nicholas Lash, 'Considering the Trinity', *Modern Theology*, 2, 3 (1986), 193.

[43] Christians should remember that what we might call 'christolatry' is as much a departure from trinitarian orthodoxy as are pantheism and what Bishop Walter Kasper has called 'the heresy of theism' (see Walter Kasper, *The God of Jesus Christ* (London: SCM Press, 1984), p. 295).

all things' inspiration. Thus, in the school of Christianity, we learn to find God's presence animating all things' fresh, surprising liveliness – for from delight all beings come, 'by joy they live and they return to joy'.[44] God is in all things joyfully alive, 'the deep delight of freedom'.[45]

To get stuck, however, in this celebration of divine identity, our hearts set absolutely on the beauty, pulse and rhythm of the world, would be to make an idol of the presence of God's self-given Spirit. All life, all freedom, is of God, but we may not make of life or freedom an object at which adoration stops. Anarchism and sensuous delight may be idolatrous. God is what God gives, but what God gives is ever being-given from the silence in which God speaks and to which all life returns: the silence that Jesus, in Gethsemane, still addressed as 'Father'.

The Christian doctrine of God, the doctrine of God's Trinity, is thus the threefold figure that furnishes the grammar for our education from threefold idolatry – from worship of the dark, from worship of the uttered word and from worship of the living world – into the freedom of confession of God's holy mystery as all things' source, and sense, and harmony; as all things' origin, and healing word, and destined peace; as Father, Son and Spirit. [46]

Whatever the merits of this approach, however, so far as Christian self-understanding is concerned, might it not hinder rather than facilitate communication between Christianity and other traditions? If, as David Burrell has reminded us, emphasis on the trinitarian character of Christianity has 'tended to create a chasm between Christians and the other two Abrahamic traditions regarding the doctrine of God',[47] might one not expect, *a fortiori*, even deeper gulfs to yawn

---

[44] *Taittiriya Upanishad*, 3.6.1.
[45] Radhakrishnan, *Principal Upanisads*, p. 557, glossing the passage just quoted (in Mascaro's translation).
[46] I have tried, in my reading of the Apostles' Creed, *Believing Three Ways in One God*, to develop this understanding of Christianity's doctrinal pattern.
[47] David B. Burrell, *Freedom and Creation in Three Traditions* (Notre Dame: University of Notre Dame Press, 1993), p. 183.

between Christianity, thus expounded, and (for example) Buddhism and Vedantic Hinduism?

Only (I suggest) to the extent that we continue to insist on squeezing different traditions of devotion, and behaviour, and reflection into the procrustean bed of early modern accounts of what constitutes 'religion', and of the relationships between religion and particular 'religions'.[48] A key feature of those accounts concerns the ways in which the distinction was drawn between God's 'nature' and the different forms of faith; between God 'in himself' and God as he appears to us to be.

In so far as this distinction was taken to be itself a fact about the world, the tendency was, then, to take 'divinity' either as the nature of a kind of being – which does not, in fact, exist – or as the symbol of our dreams. On the horns of this dilemma Feuerbach, in the nineteenth century, impaled deistic Christianity.[49]

In these lectures, however, I have attempted to pursue a different (and much older) strategy: one which takes for granted, first, that the distinction between the world and God is not itself a fact about the world and may, therefore, only appear within the world as a change in the condition of the world, which change we call the world's redemption; and, secondly, that it is from the way God deals with us that we are brought into relationship with God. It follows that all we are and think and do either expresses the reality of God within the world or, towards the world's destruction, fails to do so. From this standpoint, to 'have a doctrine of God' is to operate within a pattern of devotion, life and thought corrective of our propensities towards egotism and idolatry.

The particular features of the pattern are, of course, tradition-specific, because they are the outcome of particular histories. In the case of Christianity, they achieved their classic form in Syria and Egypt in the fourth and fifth centuries

---

[48] Procrustes, it will be remembered, was a mythical Greek robber, who put travellers in his bed, stretching or lopping off their limbs until they fitted it.

[49] See Ludwig Feuerbach, *The Essence of Christianity*, translated by George Eliot, with an introduction by Karl Barth and a foreword by H. Richard Niebuhr (New York: Harper and Row, 1957).

CE.[50] But each of the great traditions has developed similar patterns for similar purposes.[51] Hence my strategy in these lectures, the final step in which must now, therefore, be to indicate some motifs in the Upanishads that might be deemed coordinate with the Christian doctrine of God's Trinity.

SAT-CIT-ANANDA

In a talk given to the YMCA in Pune, in 1950, Bishop Lash, having remarked that 'St Thomas Aquinas would have had little difficulty in understanding the Shankaracharya, and still less in intercourse with Muslim thinkers of the same age', went on to point out that 'some recent Christian writers' have suggested that 'the Christian doctrine of the Trinity is an attempt to expand the same mystery' that finds expression in Advaita Vedanta.[52]

Nearly twenty-five years later, Panikkar announced that 'It is simply an unwarranted overstatement to affirm that the Trinitarian conception of the Ultimate, and with it of the whole of reality, is an exclusive Christian insight or revelation.'[53] My difficulty with this remark is that it is, for Panikkar, uncharacteristically slipshod. Trinities, triads and triplicities are, indeed, found in many cultures, but most of them have little or nothing to do with the distinctions that Christians painstakingly elaborated in the attempt to

[50] It bears insisting that, whatever nineteenth-century Englishmen may have supposed, and may have persuaded nineteenth-century Indians, Christianity is not, either in its origins or in its mature expression, a European religion!

[51] The context in which Burrell mentions the 'chasm' that has too often seemed to separate Christian doctrines of God from the teachings of Judaism and Islam is the conclusion of a most thoroughly documented study whose purpose is to propose that we may best bridge that chasm along the lines that I am advocating.

[52] Behind both remarks, I think that I detect the influence of his friendship with Father Mascarenhas! In fact, as early as 1882, several years before Upadhyay published his hymn (see below), Keshub Chunder Sen had observed that 'The Trinity of Christian theology corresponds strikingly with the Saccidananda' (quoted by Samuel Rayan, SJ, 'Hindu perceptions of Christ in the nineteenth century' in Leonardo Boff and Virgil Elizondo (eds.), *Any Room for Christ in Asia? Concilium*, 1993/2, 16).

[53] Panikkar, *The Trinity*, p. viii.

safeguard what they had come to understand of the mystery of God considered in the light of Christ.

Thus, for example, the Jesuit Père Bayart, in a fascinating paper on the threefold form of the divine in Hinduism, published in 1933,[54] was, on two grounds, sharply dismissive of the theological significance of the Trimurti – from upanishadic meditation upon sun and wind and fire, and other threefold features of the world, to the one reference in the *Mahabharata* to the three states of supreme reality: creating, conserving and destroying.[55] Not only would the construal of these cosmogonic motifs as expressive of God's 'nature', of 'divinity', go against the grain of the insistence that the relation of the universe to God be understood in terms of non-reciprocal dependence[56] but, in any case, these triple figures do not announce distinctions that purport to hold, even at the very heart of God, the absolute non-manifest mystery of holiness, but only in the forms of God's appearance; they are, in Christian terminology, uncompromisingly modalist. Thus, considered in itself, says Bayart brusquely, the Hindu Trimurti is a subordinationist quaternity, rather than a trinity of any kind.[57]

We move to firmer ground, however, when we turn from the Trimurti to the territory of motifs misleadingly described, in

[54] J. Bayart, 'Le triple visage du divin dans l'Hindouisme', *Nouvelle revue théologique*, 60, 3 (1933), 227–48.
[55] '"... Fire, air, sun, time, whatever it is, breath, food, Brahma, Rudra, Visnu, some meditate upon one, some upon another. Tell us which one is the best for us". Then he said to them. These are but the chief forms of the Supreme, the immortal, the bodiless *Brahman*' (*Maitri Upanishad*, 4.5, 6); 'Feminine, masculine and neuter (this) is the sex form. Fire, wind and sun; this is his light form. Brahma, Rudra and Visnu, this is his lordship form ... Earth, atmosphere and sky, this is his world form. Past, present and future, this is his time form ... Understanding, mind and self-sense, this is his thought-form' (*Maitri Upanishad*, 6.5; both in Rhadakrishnan's translation: see *Principal Upanisads*, pp. 812, 818–19); see Bayart, pp. 229–30. I have been unable to trace his reference to the *Mahabharata*, which he quotes as: 'Il y a trois états de l'Être Suprême; dans la forme de Brahmâ, il est le créateur – dans la forme de Vishnu, il est conservateur – dans la forme de Rudra, il est destructeur', giving as reference: '111, 271 (271) 47' (see p. 230).
[56] See Bayart, p. 236, and my earlier remarks on Sara Grant's treatment of this important theme.
[57] 'Considérée en elle-même, elle est une quarternité subordinatienne plutôt qu'une trinité' (p. 240).

textbooks of Christian theology, as 'psychological analogies' of trinitarian doctrine. In Hinduism, says Mascarenhas, 'the Supreme Being is proclaimed to be *Truth* itself, *Wisdom* ineffable, *Infinity* absolute. He is acknowledged to be One only, without peer, and "appropriately" spoken of as Triune (*Tri-vidham*).'[58] The reference is to the *Svetasvatara Upanishad*: 'By knowing the enjoyer, the object of enjoyment, and the mover (of all) everything has been said. This is the threefold [*Trividham*] Brahman', read in the light of other passages, from the same (fairly late) tradition, such as: 'He who knows Brahman as [reality, wisdom, and delight], placed in the secret place of the heart and in the highest heaven, realises all desires along with *Brahman*, the intelligent.'[59]

Bayart points out that although *cit* and *ananda*, consciousness and bliss, wisdom and delight, correspond quite closely to notions classically 'appropriated', in Christian theology, to God's self-unfolding, or 'procession', as (respectively) Son, or word, or wisdom, and as gift or goodness, happiness or joy, it is less usual to find reality, or being, *sat*, appropriated to God as *arche*, first, or Father. Less usual, maybe, but not quite unknown: Bayart quotes Augustine, in the *City of God*, speaking of God as 'one who most supremely is, who is supremely wise, supremely good': 'qui summe est, qui summe sapiens est, qui summe bonus est'.[60] Here, surely, we have a Christian figure closely correlative to the *Sat-Cit-Ananda*?

Bayart ended his study warmly praising Upadhyay's 'New Canticle', which he described as a veritable résumé of Catholic teaching on the Holy Trinity.[61] It would be impertinent of me

---

58 Mascarenhas, *Quintessence*, p. 25.

59 *Svetasvatara Upanishad*, 1.12 (from Rhadakrishnan, p. 717, see Mascarenhas, p. 22); *Taittiriya Upanishad*, 2.1.1 (from Rhadakrishnan, pp. 541–2, see Mascarenhas, p. 55). In the latter case, I have taken liberties with the translation: where I have 'reality, wisdom, and delight', Rhadakrishnan has 'the real, as knowledge and as the infinite', and Mascaro has 'Truth, consciousness, and infinite joy'.

60 Augustine, *De civitate Dei*, XI. 28 (CCSL, XLVIII, p. 348), cited Bayart, 'Triple visage', p. 244.

61 'Véritable résumé de la doctrine catholique de la Sainte trinité' (p. 247). Incidentally, in the light of a remark that I made earlier concerning the danger of translating *esse* into English as 'being', it is worth noticing that, perhaps following Upadhyay's own translation of his hymn, which has 'Being' for *Sat*, Bayart has

to recommend a hymn which, according to Julius Lipner, has become 'increasingly popular in Indian Christian circles'.[62] I do, however, recommend Bayart's less well-known article and Mascarenhas' little book, which introduced me to it.

'The perfect self-mirroring of Being is truth', says Panikkar, 'but even if the perfect image of Being is identical to Being, Being is not exhausted in its image. If the Logos is the transparency of Being, the Spirit is, paradoxically, its opaqueness' because the Spirit is God's freedom and, as such, is unforeseeable.[63] In his essay 'Trinity and pluralism', written in response to the paper from which that passage comes, Bishop Rowan Williams praises Panikkar for his sensitivity to what I have called the 'grammatical' character of trinitarian doctrine. Thus understood, says Williams, 'Trinitarian theology becomes not so much an attempt to say the last word about the divine nature as a prohibition against would-be final accounts of divine nature and action.'[64]

Throughout these lectures, I have tried to emphasise that it is what we do *not* know that we need to keep in mind in order that our speech about the mystery of God be, at all times, *restrained* both by recognition of the wonder, silencing our words, into which those words are uttered, and by the correlative acknowledgement that conversation between different traditions must never relax the discipline of steadying our minds as we 'set right one error of expression by another' lest ,

'Existence' (p. 248). According to Upadhyay, however, the 'equivalent [of *Sat*] in English is "Being". That which is and cannot but be is *Sat*' (see Lipner and Gispert-Sauch, *Writings of Brahmabandhab Upadhyay*, 1, pp. 126, 127; the hymn was published in *Sophia* in October 1898). But, in that case, its 'equivalent' in English would be neither 'Being', nor 'Existence', nor 'Reality', nor 'Truth' but something more like '*necessary* being' which, although perhaps preferable to philosophers, would risk hardening the arteries of analogical reflection.

62 Lipner and Gispert-Sauch, *Writings of Upadhyay*, p. 125. I have therefore been surprised to find no mention of Upadhyay's name in Michael von Brück's solid study of trinitarian motifs (written, admittedly, from the standpoint of one most at home in Lutheran dogmatics), *The Unity of Reality: God, God-Experience, and Meditation in the Hindu–Christian Dialogue*, (trans.) James V. Zeitz (New York: Paulist, 1991).

63 Panikkar, 'The Jordan, the Tiber, and the Ganges', p. 109.

64 Williams, 'Trinity and pluralism', p. 12.

in so doing, we succumb to quite unwarranted imperialistic claims to theoretical finality.[65] Whatever may be true of metaphysics, metachronics will remain, as long as there is time, unfinished!

Each tradition will have its own techniques of watchfulness, its own criteria for the purification of desire and for weaning adoration from idolatry. By way of illustration I return, once more, to the distinction between soliloquy – under which heading we might muster all science and all philosophy, all techniques of management and control – and allocution, the heart's address, without the influence of whose attentive, purifying movement all that we think and understand, desire and do, reaps bitter harvest from our egotism.

Christianity, it has been said, is not about love, but about the cost of loving. Disciples of the Crucified know that it is in darkness that light shines, from friction that fire springs from the wood. 'Prayer is the power that makes OM, [the friction-rod], turn round and then the mystery of God comes to light.'[66] Is this statement an assertion, something simply *said*, declared to be the case, or may it be itself a form of prayer? What wields the friction-rod? Whose voice utters 'OM', announces the 'Amen' that makes and heals the world? According to the Christian Scriptures, God's Spirit's groaning voices God's Word in our hearts,[67] sparks fire to light unquenchable. If that is how the passage from the Upanishad may be read, in grace-given praise of grace, then I see no reason why Christians should not make such prayers their own.

IN QUEST OF WISDOM

Having insisted on the importance of resisting claims to theoretical finality, it would be intolerably paradoxical on my

---

[65] Newman, *Theological Papers*, p. 102; see Williams, 'Trinity and pluralism', p. 8, quoted above, p. 28. One recent study which seems admirably to resist this temptation but which, unfortunately, I have been unable to consult, is Francis X. Clooney, SJ, *Theology after Vedanta. An Experiment in Comparative Theology* (New York: State University of New York Press, 1993).

[66] *Svetasvatara Upanishad*, 1.14; see John 1.1–5.   [67] See Romans 8.18–30.

part to attempt some final synthesis or grand conclusion.
Instead, I shall simply juxtapose some images of wisdom.

I remarked, at the beginning, that the crisis of our time is
characterised by the extent to which our ingenuity has outstripped our wisdom. It would therefore seem that those of us
who live, and work, and think, within the ancient schools of
wisdom that we call 'religions' bear heavy burdens of responsibility to the wider culture.

Indian wisdom knows, as does the wisdom learnt by
Christianity from Judaism, that there is a time to mourn, and
a time to dance; a time for war, and a time for peace; a time to
keep silence, and a time to speak. And Christians, as well as
Hindus, recognise that there are two ways of contemplation: in
silence and in speech.[68]

In both traditions, there is a tension between the recognition, on the one hand, that both speech and silence have
their proper time, and place, and duty, and, on the other, that
it is 'by sound we go to silence';[69] that speech, and action, and
devotion, are the way, and stillness, silence, peace, the destiny
or goal. (Nevertheless, Christianity's insistence that God's
speech, God's Word, is 'very God', and is not merely the
'appearance' of God's silence, is, I think, distinctive.)

In our unwisdom, we are, for all our ingenuity, confused;
uncertain what to say or do, unsure which way to go. We seem,
in fact, quite lost. If, however, we *are* lost then we may, perhaps,
be found. The alternative would be that humankind, and
all the world, are simply doomed. It is this nihilistic possibility which all the great traditions have, in different ways,
resisted, insisting that true wisdom sustains hope, even in the
dark.

In the Hebrew Scriptures, God's wisdom brings the world to
light from dark, chaotic waters: 'when he assigned to the sea
its limit ... when he marked out the foundations of the earth,
then I was beside him, like a master workman', delighting in

---

[68] See Ecclesiastes 3.4, 8, 7; *Maitri Upanishad*, 6.22.
[69] *Maitri Upanishad*, 6.22; Rhadakrishnan has 'by sound alone is the non-sound
revealed' (*Principal Upanisads*, p. 833).

the work.[70] (The scholars are, in fact, unable to decide whether God's world-making wisdom, in this passage, is a craftsman or a child; a child playing at its parent's side, a child, one might say, 'of the waters', God's wisdom uttered from its water-womb.)[71]

Once upon a time, a child got lost, according to Luke's Gospel. His parents sought him, sorrowing, for 'three days' and, on the third day, found him, with the wise men, in the Temple.[72] 'Christianity', says Michel de Certeau, 'was founded upon *the loss of a body* – the loss of the body of Jesus Christ, compounded with the loss of the "body" of Israel, of a "nation" and its genealogy.'[73] (Hence, incidentally, the question as to the kind of *social* fact that Christianity, the body of the risen Christ, is meant to be is, in an important sense, undecidable. It is my impression that modern Hinduism experiences a similar difficulty.)

Christianity thereby took on the nature of a quest, a pilgrimage in search of wisdom's flesh, of God's embodied Word. On the third day, Mary Magdalene 'stood weeping outside the tomb' because, she said, '"they have taken away my Lord, and I do not know where they have laid him"'.[74]

India is criss-crossed by tracks of pilgrimage, dotted with tombs and shrines, places of God's visitation. But Hinduism remains, like Christianity, a pilgrimage in quest of wisdom's place beyond the past and present forms of its appearance, a pilgrimage in which (to set Mahatma Gandhi's favourite hymn alongside the Upanishad) God's 'kindly light' leads all things to that 'end of the journey where fear and sorrow are no more'.[75]

---

[70] Proverbs, 8.29–30.

[71] For the Child of the Waters, see *Rig Veda*, 2.35; in another Vedic canticle, Speech announces: 'My womb is in the waters, within the ocean' (*Rig Veda*, 10.125.7).

[72] See Luke, 2.41–9.

[73] De Certeau, *Mystic Fable*, p. 81, his stress.

[74] John, 20.11, 13.

[75] Of the end of Gandhi's fast on 23 August 1933, C. F. Andrews wrote: 'I said Sanskrit prayers and sang his favourite hymns, "Lead, Kindly Light", and "When I Survey"' (Benarsidas Chaturvedi and Marjorie Sykes, *Charles Freer Andrews* (London: George Allen and Unwin, 1949), p. 273); *Maitri Upanishad*, 6.23.

PART II

Emerging from modernity

CHAPTER 4

Observation, revelation, and the posterity of Noah[1]

Coined in France a hundred years before, the terms 'theism' and 'deism' moved into English only at the end of the seventeenth century, remaining interchangeable until well into the eighteenth. As indicating what John Dryden called 'the principles of natural worship',[2] these terms stood doubly opposed to 'atheism', on the one hand and, on the other, to what was becoming known as 'revealed religion'.

According to the *Oxford English Dictionary*, it is in 1682, five years before the publication of Newton's *Principia*, that 'deism' makes its first appearance, in the preface to Dryden's *Religio laici*. Both poem and preface delineate, for political purposes, certain abuses of human reason. At a time of constitutional crisis Dryden, the devout Tory and (at this date) still loyal adherent of the established Church, takes issue with certain forms of dogmatism and sectarian rationalism which seem to him 'to threaten the values of human society and to menace the stability of the state'.[3]

One of his targets, then, is 'deism'. The error of the deist is 'the belief that nothing of unique value is embedded in tradition

---

[1] A paper read to a symposium held at the Vatican Observatory in September 1987, at the invitation of Pope John Paul II, to mark the third centenary of the publication of Newton's *Principia*.

[2] John Dryden, '*Religio laici*, Or, a layman's faith' in *John Dryden* (ed.) Keith Walker (Oxford: Oxford University Press, 1987), pp. 219–39.

[3] Edward N. Hooker, 'Dryden and the atoms of Epicurus' in Bernard N. Schilling (ed.), *Dryden. A Collection of Critical Essays* (Englewood Cliffs: Prentice Hall, 1963), pp. 125–35. Reprinted from *English Literary History*, 24 (1957), 177.

or history, that it is possible to wipe the slate clean (as Descartes did) and start all over again, and by the pure exercise of reason to discover "all ye know, and all ye need to know".[4]

This is not a historical paper, partly because I lack the competence to produce such a paper on the seventeenth century, and partly because the proposal I wish to offer is systematic rather than directly historical in character. Nevertheless, for reasons which I hope will eventually become clear, this little text of Dryden's may serve (especially if we keep in mind the date of its production) as an engaging parable.[5]

Dryden is not at all disposed to deny the authenticity of deist religion, the reality of communion with God according to 'the principles of natural worship'.[6] He is, however, convinced that *all* relationship with God, whatever its content or apparent structure, is in response to God's prevenient revealing grace, and not the outcome of unaided human ingenuity.

The historical character and hence the particularity of Jewish and Christian revelation is, of course, an embarrassment to the view that wherever and in whatever form we come into relationship with God, we do so in response to his revealing grace. Dryden has a marvellous conceit for disposing of the difficulty. Noah did, after all, have *three* sons. What seem to be the principles of natural worship, elaborated by unaided reason, are, in fact, 'only the faint remnant of dying flames of revealed religion in the posterity of Noah'.[7]

With the aid of this device, he is able to correct the rationalism of those 'modern philosophers' who have

> too much exalted the faculties of our souls, when they have maintained that by their force mankind has been able to find out that there is one supreme agent or intellectual being which we call God; that praise and prayer are his due worship; and the rest of those deducements, which I am confident are the remote effects of revelation, and unattainable by our discourse.[8]

[4] Hooker, p. 130.
[5] See Michael J. Buckley, SJ, *At the Origins of Modern Atheism*, in which can be found the historical warrants for several of the claims which I tentatively propose.
[6] Dryden, *'Religio laici'*, p. 220.
[7] Ibid.   [8] Dryden, pp. 220–1.

Or, as he puts it in the poem, addressing the 'Deist':

> These truths are not the product of thy mind,
> But dropped from heaven, and of a nobler kind.
> Revealed religion first informed thy sight,
> And reason saw not, till faith sprung the light.
> Hence all thy natural worship takes the source:
> 'Tis revelation what thou think'st discourse.[9]

Where our knowledge of God is concerned, are we constructors, explorers, or pupils? Dryden in 1682 was clearly concerned to exclude the first two options and keep the third alive. As the following century unfolded, however, the effort and energy and self-assurance required in order to awaken from dogmatic slumbers, finding and fashioning new worlds of knowledge and artefact and social order, rendered intolerable all acknowledgement of pupilage. But if a good part of the eighteenth century remained confident that we were not only explorers but successful explorers, discoverers of God, it seemed increasingly evident to the nineteenth (from Feuerbach to Freud) that we were constructors of all our gods.[10] We cannot now go *back* to Dryden and the dawn of the Enlightenment. And yet there may perhaps be appropriate *post*modern ways of saying, ''Tis revelation what thou think'st discourse.'

INTERACTION?

We are invited to consider aspects of 'interaction' between physics, philosophy and theology. Interaction, it seems to me, suggests (as, perhaps, does 'dialogue') something approaching parity of reciprocal influence. But is this how scientists regard the relationships between physics and philosophy? Was not

[9] Dryden, p. 229.
[10] Edward Craig, *The Mind of God*, pp. 3 and 282, argues, in a way which complements Buckley (see note 5), that two *Weltbilder* 'cover between them a large portion of the philosophy written since the time of Descartes'. In the seventeenth century we were explorers, our minds made in the image of God. Today we are constructors or, as he puts it, agents in the void.

Karl Rahner correct in saying, twenty years ago, that the
sciences today (and he had in mind the whole range of
Wissenschaften) 'take their decision about their understanding
of existence before philosophy is able to have its say. At most it
is accepted as reflection on the pluralism of these sciences and
their methods'?[11] This being the way things are (and have
been, by and large, since Hegel's owl first flew), it is hardly
surprising that there are not many learned journals or
international conferences devoted to the 'dialogue' between
philosophy and science.

Why should it be different with theology? Do scientists
really expect to have to modify their practices in the light of
what they learn from theologians? Not in my experience. And
yet, there is much talk of 'dialogue' between theology and
science.

An agenda paper for our meeting cast the 'central issues'
which we were to consider in the form of a question: 'What are
the implications of contemporary physics and cosmology for
philosophy (especially metaphysics) and theology?' Notice
that we are not asked what the implications of theology are for
physics. I make no complaint about this. I merely note, once
again, the discrepancy between fact and description where the
relationships between science and theology are concerned.
The description (whether in terms of 'dialogue' or 'interaction') suggests a reciprocity or mutuality of influence which
the facts belie. My first question, therefore, is: why should this
be so?

Theologians have perhaps not sufficiently reflected on the
fact that the factors which brought about early modern
distinctions of 'philosophy' from 'science' also helped to
generate a quite new sense of what *revelation* might mean.
(One way to watch this shift occurring would be to study, with
the tools of literary criticism, changing uses of such well-worn
metaphors of knowledge and its sources as 'light' or the 'two

---

[11] Karl Rahner, 'Philosophy and philosophising in theology' in *Theological Investigations*, IX (trans.) Graham Harrison (London: Darton, Longman and Todd, 1972), pp. 46–63.

books' – that of Scripture and that of nature or the works of God.)[12]

Consider what happens when 'observation' is made the paradigm of learning, and accuracy of representation (rather than, for example, soundness of judgement) becomes the standard of knowledge. Knowledge of nature is arrived at by looking carefully at the world. And knowledge of God? This may come either by imagining what might lie 'behind' the world and account for its configuration or, according to some people, by the careful study of data which, while constituting items on the list of things that we know, nevertheless do not simply form part of the world in which we come to know them. (And it is, of course, this last proviso which proves increasingly untenable during the eighteenth century.)

Newton, it has been said, 'revered [the two books] as separate expressions of the same divine meaning'.[13] There have, I think, been few more fateful moments in the history of Christian thought than the early modern subsumption of the whole grammar of revelation and religious belief into that 'spectatorial' model of the process of knowledge which came so to dominate the Western imagination. Before, there had been many ways of reading many texts, but few controls on interpretative ingenuity. Now, there are but two books, and both of them picture-books at that.

My suggestion, then, is that the discrepancy or inconsistency which I mentioned earlier is attributable to the enduring influence, on the imagination of scientists and

---

[12] On the former the opening lines of *Religio laici* are most interesting. Richard Rorty, *Philosophy and the Mirror of Nature* (Oxford: Basil Blackwell, 1980), pp. 12–13, is, I believe, mistaken in taking for granted that what he calls 'ocular metaphors' of cognition were as dominant before the seventeenth century as they were after it. On the latter, Arthur R. Peacocke, *Creation and the World of Science* (Oxford: Clarendon Press, 1979), p. 3, by beginning his discussion of the uses of this metaphor with Bacon, seems to miss the novelty of seventeenth-century practice. On fifteenth-century uses see Buckley, p. 69. See, also, the literature referred to by Amos Funkenstein, *Theology and the Scientific Imagination. From the Middle Ages to the Seventeenth Century* (Princeton: Princeton University Press, 1986), p. 13, n. 3.

[13] Frank E. Manuel, *The Religion of Isaac Newton* (Oxford: Clarendon Press, 1974), p. 49.

theologians alike, of seventeenth-century epistemological patterns or structuring metaphors. If there is but *one* way – namely, through disciplined observation – by which we can come to know *anything* (*sive deus, sive natura,* as it were), then we seem stuck with a tale of two sources of truth, two districts in which truths may be 'observed'. But all such dualisms eventually crumble before the practical acknowledgement of the comprehensiveness of the territory of scientific investigation. Such glimpses as we may have of the unseen, it then seems clear, can only come through observation of the visible described by science. Thus science becomes, in fact, not 'partner in dialogue' to theology, but mediator of the latter's truth. On this account, 'reductionism' and 'scientism' are symptoms rather than disease. The fundamental requirement is to come to grips with the legacy, still tenaciously exercising its influence in both theology *and* science, of early modern 'spectatorial' conceptions of human understanding.

'God', said Hegel, 'does not offer himself for observation.'[14] An eminently sensible remark, but one the significance of which is likely to be missed or misunderstood by someone who supposes that all our knowledge is, directly or indirectly, literally or metaphorically, a matter of observation: that we are simply *spectators* of our world – and of God.

But if not spectators upon our world, then what? Products of that world, undoubtedly, participants in its processes, victims and agents. And one fundamental feature of our agency is the restless quest for freedom and coherence, a quest the centrality of which is not negated by our propensity for producing hideously illiberal and incoherently oppressive caricatures of order and of liberty.

In an essay from which I quoted earlier, Rahner remarked: 'In the future, man will not objectify himself in his art and philosophy as the rational and theorising being . . . he will appear as practical man in the work of his hands, which

---

[14] G. W. F. Hegel, *Lectures on the Philosophy of Religion*, I, *Introduction and Concept of Religion*, (ed.) Peter C. Hodgson (Berkeley: University of California Press, 1984), p. 258.

changes him in a way he cannot clearly express.'[15] And again: 'In the future theology's key partner-in-dialogue . . . will no longer be philosophy in the traditional sense at all, but the "unphilosophical" pluralistic sciences and the kind of understanding which they promote either directly or indirectly.'[16]

We are a long way here from that vision of individual self-transparency and self-possession which was the ideal of Cartesian individualism. Rahner is suggesting that it was under the spell of the 'primacy of pure reason' that Neo-scholastic theology took metaphysics as its dancing-partner. Now, in contrast, it is in irreducible diversity of image and narrative, experiment, labour and technique, and not in any single, overarching description or theory of the world, that such self-understanding as we are capable of finds primary expression. This may seem a very fitful and fragmentary, confusing and dangerous thing to offer in place of that grand order, that perceived simplicity independent of ourselves, which once we thought we had discerned. Still it may at least open up fresh possibilities of fruitful interaction between scientific practice and the labour of Christian discipleship.[17]

ON JOINING THE CONVERSATION

It is nevertheless possible that such fresh forms of interaction will receive rather more philosophical assistance than Rahner expected. Writing in 1967, he could hardly foresee the remarkable extent to which an impressively diverse range of disciplines and traditions of discourse would be brought into a

---

[15] Rahner, 'Philosophy and philosophising in theology', p. 57.
[16] Rahner, p. 60.
[17] These comments may set a question mark against the suggestion (made, at Castel Gandolfo, by Professor Chris Isham) that the meeting-ground of physics and theology is philosophy. The implications, however, would seem more disturbing to our theory than our practice: at our sessions at Castel Gandolfo, for example, it did not seem in fact to be primarily (and certainly not simply) upon the ground of philosophy that such meeting as there was between physics and theology occurred. I would tentatively suggest that 'interpreter' might be a better metaphor than 'meeting-place' for the role of philosophy in the dialogue between theology and science.

common philosophical conversation (in at least some sense of 'philosophical') under the banner of 'hermeneutics'.[18]

At this point, however, the theologian wishes briefly to register a complaint. In both Europe and the United States theologians are taking an active and often well-informed part in discussion on general hermeneutics. Moreover, some of the major philosophical contributors to these debates (Gadamer and Ricoeur, for example) are sensitive to theological considerations and conversant with the literature. In the English-speaking world, however, it seems largely to be agreed that theology has about as much to contribute as does astrology to what Michael Oakeshott called 'the conversation of mankind'.[19] Newman, I think, was right when he said that 'it is not reason that is against us, but imagination'.[20] If anything, however, this merely increases the difficulty of the theologian's task. Be that as it may, what might the theologian have to contribute to what we may call the post-empiricist conversation? On this vast topic I now offer one or two suggestions.

WORDS AND STORIES

When Dryden contrasted 'discourse' (in the Johnsonian sense of *inference*: the 'course' or movement of the mind from premise to conclusion) with 'revelation', he was contrasting

---

[18] A conversation which, as Mary Hesse and others have insisted, must include the physical sciences, if only because 'the fact that a natural science requires the existence of a linguistic community of communication as an *a priori* for its own existence cannot be grasped scientifically but must be understood hermeneutically'. See Kurt Mueller-Vollmer, *The Hermeneutic Reader. Texts of the German Tradition from the Enlightenment to the Present* (New York: Continuum, 1985) p. 44; and Karl-Otto Apel, *Towards a Transformation of Philosophy* (London: Routledge and Kegan Paul, 1980). See also the discussion of Hesse's essay, 'In defence of objectivity', in Richard J. Bernstein, *Beyond Objectivism and Relativism* (Oxford: Basil Blackwell, 1983), pp. 32–4.

[19] Rorty, p. 389.

[20] John Henry Newman, *The Letters and Diaries of John Henry Newman*, xxx, (eds.) C. S. Dessain and Thomas Gornall (Oxford: Clarendon Press, 1976), p. 159. The year was 1882, and Newman was discussing the 'apparent opposition' between theology and science.

achievement with gift. And a high estimation of individual
achievement becomes the very nerve-centre of the struggle
against obscurantism: 'have courage to use your own understanding' was Kant's 'watchword' for enlightenment.[21] The
bourgeois individual, like Prometheus, is a self-made man.

When, however, that contrast was drawn in the way in which
it was then drawn, what disappeared from view was language.
Or perhaps, to be more exact, we should say, not language, but
(in a sense now very different from Dryden's) discourse: *parole*,
the spoken word; utterance as public, fleshly fact, occurring for
particular purposes in particular places and times.

In the world of the spectatorial empiricist there are only
('objective') things and ('subjective') thoughts, and endless
anxiety about their mediation.[22] The task of language is
simply to render private thoughts public and thus depict
things thought about or seen. If, in search of a slogan for the
turn to hermeneutics in recent decades, I were to speak of
'the recovery of conversation', few eyebrows would rise. But if,
instead, I spoke of the recovery of the *verbum incarnatum*, I
would probably meet with some suspicion. And yet Gadamer
himself, in a section of *Truth and Method* entitled 'Language
and *verbum*', says of 'the Christian idea of incarnation' that it
'prevented the forgetfulness of language in Western thought
from being complete'.[23] It is therefore ironic that it should now
have fallen to the philosophers to awaken theologians from
forgetfulness of the doctrine that God *is* utterance, *verbum*,
Word.

[21] Immanuel Kant, 'An answer to the question: what is Enlightenment?' in *Kant's
Political Writings*, (ed.) Hans Reiss, (trans.) H. B. Nisbet (Cambridge: Cambridge
University Press, 1970), pp. 54–60.

[22] Richard J. Bernstein, pp. 16–20, gives a masterly account of what he calls 'the
Cartesian Anxiety'.

[23] Hans-Georg Gadamer, *Truth and Method*, (trans.) Garrett Barden and John
Cumming (London: Sheed and Ward, 1975), p. 387, stresses the importance of the
fact that *verbum*, as act and event, cannot be made wholly to coincide with any Greek
philosophical account of *logos*: 'In developing the idea of the *verbum*, scholastic
thought goes beyond the idea that the formation of concepts is simply the reflection
of the order of things.' The most thorough exploration of Aquinas' contribution to
this development is Bernard J. F. Lonergan, SJ, *Verbum, Word and Idea in Aquinas*,
(ed.) David B. Burrell (London: Darton, Longman and Todd, 1968).

Because we discover this in attending to a Word once spoken in the past, the recovery of this doctrine has, of course, its dangers. A reawakened reverence for given words, inherited meaning, traditioned truth, may (if seen as simply antithetical to Enlightenment rationalism) all too easily be used to serve reactionary and most irrational purposes. However, the corrective for this tendency may be sought within that single threefold rule of speech and action which, I shall later suggest, is the Christian doctrine of God: sought, for example, in the insistence that what God 'breathes' in his self-utterance is freedom, scope, freshness, inexhaustible possibility; in a word, 'spirit'. But this is to anticipate.

One area in which the post-Heideggerian insistence on the *eventness* of utterance, the temporality of truth, puts dauntingly difficult questions to both science and theology is that of the status of our narratives. At first sight this may seem surprising, because hermeneutics at least allows us once again to take stories seriously after a long period in which one ideal of positivism had been (we could say) the suppression of story-telling, and especially of autobiography (self-involving narrative), as modes of knowledge.

And yet theologians engaged in the growth industry of 'narrative theology' ignore, at their peril, developments which reflect philosophically that declining confidence in the possibility of large-scale, purposive, 'plot-linear' narrative unity which has been one of the hallmarks of the story of the novel for nearly a hundred years. Our world is, in a phrase of Frank Kermode's, 'hopelessly plural',[24] disconnected, disoriented, fragmentary. We work (as Gadamer would say) within 'horizons'. And though horizons may be expanded, we fool ourselves if we suppose them ever to extend very far.

Cosmologists and theologians, however, not only tell stories, but have the impudence to tell stories of the *world*. And even if the cosmologists would claim that their stories are of set purpose, plotless, it seems to me that both groups could

----

[24] Frank Kermode, *The Genesis of Secrecy* (Cambridge: Harvard University Press, 1979), p. 145.

reflect with profit on the problem, not simply of what is meant by claiming that some particular story of the world is *true*, but rather of what *kind* of story a 'story of the world' might be. Who could tell it, what would it be announcing, and how would it be told?[25]

LEARNING AND LISTENING

When scientists go about their work (as Arthur Peacocke has assured us that 'the great majority' of them do and will continue to do, whatever the philosophers, sociologists and theologians may say) in a spirit of what he describes as 'sceptical and qualified realism',[26] then they do so as explorers of the world. And, in this world, they represent the only known tribe of agents and utterers, takers of initiative.

Scientists, of course, only exercise their agency effectively, are only fruitful in discovery, in the measure that they are disciplined to that passionate disinterestedness, that energetic stillness of attention, which is the hallmark of objectivity. Nevertheless, the kind of attentiveness, of listening, of contemplativity, which is in question here, seems to be qualified by the fact of our sole agency. To put it very simply: there is a difference between listening to a waterfall and listening to another person, and in the natural scientist's world there are only waterfalls.

Human persons, of course, are things, like waterfalls, and we properly treat them as such when we count them, dissect them, and so on. To say that they are not *only* things is at least to say that we deem it improper to treat them only as things. And, according to what is probably the most widespread account of the difference between treating things as things (which scientists do) and treating some things as persons, it would seem to follow that scientific attentiveness is quite

---

25 Nicholas Lash, *Theology on the Way to Emmaus*, pp. 62–74, offers some brief reflections on these questions.
26 Peacocke, p. 22. It might be more accurate to describe this spirit as one of sceptical and qualified empiricism.

unlike prayerfulness, when prayerfulness is construed as attentiveness to a personal God. Nor is it only science which is thus deemed properly to be unprayerful, but also theology, in so far as God's existence, attributes and relations with the world are treated as if 'God' were the name of a kind of natural object, a thing beyond the world, to be found, picked up and considered with conceptual tweezers.

But, whether or not natural objects are known in the way in which spectatorial empiricism supposes all objects of knowledge to be known (namely, by constructing mental representations of them), it is certain that whatever is thus known could not be God. God is not a thing, an object over against us, silently lurking in the metaphysical undergrowth, passively awaiting the services of human exploration. (I make no objection to tackling, with utmost rigour and precision, questions concerning the logic and grammar of sentences which contain the word 'God'. I am simply protesting against the fatuous illusion that we could discover or come across God as a fact about the world.)

This is, in part, the burden of Hegel's remark that God does not offer himself for observation. God, according to Hegel, can only be known *as he is*. That is to say: God can only be known in that eternally still movement of utterance and love which he *is*; known *in* that movement, not by constructing representations of it, whether these be pictorial, narrative or metaphysical (which is not to discount the pedagogic usefulness of such devices). God is known by participating in that movement which he is. And it is this participation which constitutes the reality, the life and history, of everything that is.

My purpose in so absurdly attempting a one-paragraph summary of Hegel's philosophy of religion is to ask: what notion of attentiveness is suggested by such an account? The sort of metaphors that come to mind, perhaps, are 'being in tune with', or 'being on the same wavelength as'. And could not such metaphors serve to indicate the character of fruitful attentiveness both to things *and* to persons? And, if so, would we not have begun to erode the sharp contrast between prayerfulness (which, in maturity, requires endless discipline and disinterestedness) and scientific practice? To explore this suggestion would, I think, be to engage in the *kind* of inter-action between science and theology which Rahner had in mind. To the Enlightenment, I remarked at the beginning, 'pupilage' was no longer an acceptable metaphor for our relation to the world. We had, it was thought, 'come of age'. But it is, in fact, the hallmark of the adolescent to suppose there to be no further need for teaching. To be an adult is to have discovered, often at great cost, the depth and perma-nence of the need to set ourselves at school.

Forgetful of language, inattentive to the endless diversity of linguistic practice, we set up sharp dichotomies of fact and thought, experience and idea. The religious counterpart of scientific positivism's 'brute fact' was the myth of what we might call 'brute revelation'. (Fundamentalism is not, as is sometimes supposed, an anachronistically surviving precursor of modern rationalism, but a by-product of it.) Such science and such religion both work with 'a model of truth as some-thing ultimately separable in our minds from the dialectical process of its historical reflection and appropriation'.[27] Under the influence of this model we tend to be impatient with 'ambivalence, polysemy, paradox. And this is at heart an impatience with learning, and with learning about our learning.'[28]

Williams was here reflecting on the notion of revelation, to which, he said, we have recourse in order 'to give some ground for the sense in our religious and theological language that the initiative does not ultimately lie with us; before we speak, we are addressed or called'.[29] Although it is in theology that this metaphor receives its most sustained elaboration, it is by no means only in religious language that the sense in question is discernible. According to Paul Ricoeur, it is this same sense which makes the poetic texts bearers of what he calls 'testimony' or 'witness', the appropriate response to which requires a certain docility or pupil-stance. But why, Ricoeur

---

[27] Rowan Williams, 'Trinity and revelation', *Modern Theology*, 2 (1986), 197–212.
[28] Williams, 'Trinity and revelation', p. 198.   [29] Ibid.

asks, 'is it so difficult for us to conceive of a dependence without heteronomy? Is it not because we too often and too quickly think of a will that submits and not enough of an imagination that opens itself?'[30]

Are we constructors, explorers, or pupils of the world? I have been trying to give some indication of the extent to which, in a wide variety of disciplines or cultural practices, new possibilities of 'pupilage' are opening up in the common conversation of mankind, possibilities that exist, as it were, *on the other side* of the antitheses of modernity. My question to the scientists, therefore, is this: is it of the very nature of research and experiment in the physical sciences that they should seek to stand outside such developments? Or is it possible to imagine the scientists murmuring to each other, without detriment to the rationality and autonomy of their procedures, ' 'Tis revelation what thou think'st discourse'?[31]

PROTOCOLS AGAINST IDOLATRY

How might the Christian doctrine of God be so recast or reread as not only to meet the requirements of the 'hermeneutical turn' in philosophy and social theory but also thereby to become, in fact, more faithful to the mainstream of the tradition than modern 'theism' could ever hope to be? On this vast subject, I have a proposal to make. Although it is only a proposal, I find it quite difficult to state because of the range of implications and ramifications.[32]

In the world of spectatorial empiricism, God is usually thought of as 'a' being, an object or thing standing over against us. The primary task of doctrine or theology is then the construction of conceptual representations of this thing which seek to be, so far as they go, accurate. (And as to how far they go, debate, of course, is endless!)

---

[30] Paul Ricoeur, 'Toward a hermeneutic of the idea of revelation' in Lewis S. Mudge (ed.), *Essays on Biblical Interpretation* (London: SPCK, 1981), p. 117.

[31] Dryden, p. 229.

[32] Nicholas Lash, *Easter in Ordinary. Reflections on Human Experience and the Knowledge of God* (Charlottesville: University Press of Virginia, 1988), provides a fuller version of this.

But suppose we begin, not with whatever may be abstractly considered, thought about, gazed at, but with what we do and say: with human practice. Kant's questions (What can I know? What ought I to do? What may I hope for?) are met, tackled, dealt with, in one form or another, by all normal members of all human societies. And the manner of their handling is often a matter of the patterning of thought and action in story and system, etiology and ethics, constitution, art and enquiry. Such patterns regulate speech and action not (or at least, not necessarily) in the sense of dominating them but, rather, in the sense of providing the ground-rules, the framework, of keeping the show on the road.

Where Christianity is concerned, we have such a pattern in that aspect of public pedagogy which is known as 'doctrine'. I am now taking this term to refer, not to each and every aspect of that vast diversity of practices – academic and pastoral, liturgical and catechetical – which all, in one way or another, count as 'theological', but, much more narrowly and restrictively, to the communal declaration and use of what are acknowledged to be a people's identity-sustaining rules of discourse and behaviour. In a word, the creed.

My first suggestion, then, is that the primary function of Christian doctrine is regulative rather than descriptive. As regulative, its purpose is to protect correct reference: to help us set our hearts on God (and not on some thing which we mistake for God) and make true mention of him.

We require some pattern for our pedagogy, because we are under continual pressure – from the combined forces of what Martin Buber called 'individualism' and 'collectivism', and from our own fearfulness and egotism – to seek some grasp on God, to get a 'fix' on God, by mistakenly identifying some feature of the world (some tradition, some possession, some dream, or project, or structure, or insight, or ideal) with divinity, with godness, with the 'nature' of God. But, as sensible men and women have always known, the nature of God does not lie within our grasp.

My second suggestion, then (or perhaps better, the second step in my single proposal), is that the Christian doctrine of

God, declared in the threefold structure of the single creed, protects the reference to God of Christian action and speech by simultaneously serving as a set of what I have come to call 'protocols against idolatry'.

The creed performs this single twofold service (the technical correlates of which, in theological grammar, are three 'hypostases' and one 'nature') by indicating, at each point, where God is truly to be found and then, at each point, by denying that what we find there is simply to be identified with God. Such doctrine leads, at every turn, to simultaneous affirmation and denial; it enables us to make true mention of God and, by denying that the forms of our address (our confession of God as 'gift', as *verbum* and as 'Father', for example) furnish us with some hold upon the 'nature' of God, it sustains our recognition of the absolute otherness or non-identity of the world and God.

If all this seems puzzling or somewhat unfamiliar, this is probably because, in the modern world, the tendency has been for the doctrine of God's Trinity either to be misread as the provision of further information supplementary to that contained within theism's description of the nature of God, or simply to be ignored. Thus, for example, when Walter Kasper makes the striking claim that the history of modern German thought is, at one level, a 'history of the many attempts made to reconstruct the doctrine of the Trinity', he at once acknowledges that 'the credit for having kept alive the idea of the Trinity belongs less to theology than to philosophy'.[33] As Rahner lamented in 1960, 'One might almost dare to affirm that if the doctrine of the Trinity were to be erased as false, most religious literature could be preserved almost unchanged throughout the process.'[34]

In other words, while the theologians changed the subject, and turned to arguing amongst themselves as to whether the

---

[33] Walter Kasper, *The God of Jesus Christ*, p. 264.
[34] Karl Rahner, 'Remarks on the dogmatic treatise *De Trinitate*' in *Theological Investigations*, IV, (trans.) Kevin Smyth (London: Darton, Longman and Todd, 1966), p. 79.

God of modern theism was discoverable by reason or only apprehensible by faith, inferable from the world or only visible in the light of revelation, the Christian doctrine of God (never, of course, formally denied) did not stay simply dormant, but was active in strange ways and unexpected places, shaping the dialectics of Fichte and Hegel, Feuerbach and Marx.

The next step is to take Kasper's story one stage further by noticing where Gadamer and the 'hermeneutical turn' come in. There is, I think, a tendency for much nineteenth- and early twentieth-century thought to oscillate between varieties of 'realism' and 'idealism', 'absolutism' and 'relativism', 'objectivism' and 'subjectivism', and so on. The list of labels can be extended but their referents rarely lack resonances of what, theologically, would be known as pantheism and agnosticism. And, of course, if the temper of pantheism is closest to that of the third article of the creed, the doctrine of God's indwelling, life-giving, pervading Spirit, agnosticism develops single-mindedly, undialectically, the insistence of the first article that God is unoriginate, utterly beyond all schemes and patterns of fact and explanation: that it is *ex nihilo* that God creates.

What, then, has been missing since the Enlightenment decision to excise tradition, given meaning, from the calculus of human knowing? Gadamer has already told us: *verbum*, language-as-deed, the territory of the doctrine of God's self-utterance in the world, the subject of the second article of the Christian creed.

Where the interactions between theology and philosophy are concerned, therefore, my proposal amounts to little more than the suggestion that one major school or current in recent philosophy and social theory, a current often thought to be dangerously subversive of theological discourse, is, perhaps, only lethal to that 'theism' which Newton's world invented and may, in other respects, be just what Christian theology requires to help bring it back into the conversation and put it back in touch with its own proper subject-matter.

What of the interactions between theology and science? This seems to me a much more obscure question which urgently requires a great deal of attention and hard work. The reason for the obscurity (I suspect) lies in the fact that the dialogue between theology and natural science seems so far to have gone most smoothly when both theologians and scientists operate as more or less sophisticated spectatorial empiricists!

I have no conclusion, but only two final thoughts, the first of which follows from my earlier remarks on disciplined attentiveness. My impression is that, in much of the literature, concepts such as 'scepticism' and 'agnosticism' are too easily used as blunt instruments by people apparently insensitive to the indispensability of modesty, restraint, 'unknowingness', reverence for all good conversation – whether simply amongst ourselves, or in consideration of natural objects, or in contemplating the things of God.

Secondly, it may be the residual influence on religious thought of empiricist 'exploration', but I sometimes have the impression that some people suppose that, the further we go in our discovery of 'grand unified theory' or of what went on in those initial micro-seconds, the nearer we come to the knowledge of God. Here my suspicious nose detects new seeds of gnosticism, for if we read the first article of the creed in the light of the second (or, which comes to the same thing, if we take seriously the Prologue to the Fourth Gospel) – if, in other words, we keep in mind the *singleness* of the Word which God is and utters in his stillness – then we shall be brought to acknowledge, as an implication of the Christian doctrine of God, that we are as close to the heart of the sense of creation in considering and responding to an act of human kindness as in attending to the fundamental physical structures and initial conditions of the world.

CHAPTER 5

On what kinds of things there are[1]

Religion, like art and music, is, in our culture, allowed to be about the Beautiful; sometimes it is even allowed to be about the Good. What is excluded, by the dominant ideology, is any suggestion that the business of religion, no less than that of science, is Truth. My understanding is that Alister Hardy, in whose memory we meet, devoted his life to contesting this exclusion. He did so, moreover, not by struggling against the methods and conclusions of the natural sciences, but (in David Hay's description) by 'attempting to bring about a reconciliation' between 'evolutionary theory and the spiritual awareness of humanity' that would 'satisfy the intellectual world'.[2]

Because that project seems to me as admirable as it is ambitious, I regard it as a great honour to have been invited to lecture in Alister Hardy's memory. And because I judge the strategy which he deployed in furtherance of his project to have been as philosophically muddled as it was theologically wrong-headed, we should have an interesting afternoon!

Before proceeding any further, I do want to emphasise not only that my endorsement, in principle, of Hardy's project is quite sincere, and by no means merely a gesture of ritual civility, but also that I find myself in close agreement with David Hay when he stresses the importance of teaching

---

[1] The 1992 Alister Hardy Memorial Lecture, delivered in December 1992 in Westminster College, Oxford.
[2] David Hay, *Religious Experience Today: Studying the Facts* (London: Mowbray, 1990), p. 18.

children some sense of stillness, attentiveness, or reverence, and of the need to develop in them 'an understanding of the role of language and metaphor in focusing and interpreting our experience of life'.[3] It is against this background of far from trivial agreement with the aims and purposes of those who built this Centre up that this poor Daniel now wishes to throw some morsels of contention to the lions.

THE SUBJECT-MATTER OF PHILOSOPHY,
AND OTHER STORIES

In his marvellous recent study of what he calls 'the matter of the mind', the biologist Gerald Edelman remarks: 'I used to wonder why there are so many subjects in a university catalogue. Why is knowledge so heterogeneous?'. And he goes on to suggest that, from what we now know about the processes of the human brain, about the 'recursive symbolic properties of language', and about the historical irreversibility of specific 'symbolic and artistic realisations in society and culture', it follows that 'there can be no fully reducible description of human knowledge'.[4]

Notice three features or implications of this complex and interesting claim. First, that there are many different kinds of things. Secondly, that there are many different ways in which we know the kinds of things there are. Thirdly, that competent description of kinds of things and ways of knowing demands attentiveness to the history of how things and descriptions came to be the way they are.

Suppose we stick a label on those whose task it is, in our society, to find out what kind of things there are and how they work – especially 'thick' or stuff-like things that you can weigh, and count, and measure – and call these people 'scientists'. Then we could stick another label on those who spend their time in inconclusive argument about the ways in which we

---

[3] Hay, *Religious Experience*, p. 107, cf. p. 106.
[4] Gerald M. Edelman, *Bright Air, Brilliant Fire: On the Matter of the Mind* (London: Allen Lane, The Penguin Press, 1992), p. 177.

know the things there are, calling this group 'philosophers'. This, or something like it, was the arrangement reached in Western Europe during the course of the seventeenth and eighteenth centuries.

Before long, however, the list of things there are for science to consider was extended to include 'thin' things like 'minds' and how they come to know things, and to organise their understanding in ritual and symbolic forms. Thus, in due time, 'science' came to conquer every realm and territory of the world, and could then gaze with condescension upon the remnants of 'philosophy', now banished either to the barren uplands of free-wheeling speculation unconstrained by fact (this is what they do in France and Germany) or to the dark caves in which academics quarrel, pathetically, over scraps of 'language' (this is how they live in Oxford).

Thus, in contrast to the sciences, says Gerald Edelman, 'philosophy... has no proper subject matter of its own'.[5] As my little sketch suggests, coming from some scientists such a remark would be a triumphalistic expression of scientistic fantasy. Edelman, however, understands philosophy and, in his hands, the observation is not meant to be derogatory at all. But how could it be to the credit of philosophy that it had no subject-matter of its own? With that question's help, I now want to retrace my steps behind that early modern dichotomy between physics and epistemology from which we set out.

What kinds of things are there? Nobody, in our society, would turn to the theologian for an answer to this question, and very few would turn to the philosophers. A modern government, anxious equitably to fund all areas of investigation (!) would be more likely to put the question to the Royal Society than to the British Academy.

But suppose we were to ask not just what *kinds* of things there are, but what makes a thing a 'thing'? What kinds of things should *count* as 'things'? Do numbers count as things? Do arguments and images, centuries and symphonies and weather patterns, cities and descriptions? Was Margaret

[5] Edelman, *Bright Air*, p. 158.

Thatcher right in supposing there to be no such thing as
society? And, if the market can't be bucked, is this on account
of the kind of thing it is? Is gravity a thing, is grace, and is the
human mind? Remember the police sergeant in P. D. James'
novel *Devices and Desires*: ' "For God's sake, can't we get this
thing out of here?" And then he heard Dalgliesh's voice
from the doorway, like a whiplash: "Sergeant, the word is
Body." '[6]

In my experience, scientists tend to find the detailed,
meticulous exploration of such questions irritating. And this is
interesting. At one level, they find it irritating because it
seems quite pointless, a distracting waste of time and energy.
There are, we are told, more urgent and important things to
do than worry about mere words. Perhaps, and yet the judgement that 'there's no such thing as society' expresses a view of
the unreality of social relations and responsibilities which
has wreaked havoc with our cities and the lives of their
inhabitants, and our arrogant despoliation of the planet
proceeds, in part, from the illusion that our minds are made of
such superior stuff as not to figure in the catalogue of items
that constitute the fragile, finite web of mutual dependency
which is the world of things, or matter.

Thus, at a deeper level than the mere sense of pointlessness
and triviality, such questions as 'what things should count as
things?' may disturb because they dangerously whisper the
suspicion that the scientist's cherished 'value-freedom' is, in
fact, illusory. More generally, the pressure of such questions is
towards the recognition that the scientist, far from occupying
some god-like nowhere in particular from which to contemplate the world, ineluctably endorses and inhabits (as we all
do) some ontology, some metaphysic, some story of the world
and how things go with it. And, though none of us invented for
ourselves the stories that we live and are, each of us bears some
responsibility for the narratives that we enact and illustrate.

Philosophy, said Gerald Edelman, has no proper subject-
matter of its own. 'Instead', he goes on, 'it scrutinises other

---

[6] P. D. James, *Devices and Desires* (London: Faber, 1989), p. 280.

areas of knowledge for clarity and consistency.' This view of philosophy, I would maintain, is at least within shouting distance of Aristotle's notion of metaphysics, or ontology, as 'that branch of philosophy concerned to give as comprehensive account as possible of certain concepts, involved in discourse concerning any subject-matter whatsoever, e.g. thing and quality, existence, truth, etc.'[7]

The reference to that 'branch' of philosophy reminds us that, for Aristotle, as, nearly two thousand years later, for Aquinas, the term 'philosophy' covered not only what *we* would call philosophy but also the entire range of learned practices whose descendants we now think of as the sciences. And, of course, practitioners of the physical sciences were still called 'natural philosophers' right up through the eighteenth century.

There are affinities, of concept and procedure, linking the Aristotelian distinction between physics and metaphysics, the medieval distinction between 'material' and 'formal' description, and Wittgenstein's distinction between 'empirical' and 'grammatical' investigation. To say this is not, however, to suggest unbroken continuity in the treatment of questions of ontology. Quite the contrary. In the course of the seventeenth and eighteenth centuries, *all* philosophical investigation came to be treated in the manner, and according to the criteria, of physical science or 'natural philosophy', and natural philosophy became, in turn, increasingly a matter of mechanics.[8] And if, with Kant, admiration for Newtonian mechanics is accompanied by some stirring from their slumber of formal habits of reflection, under the influence of 'Cartesian Anxiety' the concern of formal discourse shifted from what there is to know to how we come to know it: from

---

[7] Edelman, *Bright Air*, p. 158; Donald M. MacKinnon, *Themes in Theology. The Three-fold Cord*, p. 147 (see also p. 73). The MacKinnon passage, which occurs in an essay first published in 1976, paraphrases the account of Aristotle's formulation of the tasks of ontology given by Peter Geach, in 1951, in an address to the Joint Session of the Aristotelian Society and Mind Association.

[8] This is a central theme in the story told by Michael J. Buckley in his important study *At the Origins of Modern Atheism*.

metaphysics to epistemology.[9] Which brings us back to the characteristically 'modern' version of the relationship between philosophy and science from which we set out.

Some of you may be surprised by the fact that, so far, I have said nothing about religion. I have not mentioned God, and I have done little more than gesture towards the dualisms which were among my main targets in *Easter in Ordinary*. I shall touch on all these topics in due course. However, I decided to creep up on my quarry by this circuitous route because I have become increasingly convinced of three things. Human beings are things that think and have a history (not least, a history of thinking). Therefore, understanding human beings requires: first, some understanding of the kind of things that human beings are and of the ways that they relate to other things, to other facts and objects in the world; secondly, some understanding of the ways in which different things are differently known and understood; thirdly, some understanding of the ways in which things came to be the way they are and seem to be.

A measure of such understanding is, of course, acquired, sustained, distorted, deepened, through the codes and customs, narratives and symbol-systems, that constitute a culture. But our immediate concern is with what Hardy called 'the intellectual world': with, that is, the complex cluster of critical, reflective, second-order developments and appropriations of the world of commonsense which the Germans call *Wissenschaft*, the French *science*, and for which the English-speaking world (so deep and double-dyed our dualism) has no common term.

COMPETENCE AND DISAGREEMENT

My argument is not that it is desirable for scientists and philosophers, historians and (even!) theologians to take an interest in each other's work, perhaps in aid of fostering

---

[9] On 'Cartesian Anxiety', see Richard J. Bernstein, *Beyond Objectivism and Relativism*, pp. 16–20.

'reconciliation' between different elements of the intellectual world. Such common interest is undoubtedly desirable, but arguments to this effect too often give the impression that we have an option in the matter; that whether or not a scientist (for instance) touches on questions of philosophy or theology is simply a matter of individual preference. Against this, I want to argue that our options are, in fact, limited to the levels of competence that we require of ourselves and of each other.

Thus, for example, ontological 'neutrality' is an illusion: any physics or biology displays or presupposes a metaphysics of some particular kind, a story of the kinds of thing that count as things of different kinds; any philosophy of mind is incompatible with at least some accounts of the relationships of minds to brains, and brains are the business of biology; and the historian, whether of institutions or ideas, takes some position on questions of fact and value, causes and effects – on relationships between things. Finally, it would be difficult to consider 'all things' in relation to the mystery of God, who is all things' beginning and their end (to take Aquinas' description of the theologian's task) while remaining quite ignorant and ill informed about all actual kinds of thing.

It may seem perverse to put forward such a view of things in an epoch, such as ours, in which the accelerating fragmentation of specialised practices renders each of us daily more ill informed on just about everything. Paradoxically (as it may seem), not only do I accept that this is the situation, but I believe that we are much *more* ignorant than we usually suppose. We have found out so much, acquired so many skills during the past three hundred years, that we have grown most arrogant. But arrogance is not the same as self-esteem. As each advance in human knowledge and its application generates fresh devastation – for neither Aids nor famine may properly be labelled 'acts of God' – we oscillate between presumption and despair. What we quite lack is humility, which (where knowledge is concerned) I take to be an honest estimation of what it is, so far as we can see, both that we do and that we do not know and understand.

Our options, I said, are limited to the levels of competence which we require of ourselves and of each other. I am not suggesting that every biologist should be immediately eligible for election to the British Academy nor every theologian a candidate for the Nobel prize in Physics. We do, however, in the ordinary world, have quite sensible and pragmatic standards according to which we judge whether or not people are well informed and of sound judgement in matters of politics and economics, art and literature, and the history of modern times. Yet, even by such modest standards, those engaged in the quest for 'reconciliation' between science and religion still seem quite often to fall some way below the mark. Thus, for example, theologians are often told by their scientific colleagues that they are not competent to talk about the world's beginning, or its end, or how things stand with human beings (stuck, as we seem to be, some way between the angel and the ape) until they first take trouble to find out from the scientists what things there are, what they are made of and how they work.

With one quite large exception, this requirement seems to me in order. The exception is the concept of creation which, for the scientist, seems primarily to refer to the establishment of the initial conditions of the world, whereas, for the Christian theologian, it simply acknowledges all things' absolute and intimate contingency. From the physicist, the theologian learns (or should learn) something of the sheer immensity of things, the beauty and cool vastness of structures the scale of which sweeps, at both ends – from the cosmos to the particle – very far indeed beyond the modest limits of our imagination. In this strange energetic stillness, all easy and irreverent chatter about God is (or should be) silenced.

At the other end of the spectrum, the close dependence of theological interpretation upon the social sciences, history and literary criticism is (or should be) obvious – for theologians seek to understand the stories that their people tell, and to bring the fruits of their interpretation into critical correlation with other stories told by other people. Among the more interesting areas of interaction is that between theology (and philosophy), on the one hand, and biology and psychology on the other. Here, too, the scientists' description of the way things are comes first, at least in the sense that no treatment of the philosopher's distinction between mind and body, or of the theologian's distinction between the body and the soul, deserves these days to be taken very seriously if it proceeds in total disregard of the findings of biology. To adapt an argument of Gerald Edelman's: there may still be good pragmatic reasons for retaining the distinction between *Naturwissenschaften* and *Geisteswissenschaften*, but there are no good reasons for supposing that this distinction rests upon there being two kinds of 'thing', one labelled *Natur* or Matter and the other *Geist* or Spirit. We shall return to this.

Theological investigation, drawing on its own resources of suffering and celebration, narrative and symbol, thus nevertheless also depends in many different ways upon descriptions offered by the sciences of the many different things there are. And I readily admit (in public penance!) that the competence of our theology is still too often limited by neglect of this requirement. Too much theology still spins in voids of piety or disembodied biblical interpretation.

But, if we shift attention from the different kinds of things to the different ways in which we come to know them, we can begin to put some questions to the scientist. One place to start would be with the idea that there is a thing called 'scientific method', some one way 'scientists' have of doing things which other people do not. Even if we accept, for argument's sake, the regrettable contraction in the English language of the term 'science' to the business of the sciences of 'nature', and draw the boundaries of the scientific so tightly as to exclude all history, all sociology and economics, and a great part of psychology, the notion still seems highly questionable.

If, for example, the emphasis is placed upon the role played by observation and repeatable experiment, then what becomes of theoretical astronomy? And, if it is true that the structure and functions of living organisms are such that there are characteristically biological modes of thought which are not found, nor are they needed, in physics or in chemistry, then little is gained and not a little lost by obscuring these differences from view with the announcement that the particle physicist and the neuroscientist both employ 'the scientific method'.[10] Does not prediction, for example, play a very different and more central role in the physicist's work than in that of the evolutionary biologist?

Lacking competence in these matters, I can only register my impression that, far from there being any one mode of thought or manner of proceeding which might properly be called 'the scientific method', the relationship between the different instances of what might plausibly be called 'science' is, in Wittgenstein's sense and for the reasons that he gave, at most one of family resemblance. This is, I cheerfully admit, a subversive suggestion because, were it to win acceptance, then all clear distinctions between *Natur-* and *Geisteswissenschaften* would wither on the vine.

My impression is that the myth of scientific method – single, successful and austere – encourages scientists to suppose that other academic practices, being 'unscientific', are therefore less demanding, require less rigour in their prosecution. To put it very crudely: the scientists know that only the initiated can find their way around the maze of wires, valves and computer printouts – all this marvellous machinery in which the rest of us get lost – whereas it seems that, in philosophy or theology, for instance, anyone can have a go, because we only play with words.

This would, at least, be one explanation as to why it is that so many scientists treat topics in philosophy and theology with a carelessness and unconcern for competence which rightly irritates them when the boot is on the other foot. Thus, if I may stick my neck out, that 'intellectual world' with which Alister Hardy sought 'reconciliation' clearly did not number philosophers or theologians amongst its citizens, for, had it done so, he would surely have handled concepts such as 'power' and 'spirit', 'experience' and 'faith', with less blithe insouciance and inattention to the literature.

A more up-to-date example of the same insouciance would

---

[10] See Edelman, *Bright Air*, p. 73.

be the set of articles on 'Mind and brain' published, in September 1992, as a special issue of *Scientific American*. In this issue, Francis Crick and Christof Koch assured us that 'The overwhelming question in neurobiology today is the relation between the mind and the brain', yet not one of the contributors displayed a flicker of awareness of the fact that serious consideration of that question demands not only neurobiological but philosophical investigation. 'If', said Gerald Fischbach in his introductory survey, 'we agree to think of the mind as a collection of mental processes rather than as a substance or spirit, it becomes easier to get on with the necessary empirical studies.'[11] But, while wishing him every success in his prosecution of these studies, why should the rest of us agree to make life 'easier' for Professor Fischbach simply because he has not understood the incoherence of his stipulation?

Reviewing my book *Easter in Ordinary* in *Numinis*, David Hay deplored the 'intemperate' and unsympathetic character of what he called my 'strong attack on the religious ideas of William James; hence, in passing, on those of Alister Hardy'.[12] His (several times repeated) description of my critique of James as an 'attack' is interesting because it highlights some important differences in what we might call the conversational procedures of the natural sciences, on the one hand, and of philosophy or theology on the other.

Different fields of discourse have different rules of evidence, different conventions of procedure, different criteria of good performance. The physicist, we might almost say, persuades by proof, whereas it is by persuasion that the philosopher establishes her case. The natural scientist, to whom 'mere' words matter much less than measurement, looks past his language to the success of the experiment that it reports; an experiment which, if well done and then sufficiently confirmed by repetition, will not need doing again.

---

[11] Francis Crick and Christof Koch, 'The problems of consciousness', *Scientific American*, 267 (September 1992), 111; Gerald Fischbach, 'Mind and brain', ibid., 24.
[12] *Numinis*, 7 (July 1990), 11, 10.

Scientific disagreements are resolved not by force of argument, but by success or failure in prediction. Disagreement being thus, in principle, provisional, it plays an ancillary rather than a leading role in what is called research.

The philosopher does not do experiments. She reads books, a pastime which, these days, we are required by statute to describe as doing research. For the philosopher, no good words are 'mere' words. With these words, in this order, crafted with great care, she sees the world and acts in it this way. In philosophy, and in theology, disagreement is the material by means of which we come to grips with things, sharpen our wits, clarify our vision, as we struggle – on our own behalf and that of other people – to see the world and act in it less inappropriately, less clumsily, less destructively.

Nurtured, burdened and liberated as we are by memory, there is a unidirectionality, a genuine *history*, of both philosophy and theology. In each case, however, it is such as to enable and require us to keep alive the conversation with those who went before. Few physicists would expect to overturn the work of Heisenberg by taking a fresh look at Newton's *Principia*. In contrast a theologian or a philosopher might well find, in the texts of Aristotle or Aquinas, resources that would serve her well in the struggle against (to take two names at random) the worlds of Descartes or of William James.

DUALISM

This Centre, as I understand it, sets its face against what David Hay describes as 'a widespread taboo concerning religion, arising from Enlightenment ways of thinking'.[13] A key component in such ways of thinking has been that dichotomy between the individual observing mind and the realm of facts observed which is commonly referred to as 'Cartesian'.

A central issue here concerns the relationship of mind to matter. In *Easter in Ordinary*, I argued that, however hostile to

---

[13] Hay, *Religious Experience*, p. vii.

Cartesian dualism we suppose ourselves to be, it is not possible
to escape its clutches while continuing to treat the distinction
between mind and matter as empirical, as being (that is to
say) a distinction between two different kinds of 'thing' or
substance.

Throughout his philosophical career, William James' work
exhibited what I described as 'vigorous and sustained hostility
to "dualisms"' of every kind.[14] Hence Gerald Edelman has
recently suggested that James' 'greatest achievement may
have been to point out that consciousness is a process and not
a substance' or, as I put it, a thing.[15] The reason why my
discussion of James, in *Easter in Ordinary*, was so extended, and
so detailed, was that I sought to demonstrate that, notwithstanding the programmatic intention of a subtle, original and
powerful thinker, he remained trapped by the very dualisms
which he hoped to exorcise.

I took James as my conversation partner precisely because I
respected his influence, originality, and power. If James, of all
people, could be shown to be still mesmerised by the Cartesian
spell, then the power of that bewitchment's grip would have
been dramatically displayed. I was, moreover, well aware of
the fact that I was taking issue with what is probably still the
most widespread account in our culture of what is meant by
'person' and 'experience', by 'religion' and by 'God'; an
account subscribed to by both the friends of religion and its
foes. It therefore seemed to me important (on, if you like,
something like Popperian grounds) to challenge this account,
not in its casual and slipshod versions, but in the strongest,
most persuasive version that I knew. And that meant writing
seven introductory chapters on William James (although
readers of Dr Hay's review were not to discover that these
chapters were preliminary to a larger and constructive
enterprise).

Whether or not I made my case, where James' residual
Cartesianism is concerned, is up to other people to decide.
But, if I did, the chances are that those who still endorse more

[14] Nicholas Lash, *Easter in Ordinary*, p. 52.   [15] Edelman, *Bright Air*, p. 37.

or less Jamesian accounts of what is meant by 'consciousness' and by 'experience', by 'religion' and its 'objects', are still operating with Cartesian parameters. Now if (as has, I think, by now been amply demonstrated) the emergence of Cartesian dualism marked an important step along the road which led to the exclusion of religion from the realm of public truth, then the defenders of religion might be ill advised to seek its rehabilitation on the very ground and with the very weapons that drove it from the field.

One last word on dualism. Those who suppose that 'mind' (or 'consciousness', or 'spirit') and 'matter' *are* the names of different kinds of thing need to give serious consideration to this question: was there once a time when minds did not exist? If, as seems evident, there was, then how did minds first come about and of what substance were they made?

THE GRAMMAR OF 'EXPERIENCE'

Turning now to the matter of 'experience', let me ask three further questions about the kinds of things there are. How do we know what kinds of things there are? How might we decide what kinds of things there are? Third, are these two questions more or less the same? That is to say: is our knowledge of the kinds of things there are an outcome of decisions we have taken as to how things should be classified?

The answer, surely, must be 'Yes'. 'The world', says Gerald Edelman, 'with its "objects", is an unlabelled place . . . Any assignment of boundaries made by an animal is relative, not absolute, and depends on its adaptive or intended needs.'[16] All schemes of classification, all maps and names of things, are thus conventional. We assign the boundaries, and it is therefore up to us, if needs be, to redraw them differently.

It is, however, of paramount importance to insist that 'conventional' does not mean 'arbitrary'. The motorist who, having learnt that *we* decide what kinds of things there are, decides to

---

[16] Ibid., p. 28; see pp. 99, 118, 228.

treat all other objects on the road as figments of imagination would soon come to an untimely end.

How, then, might we best decide the grammar of 'experience'? To what events or processes, occurrences or undertakings, should this label be affixed, and how might the boundaries best be drawn between (for instance) 'experience' and 'language'?

In common with much writing in his particular philosophical tradition, David Hay manages throughout *Religious Experience Today* simultaneously to convey the impression that what counts as 'experience' is simply given, in the nature of things, and that decisions as to how to handle the distinction between experience and language are more or less a matter of individual taste or (as he puts it in one or two passages which misinterpret what is meant by 'hermeneutics of suspicion') temperament.[17]

Consider the following two statements which, at first sight, may seem very similar. On the one hand, David Hay: 'we need language and interpretation to mediate our experience, and these are derived from our life history'. On the other, Fergus Kerr, reflecting on postmodernism's 'rediscovery of the fact that our experience is always mediated. I see because I have been *taught* to.' The difference between these two accounts becomes apparent, however, when we notice that, for David Hay, language is liable to 'distort' the 'inner nature' of something called 'direct experience'.[18]

The myth is a familiar one: beneath, beyond, behind the images we entertain, the language that we use, there is some 'stuff' called 'pure', 'direct', or 'raw' experience.[19] Whereas, for Fergus Kerr, experience is the outcome of our education – the way we have learnt to live, and move, and have our being; what, in the long run, if we're lucky, makes us wise – James

---

[17] See Hay, *Religious Experience*, p. 39, n. 4; cf. p. 101.

[18] Hay, *Religious Experience*, p. 34; Fergus Kerr, 'Rescuing Girard's argument?', *Modern Theology*, 8 (October 1992), 388.

[19] For some references to James' talk of 'stuff', see Lash, *Easter in Ordinary*, pp. 66–7.

and his supporters attribute to an abstract noun the 'false concreteness' of the stuff of basic human sensibility.[20]

Although Oxford may be among the last places to discover this, the philosophical, psychological, sociological and now, with Edelman's work, biological criticisms of empiricist construals of the grammar of 'experience' are, by now, cumulatively so devastating as to require, at the very least, from those who wish to keep such usages alive, *arguments* and not mere expressions of preference.

Finally, as I put it in *Easter in Ordinary*, if there is now 'very little to be said in favour of, and a great deal to be said against, retaining a contracted account of experience *in general*, then there is even less to be said in favour of retaining a contracted account of *religious* experience'.[21] It is time, therefore, to say a word about the grammar of 'religion'.

THE GRAMMAR OF 'RELIGION'

If experience is not a 'thing', perhaps religion is. But, if so, what kind of thing is it? A list of what would count, for most people, as religions would include Christianity, Judaism, Buddhism, Hinduism and Islam. Yet many Jews and Muslims would deny, and with good reason, that either Judaism or Islam may properly be called 'religions'; there is a strong case for omitting from the list any movement or tradition (such as Buddhism) which has no place for adoration; and there are excellent Durkheimian grounds for classifying the ceremonies of American civic life and May Day parades in the former USSR as religious rituals.

There simply are no features common to all the main candidates for admission to the list. There is no genus, 'religion', of which particular religions are specific forms. It follows that, as with 'science', so with 'religion', the relationships between

---

[20] On 'false concreteness' see Stephen Toulmin, 'The genealogy of "consciousness"' in Paul Secord (ed.), *Explaining Human Behaviour: Consciousness, Human Action, and Social Structure* (London: Sage, 1982), pp. 53–70; Lash, *Easter in Ordinary*, p. 92.

[21] Lash, *Easter in Ordinary*, p. 92.

what might plausibly be deemed its instances are, at most, relationships of family resemblance. But, if this is right, then any quest for some kind of 'common core' is obviously doomed to failure. Here I must be careful, because your Director has identified as one of 'the two most important issues to be clarified' for the Centre's future work an issue of 'major importance to the human race', the question as to whether or not there is a 'common core . . . to all religious experience'.[22]

At the very least (to make a point similar to the one I made about the grammar of 'experience') it seems to me that the philosophical, historical, sociological and theological objections to 'genus-and-species' construals of the concept of 'religion' are, by now, cumulatively sufficiently compelling as to require, from those who wish to stand by such construals, some fresh and rigorous and detailed *arguments*, not casual expressions of hunch or personal preference.

I lay the emphasis, in each case, on the need for argument, as a reminder that to treat the issues as empirical rather than as philosophical, as questions of fact which further experiment could confirm or disconfirm, would simply display unexamined ontological commitments. And that would leave some quite important corners of 'the intellectual world' exceedingly dissatisfied.

Finally, if I have laid the emphasis on philosophical, rather than directly theological, considerations, I did so because I am convinced that it is the concept of 'experience', more fundamentally than that of 'religion', which determines what we take 'religious experience' to mean.

THE WAY AHEAD

Alister Hardy's project of bringing into common conversation evolutionary biologists and students of spirituality seems to me, as I said at the beginning, both important and exciting. (And this non-scientist's reference to the work of Gerald Edelman was intended as a modest gesture in this direction.)

---

[22] Gordon Wakefield, 'The future programme of the Centre', *Numinis*, 7 (1990), 2.

Conversation is of paramount importance because, to up-end the Jamesian slogan, language unites whereas experience divides! Therefore, I repeat my warm endorsement of David Hay's emphasis upon the need for education in attentiveness or reverence and in alertness to the languages we use. And we would all agree that much damage has been done by the exclusion of the business of religion from the realm of public truth.

I would myself prefer, however, to characterise that exclusion not as the 'censoring' or 'suppression' of religion, but rather as its displacement.[23] The secularity of our culture is an illusion, and a dangerous one at that. Almost all human beings set their hearts on something, have some object of their worship, and if they are distracted or discouraged from that laborious *ascesis* the Christians forms of which make up the costly pedagogy of discipleship, then they will set their hearts on some particular fact or thing, some dream or vision or good feeling, some institution, individual or idea. In other words, the displacement of religion from the realm of truth merely unleashes the horsemen of the Apocalypse, leaves our propensity for idolatry unchecked and unconstrained, with devastating consequences.

I mention this because no account of religious experience remotely adequate to at least the great prophetic traditions – of Judaism, Christianity and Islam – could fail to place right at the centre of its story the interconnections between duty and destiny, the cost of selflessness strenuously worked out in darkness. If, for example, Christianity has an experiential 'root' or 'core', then this is to be found not in 'fleeting' or 'puzzling' transient states of private consciousness,[24] but in the experience of Jesus in Gethsemane and on Calvary, and in the experience of his followers – at first dismayed and disoriented, later refashioned in rediscovery and worked out in courageous opposition to the authorities and in painful conflict with their fellow Jews.

Let me end, a little more light-heartedly, with a not entirely

---

[23] See Hay, *Religious Experience*, pp. 96–8.   [24] Hay, *Religious Experience*, p. 63.

frivolous proposal. What your Centre needs is a patron sage. Such a sage would, of course, have to be someone deeply versed in and appreciative of the methods and thought-forms of the natural sciences; someone with considerable competence in both philosophy and theology, who had studied the history of modern Western culture and who knew the damage done to it by the illusions of secularity; someone, above all, who set spirituality and its pedagogy at the centre of the common search for truth, and sense, and sanity. I have a candidate for the post! You have no idea how happy I would be if, next time that I came to visit you, all pictures of William James had their face turned to the wall, and there, in the entrance hall, stood a life-size statue of Baron Friedrich von Hügel.

CHAPTER 6

Contemplation, metaphor and real knowledge[1]

DOING EPISTEMOLOGY WHEN THINGS GO WRONG

We have been asked to 'focus' our deliberations on questions of epistemology. I shall begin by suggesting reasons why this request, although by no means unexpected, should neverthe-less be treated with suspicion, hence my heading for this first section: 'Doing epistemology when things go wrong'.

Next, I shall consider how things came to be the way they are, where relations between science, and philosophy, and theology are concerned. And I shall suggest that human beings might be a more fruitful topic of conversation between theology and the natural sciences than the initial conditions of the universe.

Thirdly, under the heading of 'The recovery of metaphor', I shall indicate some implications of the fact that a brief episode in the history of Western culture seems to be now drawing to a close: an episode during which great store was set on 'univocity' as paradigm strategy for straightforward speech, while metaphor was the suspect homeland of poetic licence. And as we discover, once again, that we must live and tell our stories in unlabelled places, we need to relearn ancient lessons about how we may speak of God, of God's knowledge and of our knowing God.

Finally, I shall say something about that courtesy or reticence, the 'silencing of easy speech', which is the hallmark

---

[1] This paper was originally read to an interdisciplinary symposium, entitled 'Knowing God, Christ and nature in the post-positivistic era', which took place at the University of Notre Dame in April 1993.

112

of responsible utterance not only in Christian worship and theological reflection, but across the whole range of academic or 'scientific' practices. We know best the things we know when we acknowledge all our knowing to be but educated ignorance.

D. W. Hamlyn had the Sophists in mind when he spoke of the 'general skepticism' which led to 'the beginning of epistemology as it has been traditionally known – the attempt to justify the claim that knowledge is possible'.[2] Epistemology, in other words, first came to birth at a time when things were going wrong with knowing things. And it is almost a defining feature of our modern Western philosophical imagination that all subsequent periods of comparable cognitive turbulence stand overshadowed by the upheavals of the seventeenth century. (It is, of course, too early to tell how interesting or important the epistemological confusion and cacophony of our own day will seem a hundred years from now, but at least the fog is thick enough to render the choice of focus for our conference unsurprising.)

Notwithstanding the fact, however, that epistemology, in something like Hamlyn's sense, has been an intermittently recurring preoccupation since the days of ancient Greece, it has only been 'traditionally known' as epistemology for a little over one hundred years. James Ferrier, professor of moral philosophy and political economy at St Andrews, seems to have been innovating when in his *Institutes of Metaphysic*, published in 1854, he preceded the section on ontology first by a section on 'epistemology', the 'doctrine or theory of knowing', and, secondly, by one on 'agnoiology, or theory of ignorance'.[3] The date, I think, is interesting: was this not

---

[2] D. W. Hamlyn, 'Epistemology, history of' in Paul Edwards (ed.), *The Encyclopaedia of Philosophy*, III (New York: Macmillan, 1967), p. 9.

[3] James F. Ferrier, *Institutes of Metaphysic: The Theory of Knowing and Being* (Edinburgh: William Blackwood, 1854), pp. 46, 48. John Burnet, born in 1863, the year before Ferrier's death, was to be, for over thirty years, professor of Greek at St Andrews. In May 1923 he began his Romanes Lecture, delivered before the University of Oxford and entitled 'Ignorance', 'About seventy years ago a St Andrews professor invented the word *Epistemology*. It has been immensely popular, though we could perhaps have done without it. He held, however, that the Epistemology, or Theory of

a time when a whole raft of intellectual practices sought both autonomy and cognitive respectability in seeming science-like, or *wissenschaftlich*? And so, amongst a host of other '-ologies', epistemology was born.

Ferrier's epistemology, which occupies four hundred of the five hundred pages in his book, sets out from 'the first question of philosophy – the *only* first question which it can have; and its answer is the absolute starting-point of metaphysics'. This first question is: 'what is the *one* feature which is identical, invariable, and essential in all the varieties of our knowledge?'[4]

That all the varieties of our knowledge could have or could require any such single common feature; that there could ever, in our thinking about anything, be an 'absolute' starting-point, before which nothing had been known or thought, a starting-point on which, first, epistemology and, then, ontology could be constructed; these are possibilities that it is well-nigh impossible to entertain today. Or, to be more cautious, since *everything* seems entertainable today, and there are some people who apparently succeed in entertaining just such possibilities, are they not, nevertheless, possibilities the consideration of which demands steadfast refusal to learn anything from Heidegger or Wittgenstein?[5]

If the search for single 'starting-points' or foundations and the placing of epistemology before ontology may be deemed characteristic of the 'modern' mind, then perhaps 'post-

Knowledge, was a barren thing in itself, and would not bring us a step nearer reality, unless it was supplemented by a Theory of Ignorance. That was, I think, a suggestion much to the purpose. Unhappily he thought proper to call this part of his system by the repellent name of *Agnoiology*, with the result that it has been overlooked and indeed forgotten.' (John Burnet, *Essays and Addresses* (London: Chatto and Windus, 1929), p. 236.) I am most grateful to Dr George Davie for drawing my attention to Burnet's lecture.

[4] Ferrier, *Institutes*, p. 71, his stress. The answer, given as the first 'proposition' of the *Institutes*, is: 'Along with whatever any intelligence knows, it must, as the ground or condition of its knowledge, have some cognisance of *itself*' (p. 75).

[5] As to what might be learnt, in these matters, from Heidegger and Wittgenstein, see Fergus Kerr's illuminating essay, 'Idealism and realism: an old controversy dissolved' in Kenneth Surin (ed.), *Christ, Ethics and Tragedy. Essays in Honour of Donald MacKinnon* (Cambridge: Cambridge University Press, 1989), pp. 15–33.

modernism' might mean finding Dante more congenial than Descartes, for Dante's starting-point was where we all begin: 'Nel mezzo del cammin di nostra vita';[6] in the middle of the journey of our life.

To question the priority of epistemology is not, by any means, to question the necessity of subjecting knowledge-claims to careful scrutiny and rigorous assessment. But, whereas the Cartesian supposes that establishing the possi-bility of knowledge is (as I once put it) an exercise in *engineering* – in the construction of reliable bridges between the ego or homunculus (Ferrier's 'intelligence') somewhere in my brain, and the dangerous, dark world outside – I would suggest that the appropriate investigation is ethical, rather than merely theoretical, let alone 'mechanical', in character: that is to say, it asks who, and what, and in what circumstances, and to what extent, may reasonably and responsibly be *relied* upon.[7] Whether in physics or in politics, in psychology or prayer, to grow in knowledge is to grow through trust: trust given, trust betrayed, trust risked, misplaced, sustained, received and suffered.

Hence George Steiner's emphasis, in his courageous and important essay *Real Presences*, upon what he calls 'the trust within logic itself, where "logic" is a *logos*-derivative and construct'. Contemporary nihilism is, for Steiner, a betrayal of responsibility, an 'abrogation of the contract between word and world'.[8] To many of our contemporaries, such abrogation is a game, all language merely private pastime. But suppose the broken contract was not, after all, drawn up by us? And what would it be like to trust that this were so?

Amid the suffering and confusion that surrounds us, all glib

6 Dante Alighieri, *La divina commedia. Inferno*, I.I.
7 See Nicholas Lash, *Easter in Ordinary*, pp. 69, 121, 188. 'Homunculus' is Gerald Edelman's name for the one whom I called the 'little person': see Gerald M. Edelman, *Bright Air, Brilliant Fire*, p. 28.
8 George Steiner, *Real Presences. Is There Anything IN What We Say?* (London: Faber and Faber, 1989), pp. 89, 132. 'The broken contract' is the title of the second of the three parts of Steiner's study (pp. 53–134). For some reflections on the theological implications of Steiner's argument, see my 1990 Aquinas Lecture, 'Friday, Saturday, Sunday', *New Blackfriars*, 71 (1990), 109–19.

and easy answers to such questions verge on the obscene. It is incumbent upon Christians to react with caution to the remarkable burgeoning of interest in 'religion' we have seen these last few years. Suddenly, at what had seemed the hour of the final triumph of 'secularisation', literary critics and philosophers, physicists and social scientists have started speaking with enthusiasm about 'spirit' and 'transcendence', 'god' and 'gaia', while the shelves of bookstores groan with titles listed under 'mysticism', 'spirituality', 'the supernatural' and 'occult'. This last fact alone should give us pause for thought.

The nihilism which insists we have no grounds for trust may take two forms: one brightly chattering before the lights go out, the other silent on all questions other than those concerning short-term calculi of ownership and power. We are not constrained, however, either to easy speech or to silence. There remains a different possibility, another route for testing knowledge-claims, along which the rigorously disciplined attentiveness of science well done might be surprised by its proximity to the entirely non-esoteric reticence, the *'docta ignorantia'* (as Rahner loved to call it), of Christian faith's cognitive relationship to the mystery of God.

STORIES OF SCIENCE

The plausibility of this suggestion depends, in part, upon our view of how things came to be the way they are. So, let us go back to the beginning (!) and ask: where were 'science' and 'philosophy' before the great transitions of the seventeenth and eighteenth centuries, and how did things then go from there? Vastly to simplify a very complex story, we might say that, whereas the sense of 'science' (which most of philosophy once was) contracted from *all* kinds of knowledge to become, by the later nineteenth century, the name of that *one* kind of knowledge to which our knowledge of all kinds of things should (in principle) aspire, 'philosophy' (which once was most of science) shifted from being ordered knowledge via an under-standing of the concatenation of particular knowledges, which bifurcated into 'natural' and 'moral' philosophy before coming to mean, first and foremost, our grasp of the conditions of knowledge of all kinds.[9] Or, as non-philosophers might prefer to put it, once natural philosophy had become natural science, philosophers had little left to do except to think non-scientifically about nothing in particular.

Thus, 'scientists' became the name for those whose task it is to find out what kinds of things there are and how they work. Quite soon, with no exceptions left to the list of things that could be thought of in the way that 'science' considers things, the scientists began to gaze with condescension upon the remnants of 'philosophy', the scope of which was now reduced to 'the analysis of language. What a comedown from the great tradition of philosophy from Aristotle to Kant!'[10]

Let me try to put my finger on one key factor underlying the irritated incomprehension with which many scientists (by no means only Lewis Wolpert) regard philosophy. There are significant affinities linking medieval distinctions between 'material' and 'formal' description (and their classical precursors) to Wittgenstein's distinction between 'empirical' and 'grammatical' investigation. In the course of the seventeenth and eighteenth centuries, however, such distinctions were lost sight of as all philosophical investigation came to take the form of 'natural' philosophy which, in turn, became mechanics. And if, with Kant, admiration for Newtonian mechanics was accompanied by some stirring from their slumber of formal habits of reflection, the focus of concern of formal discourse had now shifted to epistemology thus, as it were, abdicating the territory of ontology to natural scientists.

My suggestion, in other words, is that the dismissiveness displayed by scientists towards philosophy is due, in part, to the extent to which, in our culture, philosophers are (with mathematicians and linguistic theorists) among the few

[9] For the history of the relations between science, philosophy and theology, I am especially indebted to Michael J. Buckley, *At the Origins of Modern Atheism*, and Amos Funkenstein, *Theology and the Scientific Imagination*.

[10] Stephen W. Hawking, *A Brief History of Time* (London: Bantam Press, 1988), p. 175.

people still educated to appreciate distinctions between empirical and 'grammatical' procedures. It is, therefore, not surprising that most people deem it a pointless waste of time and energy to consider questions such as: what makes a thing a 'thing'? What kinds of things should *count* as 'things'?[11]

To put it slightly differently: in a culture which supposes all such questions to be questions of the kind 'and is there honey still for tea?', the theologian who suggests that grace is *not* a thing, and neither is God, nor is the human mind, will find that such suggestions are comprehensively misunderstood as denials of the reality of mind, and grace, and God.

In the interest of clarifying, a little, this confusing history of the ways in which we think of things, I propose a modest thesis: that human beings are things that think and have a history (not least, a history of thinking). This may seem uncontentious. However, it implies that understanding human beings requires, first, some understanding of the kind of things that human beings are and of the ways that they relate to other things, to other facts and objects in the world; secondly, it requires some understanding of the ways in which different things are differently known and understood; thirdly, it requires some understanding of the ways in which things came to be the way they are or seem to be.

A measure of such understanding is of course, acquired, sustained, distorted, deepened, through the codes and customs, narratives and symbol-systems, that constitute a culture. But, where those reflective appropriations of the world of common sense known in Germany as *Wissenschaft* and in France as *science* are concerned, my thesis implies that the practices which we call 'history' and 'philosophy' and 'science' are interdependent elements of a single structure. Notwithstanding the accelerated fragmentation of specialised academic activities, we trample in each other's territory, sing each other's songs, whether we want to or not. This being the case, it would seem sensible of us to minimise our

---

[11] See above, Chapter Five, pp. 95–6.

incompetence in respect of those elements of the structure in which we are not specialists.

For example: any philosophy of mind is incompatible with at least some accounts of the relationships of mind to brains, and brains are the business of biology; any physics or biology incorporates some story of the kinds of thing that count as things of different kinds; and any historian takes some position on causes and effects, on relationships between things. The maps we draw of academic practices illustrate, quite neatly, the interdependence that I have in mind. Distinctions between *Naturwissenschaften* and *Geisteswissenschaften* were not drawn by procedures characterisable, in modern English, as 'scientific'. These distinctions are, rather, the historical outworkings of early modern philosophical distinctions between *Natur* and *Geist*.

It is a pity that the conversation between science and religion should be so much more lively in the United States and Britain than it is elsewhere. A pity, because we all speak English. And the inconvenience of enduring distinctions between *Natur* and *Geist* pales into insignificance when compared with the disastrous consequences of our surrender (in English) of *scientia* to one small, though most distinguished, corner of the wide world of *Wissenschaft*. In becoming the paradigm of 'science', first physics and then chemistry and biology became the quite unwarranted paradigm of all rigorously ordered public knowledge. Even today, when the remaining spokesmen for scientistic imperialism sound more like dinosaurs than voices of the future, the myth of 'arts and sciences' still exhibits most depressing strength (in its hold not only over our imaginations but, which is almost as important, over funding policy!)

On this myth I have three brief remarks to make. First, even were we to allow the restriction of the realm of 'science' to so-called physical sciences, or sciences of nature, there still would not be just one thing called 'science' performed by one type of procedure known as 'scientific method'. If, for example, the emphasis is placed upon repeatable experiment, then what becomes of theoretical cosmology? Or, again, am I wrong to be persuaded by Gerald Edelman that the structure and functions of living organisms are such that there are characteristically biological modes of thought which are neither found nor needed in physics or in chemistry? Does not prediction play a very different role in the physicist's work than in that of the evolutionary biologist?[12]

In the second place, whereas Wittgenstein's notion of family resemblance is flexible enough to cover the complex networks of affinity and influence, difference and derivation, which characterise the actual relationships between the vastly diverse sets of intellectual practices accommodated by a modern university, under the influence of the 'arts and sciences' myth discussion of comparative method or epistemology is too often marked by an extraordinary lack of interest in the things that some three-quarters of our colleagues do: in law and economics, for example, in history and engineering, psychology and textual criticism, archaeology and medicine.

In the third place, however, it is not my intention, in thus emphasising the sheer diversity of the forms of disciplined enquiry, to deny that there are common features shared (for example) by philosophy and theology, on the one hand, and, on the other, by physics, biology and chemistry. Consider, for instance, the part played by disagreement. The natural scientist, to whom 'mere' words matter much less than measurement, looks past his language to the success of the experiment that it reports; an experiment which, if well done, and then sufficiently confirmed by repetition, will not need doing again. Scientific disagreements are not resolved by force of argument, but by success or failure in prediction. Disagreement being thus, in principle, provisional, it plays an ancillary rather than a leading role in what is called research.[13]

I have been asked to keep in mind Karl Rahner's contribution to the conversation between theology and science. At

[12] See, e.g., Edelman, *Bright Air*, pp. 73 ff. Moreover, unlike physics, 'biology is historical' (Edelman, p. 239).

[13] See above, Chapter Five, p. 103.

this point, I simply draw attention to the fact that he had far less to say about these things than we, with our contracted sense of 'science', might suppose. Thus, for example, only one of the nineteen essays in a volume entitled *Science and Christian Faith* is directly concerned with the subject-matter of this symposium. The reason is, of course, that most of those of his essays which might seem (from their English titles) to be about relations between theology and science are, in fact, concerned with the relationships between the life of faith and scholarly reflection, of whatever kind. Thus, for example, 'Science as a "confession"?', the title of a well-known essay dating from 1954, in fact translates 'Wissenschaft als "Konfession"?'.[14]

Karl Rahner never doubted that we are entitled, indeed required, to demand that the standards of *Wissenschaft* be set as high in theology as in any other field of erudite endeavour. But, especially in his later writings, he insisted that *Wissenschaft* alone is not enough. The academic theologian is, we might say, the literary critic of faith's autobiographical performance of the Christian story of the world.[15] The critic may not, however, take the telling of the tale for granted, leaving it to other people or to another time. In speaking of what he called a 'missionary and mystagogic' element necessary in theology today, Rahner was insisting that even the most rigorous and technical academic theology must itself exhibit something of the message, the announcement, *God's* announcement, to which it points and of which it seeks some understanding.[16] To vary my earlier metaphor, we might say

---

14 See Karl Rahner, 'Natural science and reasonable faith' in *Theological Investigations*, XXI, *Science and Christian Faith* in (trans.) Hugh M. Riley (London: Darton, Longman and Todd, 1988), pp. 16–55; 'Science as a "confession"?' in *Theological Investigations*, III, *The Theology of the Spiritual Life*, (trans.) Karl-H. and Boniface Kruger (London: Darton, Longman and Todd, 1967), pp. 385–400; 'Wissenschaft als "Konfession"?' in *Schriften zur Theologie*, III, *Zur Theologie des Geistlichen Lebens* (Einsiedeln: Benziger, 1962), pp. 455–72.

15 On faith as autobiographical and as performance, respectively, see Nicholas Lash, 'Ideology, metaphor and analogy' and 'Performing the Scriptures' in *Theology on the Way to Emmaus*, pp. 95–119, 37–46.

16 See, e.g., Karl Rahner, 'Possible courses for the theology of the future' in *Theological Investigations*, XIII, *Theology, Anthropology, Christology*, (trans.) David Bourke (London: Darton, Longman and Todd, 1975), pp. 40–2.

that the theologian, as music critic of the song of songs, must also – in the very texture of her critical activity – make some contribution to its singing. My own view is that, if we took this requirement seriously, we would be far more concerned than we seem to be at present with the *poetics* of theology. It is a necessary condition of theology well done that it be not merely erudite and rigorous and accurate in argument and in the handling of evidence, but also that it be well written. God's beauty is not well served by ugly prose.

'The world, with its "objects"', says Gerald Edelman, 'is an unlabelled place.'[17] We put the labels on, assign the boundaries, and it is up to us, if need be, to redraw them differently. However, although I have regretted the contraction of the territory of 'science' (in English) to one small segment of the world of *Wissenschaft*, merely to relabel things would, in itself, serve little useful purpose. (After all, labelling sociology and economics as 'social sciences' simply reinforces some people's prejudices that social sciences are not 'really' sciences at all!)

I have, however, made two positive proposals: that Wittgenstein's notion of family resemblance would be a good heuristic guide to the geography of intellectual practices, and that all of us might benefit from thinking through the epistemological implications of the fact that human beings are things that think and have a history. To conclude this section of my remarks, let me suggest four reasons why *human being* (human 'nature', if you will) may be the most fruitful focus for conversation between theology and the natural sciences.

In the first place, it might help to counteract the widespread and unfortunate impression that, because God is 'beyond' the world we know, therefore the further that we move from where we are – in space, or time, or understanding – the nearer we may get to God. I have a hunch that this strange view of things has been a factor in the sales of Stephen Hawking's *Brief History of Time*.

In the second place, whereas only a quite small band of

---

[17] Edelman, *Bright Air*, p. 28.

specialists are competent to consider the initial conditions of the world, human beings are a proper subject of scrutiny by everyone: biologists and philosophers, lawyers and linguists, psychologists and animal ethologists, archaeologists and historians of art, economists – and even theologians! – may all have something to contribute.

In the third place, Christopher Mooney, making a similar suggestion in *Theological Studies* two years ago, quoted the late Heinz Pagels to the effect that 'Science has explored the microcosmos and the macrocosmos; we have a good sense of the lay of the land. The great unexplored frontier is complexity. Complex systems include the body and its organs, especially the brain.'[18]

In the fourth place, the recent assertion, by Francis Crick and Christof Koch, that 'the overwhelming question in neurobiology today is the relation between the mind and the brain',[19] suggests that the interdisciplinary study of human being might prove a fruitful context in which to start unscrambling the dualisms which, since the seventeenth century, have done such damage to our understanding of ourselves, the world of which we form a part, and our relationship to the mystery of God.

THE RECOVERY OF METAPHOR

At one point in an interesting paper, Mooney nods. 'Theologians', he tells us, 'have in the past *always* held some version of spirit/matter dualism'. There are two things wrong with this generalisation. The first is that it is promptly contradicted by his own addition: 'Clearly there is no such dichotomy in the Bible.'[20] But the second is the distressingly casual

---

[18] Heinz R. Pagels, *The Dreams of Reason* (New York: Bantam, 1989), p. 12, quoted from Christopher F. Mooney, 'Theology and science: a new commitment to dialogue', *Theological Studies*, 52 (1991), 320.

[19] Francis Crick and Christof Koch, 'The problems of consciousness', *Scientific American*, 267 (1992), 111.

[20] Mooney, 'Theology and science', p. 325, my stress. Contradicted, that is, on the supposition that Isaiah and Paul and the author of the Fourth Gospel (for example) are not to be excluded from the ranks of the theologians!

nature of the claim. Far too often, discussion of these questions seems to proceed on a twofold assumption, firstly, that distinctions between mind and body, spirit and flesh, *Geist* and *Natur*, 'subjective value' and 'objective truth', the 'private' and the 'public' realms, are, at the end of the day, all more or less the same and, secondly, that it is not possible to insist on the irreducibility of one or more of these distinctions without thereby endorsing a 'dualism' of some kind that is to be deplored.[21]

The first of these assumptions will not bear a moment's serious consideration. Thus, for example, the distinction between *Geist* and *Natur*, drawn at a time when people had lost sight of the fact that human culture forms part of human nature, being the production and expression of the kind of thing we are, has almost nothing in common with biblical distinctions between the spirit that gives life and not-life, or lesser life, or life gone wrong.[22] Nor are there inferences legitimately to be drawn, from either of these two distinctions, which would warrant claims that the knowledge gained by science is public, whereas our knowledge of each other and of the things of God pertains to something called the 'private world'.

Perhaps the most straightforward kind of dualism is that according to which the items which constitute the furniture of the world fall into two irreducibly distinct classes or kinds of thing. Gerald Edelman, who calls this 'substance dualism', distinguishes it from 'property dualism (the notion that psychology can be satisfactorily described only in its own terms)'.[23]

---

[21] According to Michael Buckley, Max Planck believed that science and religion were compatible because 'science deals with objective truth, while religion is concerned with subjective value' (Michael J. Buckley, 'Religion and science: Paul Davies and John Paul II', *Theological Studies*, 51 (1990), 312). In his 1988 Eddington Lecture, my colleague Sir Brian Pippard said of 'The knowledge of the private world' that it is 'the knowledge gained by mystics and musicians and lovers, knowledge which stands outside words and logic . . . it is precisely here, in the contemplative role of the conscious mind, that science has nothing to say' (Brian Pippard, 'The invincible ignorance of science', *Contemporary Physics*, 29 (1988), 404).

[22] See Lash, *Believing Three Ways*, pp. 83–5.   [23] Edelman, *Bright Air*, p. 190.

There are still substance dualists around but, as it seems to me, there are two questions which they need to answer. Was there a time when minds did not exist? And if, as seems quite evident, there was, then how did minds first come about and of what substance were they made? Incidentally, substance dualism is not required by the belief that each individual human being is unique, and in unique relationship to the mystery of God, because, on a non-dualistic version of the biological story such as Edelman's, 'each individual person is like no other and is not a machine'.[24]

Property dualisms are not so easily disposed of, but I am persuaded by Edelman's account of the emergence and development of human consciousness, according to which 'That [consciousness] emerges from definite material arrangements in the brain does not mean that it is identical to them, for . . . consciousness depends on relations with the environment and, in its highest order, on symbols and language in a society.'[25] There are, I think, exciting possibilities for conversation between this view of the relations between biology and human sociality and (for example) Rahner's insistence that, in both philosophy and theology, we are 'going to have to realise more clearly and more radically that [our] very recognition and acceptance of the fact of being lost in the cosmos actually raises [us] above it'.[26]

So far, I have not indicated why this section is headed 'The recovery of metaphor'. Let us turn back, then, for a moment, to the seventeenth century, the heyday of substance dualisms drawn between describers and the things described. According to Amos Funkenstein, only in the seventeenth century was the late scholastic ambition to purify scientific discourse of all ambiguity fused with the Renaissance goal (learned from the Stoics) of finding in nature 'homogeneity . . . in all its parts, a

---

[24] Edelman, *Bright Air*, p. 171. A large part of his argument is devoted to furnishing the warrants for the latter judgement. The guiding principle of his study is that 'there must be ways to put the mind back into nature that are concordant with how it got there in the first place' (p. 15).

[25] Edelman, *Bright Air*, p. 198.

[26] Rahner, 'Natural science and reasonable faith', p. 50.

nature constructed of one matter and of one set of forces'. With this fusion there came a new ideal: 'a science that has an unequivocal language with which it speaks and uniform objects of which it speaks'. The pursuit of this ideal left no time for narrative, no patience with poetry, polysemy, paradox, echo and allusion. As a result, both 'scientists and theologians in the seventeenth century spoke pure prose; but, unlike Mr Jourdain, they knew it'. Thus, in a world in which univocity was the ideal of description and homogeneity the character of things described, Descartes and More and Leibniz 'and most of the others believed that the subject of theology and science alike can be absolutely de-metaphorized and de-symbolized'.[27]

Our world, in these last years of the twentieth century, with all discourse, as it sometimes seems, rudderless in storm-tossed seas of 'pluralism' and postmodern *différance*, contrasts dramatically with that described by Funkenstein. It is as if the ideals of the seventeenth century had been reversed: no longer imagining that we are made of different and superior stuff or that we stand aloof from all the things that we describe, increasingly amazed by their exuberant diversity and fascinated by their interaction, we find ourselves enmeshed in endless labours of interpretation, all discourse seemingly unstable, pregnant with possibility and unforeseen disaster, heavy with allusions, dreams and nightmares. It is now plain speech and uncontrovertible straightforwardness, univocity and literal description, not metaphor and ambiguity, that are the exception rather than the rule – at best, perhaps, fleeing moments of stability in the confusion and the flux of things.

In thus impressionistically evoking a widespread climate of belief, I am not recommending that we lose our nerve, succumb to the temptation of supposing that it does not really matter what we say. On the contrary, it matters a great deal, for the ways in which we speak and think, argue, imagine and narrate are the ways in which we nurture or destroy the world, each other and ourselves; the ways in which we either learn attentiveness to the peremptory stillness of God's Word or

---

[27] Funkenstein, *Theology and the Scientific Imagination*, pp. 41, 72, 116.

close our hearts and minds, chattering light-heartedly towards despair. 'It is simply *not* self-evident', says John Milbank, 'that every game of truth is but a local ritual', an arbitrary pastime.[28] But, for it to be more, for the word-games that we play to dramatise, exhibit, bring to speech some larger truth not of our invention, requires of us not merely the passionate attentiveness, the loving and disinterested contemplativity, that is, for science and theology alike, the heartbeat of all serious investigation, but also an unending discipline in learning how to speak. And there is no word that is more difficult to use appropriately than 'God'.

THE SILENCING OF EASY SPEECH

I keep, at home, a poster, one of a series issued by the British Government, during the Second World War, in order to sustain high levels of public vigilance. Its message: 'Careless talk costs lives.' Precision, rigour, accuracy, *akribeia* (as Aristotle might say), is a concept the instances of which, differently applicable in different fields of discourse, are (once again) best mapped by family resemblance. There are affinities, discernible relationships, between (for instance) what counts as courtesy and sensitivity in informal conversation, as unambiguous and lucid technicality in law, precision in diplomacy, appropriate accuracy in economics, poetry, or mathematics; as faith and hope well brought to speech in prayer.

Where measurement, direct description and mathematical expression are concerned, physical scientists are trained to high standards of disciplined precision. It is, however, an implication of my reminder that questions of empirical description, ontology and history are inextricably intertwined, that scientists (like everybody else) would do well to watch the larger framework of their thinking and imagining with comparable care. As Mary Midgley has often pointed out,

---

[28] John Milbank, 'The end of enlightenment: post-modern or post-secular?' in Claude Geffré and Jean-Pierre Jossua (eds.), *The Debate on Modernity. Concilium*, 1992/6, 42.

however, many quite serious scientific works, going all unbuttoned in their final chapters, display, in a surprisingly undisciplined and casual manner, the sometimes quite disturbing metaphysical assumptions on which they are constructed.[29]

There is nothing whatsoever, no fact or circumstance, no person, feeling, need, or feature of the world, that it is an *easy* thing to speak of well. And, of all the words we use, there is none whose use requires more careful crafting than the 'almost ridiculously exhausting and demanding word' – God.[30] That the holy mystery which we call God is only named with difficulty, only approached in fear and trembling, has been, from the beginning, a commonplace of Judaism, Christianity and Islam. There seem to have been few if any precedents for the strange situation which arose, quite recently, when early modern ideals of 'pure prose' were brought to bear even upon the way in which we speak of God. Where what we might call philosophical strategies in these matters are concerned, few divisions run as deep as that between those, on the one hand, who still stand in this seventeenth-century tradition of plain

---

[29] See Mary Midgley, 'Fancies about human immortality', *The Month*, 251 (1990), 458–66; in general, Midgley, *Science as Salvation. A Modern Myth and its Meaning* (London: Routledge and Kegan Paul, 1992). 'Sometimes quite disturbing' because, as she points out, much of this material appears to spring from quite old-fashioned dread of death, of flesh, of our contingency; see Lash, *Believing Three Ways*, p. 41. In a popular work, Heinz Pagels distinguished what he called 'third-person science', the picture of the world that results from scientific inquiry, from 'first-person science', by which he meant the 'personal thoughts of an individual interpreting and responding to the reality of the world discovered by science' (Heinz R. Pagels, *Perfect Symmetry. The Search for the Beginning of Time* (London: Michael Joseph, 1985), p. 362). If a banker or an archaeologist were to offer their homespun personal thoughts about the world, I doubt whether they would preposterously describe such discourse as first-person banking or archaeology! Moreover, like many scientists, Pagels' innocence extended to the history of science: 'Centuries ago, when some people suspended their search for absolute truth and began instead to ask how things worked, modern science was born.' (*Perfect Symmetry*, p. 370.)

[30] Karl Rahner, *Foundations of Christian Faith. An Introduction to the Idea of Christianity*, (trans.) William V. Dych (London: Darton, Longman and Todd, 1978), p. 51. With my earlier remarks about 'starting-points' and 'foundations' in mind, it may be worth mentioning how poorly 'foundations' translates *Grundkurs* in the title of this work by one who was, after all, a pupil of Martin Heidegger. 'Five-finger exercises' might be nearer the mark!

speech, and those who find 'God' the most important but most *burdensome* of all our words.[31]

In a most interesting paper read on the last occasion that he and I were here together at Notre Dame, Professor William Alston said: 'I think of God as literally a "personal agent".' He explained that 'In saying that God *literally* acts in the light of knowledge and purposes' he meant that recognition of whatever differences there may be between 'what it is for God to intend something' and 'what it is for a human being to intend something' is 'quite compatible with the basic sense of terms like "know" and "intend" holding constant across the divine–human gap'.[32]

I have two main misgivings about Alston's way of setting up the issues. In the first place, the supposition that there could be a single 'basic sense' of 'know', held constant 'across the divine–human gap', risks giving the impression that bodiliness is, in the last analysis, incidental to what, in human beings, knowledge means, and to how we come to know things. It is, after all, our being in the body, being in time, being historically, socially and culturally produced and nurtured, which makes human knowing the experientially grounded interpretative and responsive negotiation of circumstances not of our creating. Whereas God's knowledge lovingly and gratuitously creates the things God knows, *ex nihilo*, ours does not.

In the second place, I am unhappy about suggestions that God 'literally' acts, or knows, or speaks, or loves the world, not because we may not properly and truly say God really does these things, but because 'literally' may too easily be taken to imply that, in saying them, we know what we are doing. It is a pity that Aquinas' distinction between what is said 'metaphorice' of God, and what is said 'proprie' is usually

[31] On knowledge of God as knowledge of 'holy mystery', see Rahner, *Foundations*, pp. 51–71. On Rahner on this issue, and on the division between philosophical strategies, see Lash, *Easter in Ordinary*, pp. 231–42.
[32] William P. Alston, 'God's action in the world' in Ernan McMullin (ed.), *Evolution and Creation* (Notre Dame: University of Notre Dame Press, 1985), pp. 197–8, his stress.

translated as a distinction between metaphorical and literal speech.[33] 'Literally' seems to carry unfortunate connotations of straightforwardness, of knowing without too much difficulty what we mean 'across the gap', which 'appropriately' or 'properly' might not.

Where Christianity is concerned, there is, of course, a further and quite fundamental reason for being suspicious of the epistemic strategies of early modern theism, and it is that all we say of God is said of one confessed as Father, Son and Spirit, one of whom we cannot *simultaneously* say the three things we have learned to say about the holy mystery that makes and heals the world.[34]

The price paid for habits of speech derived from early modern ideals of 'pure prose' has been to foster a climate of intellectual irreverence, a forgetfulness, in practice, of the insurpassable and enduring primacy of the apophatic. It is not enough to pay lip-service to the otherness of God, to reduce divine transcendence to life lived 'across the gap'. We are on surer ground, it seems to me, in closer contact with both the instincts of Christian Neoplatonism and our development of the Jewish prohibition against making images of God, if we acknowledge, with Mark Jordan, that 'If one could see why human names fail to name God, then one would understand as much of the divine nature as can be *known* outside beatitude . . . the surest approach to the divine is by the scrutiny of linguistic failure.'[35]

Karl Rahner would have understood this and, being a Jesuit, would have set it under the standard of the *Deus semper major*:

---

[33] Thus, to take one key text, *Summa theologiae* 1a, 13.3, the current Dominican edition translates 'utrum aliquid nomen dicatur de Deo proprie' as 'can we say anything literally about God?' (*St Thomas Aquinas. Summa theologiae*, III, *Knowing and Naming God*, (trans.) Herbert McCabe (London, Eyre and Spottiswoode, 1964), pp. 56, 57).

[34] This bold assertion I have spelt out a little in the closing chapters of *Easter in Ordinary* and in *Believing Three Ways in One God* (a title intended to indicate not only that we believe, three ways, in God but that there are, in God, three ways to be believed).

[35] Mark D. Jordan, 'The names of God and the being of names' in Alfred J. Freddoso (ed.), *The Existence and Nature of God* (Notre Dame: University of Notre Dame Press, 1983), p. 161, his stress.

'God becomes greater . . . We Christians can be bound by a feeling of brotherhood, not to the militant atheists, but quite certainly to those who are agonised by the question of God, those who are silent, reserved, averse to noisy conviction.' Hence his belief that it is as 'the guardian of the *"docta ignorantia futuri"* for the history of mankind in general' that Christianity may best contribute to the development, in every field of discourse, of real knowledge: knowledge, that is to say, patiently and truthfully and penitently recognisant of human finitude, of our contingency. It follows, moreover, that there should always be an element of provisionality and incompleteness, a resistance to premature totalisation, in the relationships between particular discourses and traditions and, not least, between Christian theology and natural science: 'there will never be a single, all-inclusive formula in this history of knowledge; and the ultimate unity to be granted to man . . . is the surrender of all knowledge in a *docta ignorantia* to the eternally abiding mystery of God and his underivable will'.[36]

In conclusion, then, a theology which remains always acutely conscious of the need both to sustain close contacts with its roots in contemplation and of the need to learn, from science, particular details of the features of the world, should not find it too difficult to develop habits of mutually corrective and fruitful conversation with sciences grown more aware of the need not only to be watchful of their language, but also sensitive to their contingency as particular products and expressions of specific sets of historical circumstance.

[36] Rahner, 'Science as a "confession"?', p. 392; 'Theology as engaged in an inter-disciplinary dialogue with the sciences' in *Theological Investigations*, xiii, p. 33; 'On the relationship between natural science and theology' in *Theological Investigations*, xix, *Faith and Ministry*, (trans.) Edward Quinn (London: Darton, Longman and Todd, 1984), p. 21.

CHAPTER 7

When did the theologians lose interest in theology?[1]

INTRODUCTION

Consideration of how the word 'God' goes, of the grammar of its usage, is of central concern to any tradition of theological investigation. And it would surely not be quite arbitrary to propose that consideration of the uses of 'God' is not to be counted *Christian* unless it includes some mention of, or reference to, the figure of Jesus. In this sense, at least, a theological tradition whose doctrine of God lacked any christological component might be said to have 'lost interest' in the proper subject-matter of Christian theology. And yet Michael Buckley's magisterial study of the origins of modern atheism has shown that already in the early seventeenth century, thirty years before Newton's birth and within half a century of Calvin's death, patterns of theological enquiry were being laid down which 'abstracted God from Christ as either definition or manifestation'. In their developed forms, these patterns of enquiry took Jesus as a teacher of morals, while looking to nature and the cosmos alone to teach us about God.[2] Even to this day, ask almost any unsuspecting passer-by what they take the word 'God' to mean and the likelihood is that the

---

[1] This chapter was originally a contribution to a *Festschrift* for George Lindbeck which appeared as *Theology and Dialogue. Essays in Conversation with George Lindbeck*, (ed.) Bruce Marshall (Notre Dame: University of Notre Dame Press, 1990).

[2] Michael J. Buckley, *At the Origins of Modern Atheism*, p. 346; cf. p. 55. Leonard Lessius' *De providentia numinis et animi immortalitate. Libri duo adversus atheos et politicos* was first published in 1613 (see Buckley, p. 42).

answer (even from quite conservative Christians) will make no mention of Jesus.

Now, a state of affairs in which it is possible for people not only to indicate what they mean by 'God', but also to specify the ways in which we come to know whatever we know of God, without reference to Jesus, would seem at least prima facie incompatible with the effective operation of the three 'regulative principles' which, according to George Lindbeck, were at work in the elaboration of the ancient creeds.[3] And some such state of affairs was widespread by the end of the seventeenth century. But when did the rot set in? According to Buckley, the answer is to be sought as far back as the thirteenth century, with Aquinas' momentous decision, when designing the *Summa theologiae*, to consider what can and cannot be said concerning 'divina essentia' before discussing those things which pertain to the distinction of persons in God (as Aquinas himself put it in the Prologue to the 'Prima pars').

In this chapter, offered in celebration of Lindbeck's work and in gratitude for his friendship, I propose, after some introductory remarks on the regulative character of Christian doctrine, to challenge Buckley's interpretation of Aquinas. My aim in so doing is constructive: freed from the spurious support of the sub-plot, Buckley's main argument, concerning the sea change in both method and content which Christian theology underwent in the seventeenth and eighteenth centuries, stands out with greater force and freshness.

---

[3] 'Three regulative principles at least were obviously at work. First, there is the monotheistic principle: there is only one God, the God of Abraham, Isaac, Jacob, and Jesus. Second, there is the principle of historical specificity: the stories of Jesus refer to a genuine human being who was born, lived, and died in a particular time and place. Third, there is the principle of what may be infelicitously called Christological maximalism: every possible importance is to be ascribed to Jesus that is not inconsistent with the first rules' (George A. Lindbeck, *The Nature of Doctrine. Religion and Theology in a Postliberal Age* (London: SPCK, 1984), p. 94). For some critical comment on these principles, as stated, and especially on the third, see Lee C. Barrett, 'Theology as grammar: regulative principles or paradigms and practices?', *Modern Theology*, 4 (January 1988), 167–71; Stephen Williams, 'Lindbeck's regulative christology', *Modern Theology*, 4 (January 1988), 183–4.

PATTERNS OF SPEECH

The concept of 'the Christian doctrine of God' is, I suggest, best taken as referring to the declaration, by the Christian community, of identity-sustaining rules of discourse and behaviour governing Christian uses of the word 'God'. In a nutshell: the concept of the Christian doctrine of God refers to the use of the creed as *regula fidei*. This account of the regulative character of Christian doctrine has evident affinities with that offered by Lindbeck in *The Nature of Doctrine*. For the purposes of this chapter, it is not necessary to examine in any detail the similarities and differences between our two accounts.[4] There are, however, two points that need to be made.

In the first place, without wishing to open the Pandora's box of questions concerning the ways in which metaphors of 'intra-' and 'extratextuality' are best construed, there is a word to be said about *reference*. If God is not a figment of our imagination, then in our worship of God, our address to God, we may hope successfully to refer to him, to make true mention of him. Our worship, in other words, has cognitive implications: it entails the conviction that there is something that we can truly say of God. And this conviction is quite compatible with insistent nescience so far as our knowledge of 'the nature' of God is concerned. On this account, one of the principal functions of doctrine, as regulative of Christian speech and action, would be to help protect correct reference by disciplining our manifold propensity toward idolatry. Idolatry is a matter of getting the reference wrong: of taking that to be God which is not God, of mistaking some fact or thing or nation or person or dream or possession or ideal for our heart's need and the mystery 'that moves the sun and other stars'.

In other words, I set as much store by the distinction between reference and description as Lindbeck does by that

---

[4] See Nicholas Lash, *Easter in Ordinary*. For my general reactions to *The Nature of Doctrine*, see my review in *New Blackfriars*, 66 (November 1985), 609–10. I am unpersuaded by the claim that the functions of church teaching can be *confined*, as Lindbeck proposes, to the regulative: see Avery Dulles, 'Paths to doctrinal agreement: ten theses', *Theological Studies*, 47 (1986), 32–47.

between description and regulation. But whereas I see these two distinctions as lying along different axes, much that Lindbeck has to say about cognition, about propositions, and about what he sometimes calls 'ontological reference' leads me to suspect that, in his concern to secure the second distinction, he has overlooked the importance of the first.[5]

In the second place, there is the matter of what I will call the *pattern* of Christian doctrine. This is an issue barely touched on in *The Nature of Doctrine*. There, in spite of the emphasis on the comprehensively regulative character of doctrine, the emphasis is on 'doctrines', in the plural, rather than on their unity and the forms of their coherence.[6]

The Christian doctrine of God is the doctrine of God's Trinity, which serves, in Walter Kasper's admirable description, as 'the grammar and summation of the entire Christian mystery of salvation'.[7] I have tried elsewhere to show how it is that the creed, as paradigmatic expression of Christian doctrine, provides a pattern of self-correction for each of the three principal modes of our propensity to freeze the form of relation with God into an object or imagined possessed description of the divine nature.[8] The unceasing dialectically corrective movement, which the pattern requires, between the three fundamental regulations for Christian speech and action that are indicated in the three articles of the creed, is, we might say, a matter of *perichoresis*. It is only in this movement, and not apart from it, that the oneness or unity of him whom we triply worship is apprehended. It does not follow that there is nothing to be said about 'godness' – or what Aquinas called 'divina essentia' – nothing to be said about God in abstraction from consideration of the three modes or aspects

---

5 On 'ontological reference', see Lindbeck, *The Nature of Doctrine*, p. 106. William Placher is, I think, making a point similar to mine when he suggests that, on this crucial question of reference, Lindbeck is strangely ambivalent: see William C. Placher, 'Paul Ricoeur and postliberal theology: a conflict of interpretations?', *Modern Theology*, 4 (October 1987), 47–8.

6 See, for example, the discussion of a 'taxonomy of doctrines' (pp. 84–8).

7 Walter Kasper, *The God of Jesus Christ*, p. 311.

8 See Nicholas Lash, *Believing Three Ways*.

of our relationship to him. But whatever is thus said is said, precisely, in *abstraction*. To put it with perhaps misleading brevity: God is not an object whose nature we are capable of describing.

Such thoughts will hold no surprises for George Lindbeck, no more than they would have done for theologians during the first 1,600 years of Christian history. And if they seem, to many people today, obscure, eccentric, bordering on the unintelligible, this is perhaps because our modern imagination is still so dominated by a quite different account of what a doctrine of God might be and of the functions that it might perform, an account first formulated in the seventeenth century.

CHANGING THE SUBJECT

Michael Buckley's study is so rich in detail and elegant in design that summary of its aims and argument can hardly fail to be misleadingly banal. The enquiry proceeds on the assumption that 'The emergence of modern atheism lies with Diderot and d'Holbach', to the discussion of whom nearly one-third of the book is devoted. But what processes and what factors *account* for this emergence, in the precise form that it took? From the confused contradictions (as he saw them) of theology, d'Holbach, systematising Diderot's more eclectic achievement, singled out two theologians of indisputable significance: 'Dr Samuel Clarke of England and Father Nicholas Malebranche of France. Both of these theologians are descended from figures that dominated the European philosophic and scientific world: Clarke sits at the feet of Newton and Malebranche on every page bears witness to his extraordinary conversion to Descartes.' The chapter on Malebranche and Clarke, which precedes those on Diderot and d'Holbach, is, therefore, in turn preceded by a chapter on Descartes and Newton.[9]

---

[9] Buckley, *Origins*, pp. 34, 32. Newton figures largely in an earlier study: see Michael J. Buckley, *Motion and Motions's God: Thematic Variations in Aristotle, Cicero, Newton and Hegel* (Princeton, NJ: Princeton University Press, 1971).

The enquiry is not yet at an end, however, because it has not yet accounted for the most surprising characteristic of 'this emergence of the denial of the Christian God', which is that 'Christianity as such, more specifically the person and teaching of Jesus or the experience and history of the Christian church, did not enter the discussion.'[10]

In order, therefore, to answer the question, 'how did the issue of Christianity and atheism become purely philosophical?', Buckley takes the enquiry a stage further back to the early years of the seventeenth century. Then, the Louvain Jesuit Leonard Lessius and the prodigiously polymathic Parisian Franciscan Marin Mersenne

treated the atheistic question as if it were a philosophic issue, not a religious one. Both acted as if the rising movement were not a rejection of Jesus Christ as the supreme presence of God in human history, whose spirit continued that presence and made it abidingly evocative, but a philosophic stance toward life brought about by either the scandal of the state of the world, the personal dissolution of the moral virtues, or the collapse of religious unity and the horror of the religious wars.

Buckley urges the importance of remembering that, in their repudiation of atheism, the major figures of the Enlightenment 'counted the Church and confessional religion not as allies, but as adversaries'. As Thomas Jefferson was eventually to argue, since only one-sixth of the known world is Christian, to affirm revelation in Christ as necessary for knowledge of God is to deny human beings that awareness which underlies the argument from universal consent and thus to encourage atheism and unrest.[11] The theologians agreed with the philosophers that the evidence for the reality of God, evidence the buzzword for which as early as the first decades of the seventeenth century is 'design', must be obtained – independently of any religious community or tradition of discourse – from a philosophical consideration of the world.

As Buckley traces the discussions and debates from Lessius

10 Buckley, *Origins*, p. 33.   11 Buckley, *Origins*, pp. 33, 65–6, 38; see p. 40.

to d'Holbach by way of Newton's Cambridge, we see that the original resolute dissociation of apologetics from spirituality (both of which flourished in the same place and often in the same hands, yet 'never intersected except in a genius such as Blaise Pascal') constructs the elements for its own subversion. Thus, for example, in the mid eighteenth century, 'Diderot's *Pensées* exhibit in miniature the development of natural theology since the days of Lessius and Mersenne. Theology gives way to Cartesianism, which gives way to Newtonian mechanics. The great argument, the only evidence for theism, is design, and experimental physics reveals that design.' All Diderot had to do was take weapons from Newton and Descartes and turn them against their forgers, 'mingling the method of Newton with the issues and principles posed by Descartes'.[12] There are several ways in which the story might be summarised. The theologians begin to tackle the question of God as a philosophical, and not a theological, question. But philosophical questions become, increasingly, questions in natural philosophy, which is to say, questions in science (and specifically, in mechanics). But scientific questions came increasingly, and quite properly, to receive only scientific answers. Or, as Buckley himself put it:

Theology alienated its own nature by generating a philosophy that functioned as apologetics. Philosophy eventually developed into natural philosophy, which became mechanics. And mechanics established its own nature by denying that its evidence possessed any theological significance and by negating any theological interest ... The origin of atheism in the intellectual culture of the West lies thus with the self-alienation of religion itself.[13]

PHILOSOPHY AND THE PHILOSOPHICAL

At the heart of that self-alienation which generated modern atheism, then, there lay the treatment of what is at issue between Christianity and atheism as a 'purely philosophical' affair. But what are the parameters of that 'philosophical'?

[12] Buckley, *Origins*, pp. 345, 202, 269.   [13] Buckley, *Origins*, pp. 358, 363.

What is it about the subject-matter of a question, or about the manner in which that question is treated, which renders the question (or at least its treatment) 'philosophical'?

At the period which marks the *end* of Buckley's story, such questions receive fairly clear answers. Thus, for example, with metaphysics transmuted into Newtonian mechanics, the stage is set for Kant, who was 'heart and soul a Newtonian', to shift the territory of the philosophical from ontology to epistemology and ethics.[14] But what was the state of affairs at the *outset*? How are distinctions between theology and philosophy to be drawn in respect of the early seventeenth century?

I have already indicated the negative component in Buckley's answer: Lessius' treatment of the question of God was not theological, because it lacked any christological dimension and drew not at all upon the experience of Christ's followers. Positively, his reply has two main elements. 'The attack mounted against the atheists is fought for mind over nature as the final explanation of things.' Lessius' apologetic is philosophical in that the sources of its arguments are, in respect of both structure and vocabulary, not Christian but Stoic. Mersenne drew largely upon more recent sources, but it was equally true of him that the battle with atheism was to be fought on 'common ground . . . provided by the cosmos'[15] and not in respect of anything specific to Christian life or memory.

Over and above this decision to take the question of the world's design as battleground, however, there was a further component to the 'philosophical' character of seventeenth-century apologetic. There occurred, during this period, a 'textbook revolution' in the theological schools. Lessius brought to Louvain an innovation which Francisco de Vitoria had introduced in Salamanca in 1526: the replacement of Peter Lombard's *Sentences* by Aquinas' *Summa theologiae* as matter for magisterial commentary.[16]

Commenting, twenty years ago, on Herbert Butterfield's

---

[14] See Buckley, *Origins*, pp. 326–8.
[15] Buckley, *Origins*, pp. 48, 345.   [16] Buckley, *Origins*, pp. 341, 343.

claim that the rise of modern science in the seventeenth century 'outshines everything since the rise of Christianity and reduces the Renaissance and the Reformation to the ranks of mere episodes, mere internal displacements, within the system of medieval Christendom', Bernard Lonergan said of the theologians of the period that they 'replaced the inquiry of the *question* by the pedagogy of the thesis'. Buckley registers this shift (so central to the burgeoning apologetic obsessions of the new theology) and also the transposition of Aquinas' arguments concerning 'divina essentia' from 'metaphysics, which is obscure, to the more evident data of the universe of Tycho Brahe . . . and the biological measurements of the human body'. Notwithstanding these profound displacements of topic and treatment, however, Buckley takes it for granted that a fundamental continuity still obtained between Lessius and Aquinas. For both men, questions concerning the existence and attributes of God pertain to 'praeambula fidei': they 'provide a preamble to Christian convictions about God which does not include Christ'.[17] That Lessius read Aquinas this way, I have no reason to doubt. But I do now want to challenge the view that thus to read Aquinas is to read him well.

AQUINAS: GODFATHER OF THE ENLIGHTENMENT?

The claim that 'Lessius took from the Thomistic tradition . . . the persuasion that the existence of God was essentially a philosophical problem rather than a theological or religious one' is vague enough to be unexceptionable. And the historian exhibits admirable caution when he says that 'The theologians followed the Thomistic lead, or what they understood as the Thomistic lead.' Elsewhere, the cat gets out of the bag, as with the claim that 'the surrender to natural philosophy of the

---

[17] Herbert Butterfield, *The Origins of Modern Science, 1300–1800* (London: G. Bell, 1968), p. vii; Bernard J. F. Lonergan, 'Theology in its new context' in Lonergan, *A Second Collection*, (eds.) William J. F. Ryan and Bernard J. Tyrrell (London: Darton, Longman & Todd, 1974), p. 57; Buckley, *Origins*, p. 55.

foundations of religion' occurred not in the seventeenth century, but *'many centuries* before the Enlightenment'.[18] In context, this can only mean that the surrender occurred in the thirteenth century.

There are two distinct components to the well-known suspicion that Aquinas' doctrine of God is 'philosophical', and hence not properly 'theological', in character. The first concerns the relationship between the consideration of 'divina essentia' ('Prima pars', qq. 2–26) and the discussion of God's Trinity (qq. 27–43). The second arises from the belief that 'In the *Summa theologiae*, Christ makes a central appearance only in the third part – after the doctrines of God, providence, the nature of the human person, creation, and human finality have already been defined.'[19] The implication, it seems clear, is that all these other topics have been 'defined' without reference to Christ.

For all its undoubted importance, the second of these problems is far too complex to be treated here. Suffice it to say that, in order to understand the design of the *Summa*, it is necessary, firstly, to take serious account of what Aquinas himself has to say in his opening question about the character and subject-matter of 'that theology which pertains to holy teaching'[20] and, secondly, to bear in mind how deeply Neoplatonic remained the scheme with which he worked. We might almost say that, for Aquinas, the 'soundness' of his 'educational method'[21] depended upon the extent to which the movement of his exposition reflected the rhythms of God's own act and movement: that self-movement 'outwards' from divine simplicity to the utterance of the Word and breathing of the Gift which God is, to the 'overflowing' of God's goodness in the work of his creation ('Prima pars'); the 'return' to God along that one way of the world's healing which is Christ ('Tertia pars'); and, because there lies across this movement

---

[18] Buckley, *Origins*, pp. 341, 354, 283 (emphasis added).
[19] Buckley, *Origins*, p. 55.   [20] Thomas Aquinas, *Summa theologiae*, 1a, 1, 1 ad 2.
[21] The reference is to the Prologue to the *Summa*, on which see Victor White, *Holy Teaching: The Idea of Theology According to St Thomas Aquinas* (London: Blackfriars, 1958).

the shadow of the mystery of sin, we find, between his treatment of the whence and whither, the 'outgoing' and 'return', of creaturely existence, the drama of conversion, of sin and virtue, of rejection or acceptance of God's grace ('Secunda pars').[22]

When Aquinas speaks of the effect of 'holy teaching' (which is first to last *God's* teaching and only by his free grace our human participation in such pedagogy) as being to set a kind of 'imprint' on our minds of God's own knowledge, he is speaking in a different figure of putting on the mind of Christ.[23] *Everything* in the Summa 'pertains to holy teaching'. I see no reason, whether of topic or treatment, to doubt that Aquinas meant what he said when he asserted that such theology differs root and branch ('differt secundum genus') from that theology which ranks as a part of philosophy.[24] But if this *is* true, not only of the *Summa* as a whole, but also of each of its constituent parts, then what are we to make of the apparently purely 'philosophical' consideration of 'divina essentia' in questions 2 to 26? Even if these questions are, as Buckley allows, 'integrated into theology as a moment within theology', are they not nevertheless (as he also says) 'philosophical in their issues and methods'?[25]

Buckley calls on no less authoritative a witness than Etienne Gilson, according to whom 'The existence of God is a philosophical problem' concerning which 'a theologian cannot

---

[22] See W. M. Hankey, *God in Himself: Aquinas' Doctrine of God as Expounded in the Summa Theologiae* (Oxford: Oxford University Press, 1987). Hankey is concerned, above all, to demonstrate the Neoplatonic background and structure of Aquinas' doctrine of God. He is sometimes overzealous in distinguishing his views from those of earlier commentators. For example: I would still recommend M.-D. Chenu's account of 'the construction of the *Summa*' in his *Toward Understanding St Thomas*, (trans.) A. M. Landry and D. Hughes (Chicago: Henry Regnery, 1963), pp. 310–17. It is grossly misleading to present Chenu's distinction between the 'structure' and 'history' of our return to God in Christ as a story of '*two* returns', one of nature, the other of grace (see Hankey, pp. 34, 139). There are important differences between Chenu's account and Hankey's, but they are not, I believe, as dramatic as the latter would have us suppose.

[23] See *S. T.*, 1a, 1, 3 ad 2.

[24] 'Theologia quae ad sacram doctrinam pertinet differt secundum genus ab illa theologiae quae pars philosophiae ponitur' (*S.T.*, 1a, 1, 1 ad 2).

[25] Buckley, *Origins*, p. 55.

do much more than apply to the philosopher for philosophical information'.[26] When, however, we remember that Gilson was a doughty advocate of the concept of 'Christian philosophy', we are alerted to the possibility that the sense, in his thought, of both 'philosophy' and 'theology', and hence also his account of the relationships between these two enterprises, may have been very different from that entertained by those for whom the notion of a 'Christian' *philosophy* would seem quite evidently mistaken or confused.

We touch at this point on a general issue of quite fundamental importance. I earlier referred to the suspicion that Aquinas' doctrine of God is philosophical and *hence* not properly theological in character. That way of putting the matter, however, presupposes that no text or argument could be, at one and the same time, thoroughly and quite properly theological and also philosophical in character. I shall suggest in due course that this presupposition is crucial to Buckley's misreading of Aquinas. For the time being, however, I do no more than register the possibility that not all philosophical investigation is necessarily untheological or irreligious.

When undertaking the massive redistribution of material which differentiates the *Summa theologiae* from Peter Lombard's *Sentences* (and from his own earlier *Commentary* on those *Sentences*), why did Aquinas divide 'what in Peter Lombard is the "de mysterio Trinitatis" into a *de deo uno* and a *de deo trino*',[27] taking the former topic first? Was it because he sought, apologetically, to provide some areligious 'preamble' to the consideration of Christian beliefs, or had he quite different aims in view? The third article of question 2 is quite certainly the best-known item in the *Summa*. It considers whether God exists: 'utrum Deus sit'. Philosophers, rushing to consider the 'five ways' outlined in reply, seldom pause to notice where the argument begins: namely from God's pronouncement (reported in Exodus 3:14) 'Ego sum qui sum.' Aquinas, in other words, 'starts from what God in his own

---

[26] Etienne Gilson, *Elements of Christian Philosophy*, cited from Buckley, *Origins*, p. 341.
[27] Hankey, *God in Himself*, p. 23.

person says; he begins treating God's existence from what we have been told'. If, from this starting-point, he then proceeds to work with what he takes to be familiar features of common human experience, he does so (in Cornelius Ernst's felicitous description of the 'five ways') 'to show how one might *go on* speaking of God in the ordinary world'.[28]

The fundamental reason, according to Aquinas, for beginning theology with the *unity* of God, rather than with God's Trinity, is 'because the one is by nature principle'.[29] The sequence of topics in the 'Prima pars' follows 'the step-by-step derivation of multiplicity from the divine unity', it moves from the 'simpleness' of God's being through increasing complexity (even in God himself) to the scattered diversity of his creatures. Hence, on the specific question of the relationship between the treatment of God's being and the consideration of God's Trinity, we can say that 'the *de deo trino* communicates with the *de deo uno* in virtue of the gradual development toward greater distinction in the terms of the various forms of self-relation in the divine.'[30]

The structure of the *Sentences* derived (as Aquinas knew and pointed out) from the *exitus–reditus* rhythms of Augustinian Neoplatonism. Paradoxical as it may seem, the effect of Aquinas' refashioning of that structure was to make the *Summa theologiae* more, not less, Neoplatonic than the work it superseded. The subject-matter of the *Summa*, its 'formal object', is God himself and all things in relation to God, their origin and end. The design of Aquinas' doctrine of God comes to him 'through Dionysius and is Proclan in its philosophical origins. The step-by-step development from the unity of substance through the conceptual division of the operations to the real relation and opposition of the persons also has a late Neoplatonic logic behind it.'[31]

---

[28] *God in Himself*, pp. 33–7; Cornelius Ernst, 'Metaphor and ontology in *Sacra Doctrina*' in Fergus Kerr and Timothy Radcliffe (eds.), *Multiple Echo* (London: Darton, Longman and Todd, 1979), p. 74, his emphasis.

[29] For references, see Hankey, *God in Himself*, pp. 10, 37.

[30] Hankey, *God in Himself*, pp. 39, 131.

[31] See *S.T.*, 1a, 1, 3 ad 2; Hankey, *God in Himself*, p. 23.

I hope already to have provided some indication as to why the technicality and formal abstractness of Aquinas' doctrine of God is better read as being 'for the sake of making God's revelation thinkable' than as providing a 'preamble to Christian convictions about God', let alone as marking the 'surrender to natural philosophy of the foundations of religion'.[32] Nevertheless, it is still necessary to focus more exactly on the question of what the relationship between 'theology' and 'philosophy' in his texts might be.

According to Hankey, the Neoplatonic rhythms beat not merely in the structure of the *Summa* as a whole, but in the movement of its every part. 'Not only is the whole a movement from God to material creation and back through man, but this pulse of going out and return runs through the individual parts of the work.'[33] Nor are the relationships between 'outgoing' and 'return', between God's self-gift and our appropriation of it, between God's reaching down to us and our raising of our minds and hearts to him, between (to risk the slogan words worn most misleading through subsequent sea changes in their use) 'grace' and 'nature', 'revelation' and 'reason', to be thought of simply as *successive*. On the contrary, we only get near the heart of the matter when we notice Aquinas' concern to hold both 'beats' in some approximation to divine simultaneity, such that all our language is wholly fashioned to the pressures of God's grace while grace comes visible in wholly human speech: 'Natural reason moves up to knowledge of God through creatures; conversely, knowledge of faith moves down from God to us by divine revelation; the *upward and the downward path are but one way.*'[34] And, even if Neoplatonic thought, both within and without Christianity, furnished Aquinas with the conceptual apparatus for this view of the

---

[32] Hankey, *God in Himself*, p. 41; Buckley, *Origins*, pp. 55, 283.

[33] Hankey, *God in Himself*, p. 54.

[34] 'Quia vero naturalis ratio per creaturas in Dei cognitionem ascendit, fidei vero cognitio a Deo in nos e converso divina revelatione descendit; est autem eadem via ascensus et descensus' (Thomas Aquinas, *Summa contra gentiles*, Bk. IV, ch. 1; cited from Hankey's discussion of this 'epigrammatic formula' in *God in Himself*, pp. 35, 31).

matter, it was a view controlled and radicalised by the conviction that that 'one way' has now a name, a date, a history, a cloud of witnesses.[35]

Let us go back for a moment to that second question of the *Summa*: 'utrum Deus sit'. To many of our contemporaries, the question as to whether or not 'God is' is an empirical question, a matter of fact. And, according to some people, it is important to settle this question, to ascertain whether or not God exists, before moving on to the riskier business of religious belief (hence the notion of 'preambles' to faith).

Aquinas, however, was not asking an empirical question, nor seeking to settle some question of fact. His enquiry was much more limited in scope and quite different in character. It was grammatical; it concerned, we might say, our handling of 'existence talk' in respect of God. (It was, in other words, more like a discussion of whether numbers 'exist' than like an enquiry as to whether you have any cousins.)

Now if, by 'philosophical issues and methods' one means the kinds of questions which invite – and best receive – grammatical rather than empirical investigation, then, in *this* sense it seems correct to say (as Gilson did) that the existence of God is treated by Aquinas as a philosophical question. But this says nothing either way concerning the kind of place, if any, which such grammatical consideration might occupy within the loving obedience of faith in quest of understanding. In other words, whether consideration of God's existence which is, in *this* sense, 'philosophical' is or is not also properly theological will depend, not upon the pattern of words on the page, but upon the context and climate of their use.

We tend to consider contemplative wonder, the docility of faith, as standing in sharp contrast to the requirements of critical rationality. The prie-dieu, we imagine, is not the place

---

[35] 'Over and over again Christ is called the *Via*', 'Christianity is able to find in Christ's union of God and man a point upon which to move the universe, which fulcrum is lacking in the Neoplatonism supplying the philosophical logic for the development' (Hankey, *God in Himself*, pp. 35, 31).

to do philosophy. A glance at Anselm's *Proslogion*, however, should be sufficient to remind us that there have been *other* ways of handling the relationship between 'faith' and 'reason'.[36] (Both words are set in quotation marks as a reminder, once again, that *none* of the key terms in this discussion, nor any of the relationships between them, have constant sense or connotation.)

Eventually, of course, a day was to dawn when the question of God's existence would become an empirical question, a matter of fact, if only for the excellent reason that, at this time, *all* philosophical questions were on their way to becoming matters of fact, matters of natural philosophy, matters of terrestrial, celestial or transcelestial mechanics. But, for that shift, it would be less than reasonable to blame Aquinas' Neoplatonism!

Michael Buckley takes Descartes and Newton, 'the most influential thinkers at the dawn of modernity', as the best examples going 'of what Martin Heidegger characterises as the malaise of our world: *Seinsvergessenheit* – a forgetfulness of being, with its concomitant inability to ask the question of God at the depth which alone can give any theological sense to the content of the answer'. Both Descartes and Newton, he goes on, 'achieved a god commensurate with the evidence they explored . . . an explanatory factor in a larger, more complete system'.[37] All that I have tried to indicate is that such 'forgetfulness' may not plausibly be laid at Aquinas' door.

DATING THE GREAT REVERSAL

'What Lessius presents', in the *De providentia numinis*, 'is not the person and message of Jesus, but those cosmological

---

[36] I have in mind the smoothness of transition between daunting logical brain-twisters such as 'Something-than-which-a-greater-cannot-be-thought exists so truly then, that it cannot be even thought not to exist' and (the very next words) the language of prayerful address: 'And You, Lord our God, are this being . . . ' (*Proslogion*, chapter 3, translation from M. J. Charlesworth's edition, p. 119).

[37] Buckley, *Origins*, pp. 348–9.

and historical experiences which are open to any human being.' Here, in 1613, we are evidently already in the presence of what Hans Frei called the 'great reversal', that shift in interpretative strategy as a result of which theological interpretation became 'a matter of fitting the biblical story into another world' (namely, the world now taken to be constituted by those ranges of experience deemed open to any human being) 'rather than incorporating that world into the biblical story'.[38] In the self-assured world of modernity, people seek to make sense of the Scriptures, instead of hoping, with the aid of the Scriptures, to make some sense of themselves.

Although Frei mentions, in passing, the possibility that the 'roots' of this modern world's theology go back to the seventeenth century, he firmly dated the great reversal somewhat later: 'If historical periods may be said to have a single chronological and geographical starting-point, modern theology began in England at the turn from the seventeenth to the eighteenth century.'[39] (That there is some implausibility in this account might have been suspected from the fact that the characteristic watchwords of the new theology, 'theism' and 'deism', were coined in *France* several decades before they were taken up in England.)

When did the theologians lose interest in theology? If we take my title as polemical paraphrase of that revolution in method and subject matter which marked, for good and ill, the 'great reversal', then the answer, I suggest, is: not in early eighteenth-century England, as Frei proposed, nor in the thirteenth-century Parisian schools, as Buckley assumes (misled by modern Thomism's enduring tendency to read the thirteenth century through spectacles fashioned in the seventeenth), but in the France and Low Countries of the early seventeenth century, the world of Lessius and Mersenne. The

---

[38] *Origins*, p. 54; Hans W. Frei, *The Eclipse of Biblical Narrative: A Study in Eighteenth and Nineteenth Century Hermeneutics* (New Haven, CT: Yale University Press, 1974), p. 130.

[39] *Eclipse*, p. 51; see p. 325.

weight of argument of Buckley's splendid study points massively to this conclusion. All that I have tried to do is to scrape one barnacle off the hull.[40]

---

[40] Since this paper was first written, I have had an opportunity to discuss it with Michael Buckley, who is alarmed to find me ascribing to him a particular view concerning how Aquinas is best read, on which he had in fact intended to keep his options open. Whether he was, in the event, entirely successful, I leave to our readers to decide.

CHAPTER 8

Anselm seeking[1]

STRANGER OR GUIDE?

The curriculum of theological education in English universities is still subject to the malign influence of what I call
'the myth of the missing millennium'. According to this myth,
little or nothing of abiding theological interest was said or
done between the year 450 and about 1450 CE. We still treat the
intervening centuries as something called the 'Middle Ages',
the great inertia, wilderness of spirit, between the Fathers and
the Renaissance. (And you will have noticed that the media
always refer to some particularly mindless piece of civil strife
as 'medieval' behaviour.) Sustained by the myth, we are not
too much troubled by the consequent inexplicability of works
of sensitive intelligence as various as Dante's *Divine Comedy* or
this incomparable building in which we meet.

The myth, as regularly propagated, does allow of two
exceptions: Thomas Aquinas and Anselm of Canterbury.
(Actually, this list of two names has recently been extended to
four, with the addition of Julian of Norwich and Hildegard of
Bingen. It is a triumph of feminism to have persuaded us that,
during this thousand years of European history, there were not
only two intelligent men, but two intelligent women as well!)
Quite how Aquinas' reputation is maintained, I have
absolutely no idea, because few English theologians seem ever

---

[1] A lecture given in Canterbury Cathedral on 27 September 1993 as part of the
celebrations of the 900th anniversary of St Anselm's enthronement as Archbishop
of Canterbury.

to have studied more than a tiny handful of his texts and, as usually presented in the textbooks of theology, St Thomas seems to have sustained a concatenation of absurd opinions in a singularly dry and unappealing manner.

The reverence shown to Anselm is a little more intelligible. On the one hand, he is much esteemed by philosophers in Oxford and, on the other, the greatest Protestant theologian of this century wrote a most admiring book about him. Even so, my guess is that, as a 'monastic' theologian of the 'Middle Ages', Anselm seems, to most English Christians, a figure from a very strange and distant world.

My ambition in this lecture, however, is to try to strip away one or two of the distorting filters through which we tend to view him. If I succeed, then perhaps he may begin to speak with quite surprising aptness and attractiveness to our contemporary predicament. Anselm (I shall argue) stands closer to our needs and circumstances than do those later thinkers of the seventeenth and eighteenth centuries, those makers of the modern world, under whose influence we have learned to deem the 'Middle Ages' alien.

I thought of subtitling my lecture 'A tale of two mottoes'. One of my mottoes would have been that three-word phrase, the best-known phrase in Anselm's writings: 'Credo ut intelligam'; 'I believe so that I may understand.'[2] If, when considering this phrase, you find yourself drawn into a discussion in which all sides take for granted that either 'faith' or 'reason', either received tradition or our individual attempts to make some sense of things, must gain the upper hand, then Anselm will stay a stranger to your world. If, on the other hand, you find yourself muttering, without pain or effort, complacent bromides about 'of course we need both "faith" and "reason"', then not only Anselm's writings, but those of all great Christian thinkers, will remain closed books gathering dust in the shuttered attic of your sleeping mind.

---

[2] *St Anselm's Proslogion*, (trans.) Charlesworth, pp. 114, 115.

KARL BARTH AND UPDIKE'S GAP

Karl Barth was born in 1886. In November 1963, still very sprightly at the age of seventy-seven, he wrote to a friend at Princeton: 'Will you give my greetings, please, to President McCord. He told me about a review of my book on Anselm by the novelist John Updike. I am wondering what he may have said.'[3]

The book on Anselm, arising indirectly from a seminar on the *Cur Deus Homo* which Barth had held in Bonn in 1930, was first published in 1931. In fact, Barth's love for Anselm dates even further back. In his first lectures on dogmatics, in 1925, he warmly recommended Anselm's method and (as he tells us) 'as a result was promptly accused of Roman Catholicism and Schleiermacherism'.[4]

Though Barth continued to think highly of the little book he published in 1931, it was not translated into English until 1960, when it appeared with the daunting title *Anselm: Fides Quaerens Intellectum. Anselm's Proof of the Existence of God in the Context of his Theological Scheme*. Three years later, John Updike, for whom Barth was 'the most prominent, prolific, and (it seems to me) persuasive of twentieth-century theologians', reviewed the book in the *New Yorker*. Updike's admiration, though considerable, was not unqualified. 'This essay on Anselm', he wrote, 'is, even for a piece of theology, uncommonly tedious and difficult, replete with untranslated passages of Latin, English words like "ontic", "noetic", and "aseity", and non-stop sentences of granitic opacity'.[5]

Where, then, does Barth's attraction and importance lie? Let us go to the heart of things and think of faith and unbelief. Suppose it is by God's free gift of faith that we are saved, brought into life in him. If so, then it would be by unfaith,

---

[3] Geoffrey W. Bromiley (ed.), *Karl Barth. Letters 1961–1968* (Edinburgh: T. & T. Clark, 1981), p. 139.

[4] Karl Barth, *Anselm: Fides Quaerens Intellectum. Anselm's Proof of the Existence of God in the Context of his Theological Scheme* (London: SCM Press, 1960), p. 7.

[5] John Updike, *Assorted Prose* (London: Andre Deutsch, 1965), pp. 173, 174. (The review first appeared in the *New Yorker*, 12 October 1963, 203–10.)

unbelief, that, resisting God's self-gift, we would be lost. Much of Anselm's argument, in the *Proslogion*, concerns the 'unwise' one, the *insipiens*, the 'fool', who (according to the psalmist) 'says in his heart, "There is no God."' It is this unwisdom which Barth has in mind when, near the end of his little book, he says: 'By the miracle of foolishness it is possible to think of God as not existing. But only by this miracle. Anselm had certainly not reckoned with this.'[6]

Quite what Barth meant by that last remark is not entirely clear. He certainly did not mean that Anselm had not reckoned with the mere fact of disbelief in God. I rather think he meant that Anselm's thinking flowed from such deep tranquillity of faith that he was *not troubled* by the paradox of unbelief. This, at least, is how John Updike read him. Here are Updike's reflections on the remark, which I just quoted, about Anselm not having reckoned with the 'miracle of foolishness': 'There is, then, a difference between the modern and the medieval theologian – the theologian of crisis and the theologian without a sense of crisis. They are separated by nine centuries in which the miracle of disbelief has so often recurred that to call it a miracle seems an irony. The gap between *credere* and *intelligere* across which Anselm slung his syllogism has grown so broad' that human ingenuity can no longer bridge it.[7]

'Across which Anselm slung his syllogism': the metaphor is of a bridge or, perhaps, a hammock. Updike's Anselm, medieval man, snoozes across the gap between belief and understanding, finding faith no problem. Hence his description of Anselm as 'the theologian without a sense of crisis'; no shred of evidence is offered for this patronising view. Why on earth should we suppose that eleventh-century Christians found it easier than we do to bear the silence of Gethsemane? It may have been easier for the people of Anselm's day to say 'Lord, Lord', but (if so) should we envy them that dangerous simplicity?

On the one hand, then, I see no reason to suppose that faith,

---

[6] Psalm 14.1; 53.1; Barth, *Fides Quaerens*, p. 165.　　[7] Updike, *Assorted Prose*, p. 181.

true faith, the fruitfulness of grace in open-eyed discipleship of the Crucified and Risen One, came easier in Anselm's day than it may do in ours. The other side of the coin is Updike's remark that, during the nine centuries which separate our time from Anselm's, 'the miracle of disbelief has so often recurred that to call it a miracle seems an irony'. But this is to reduce the mystery of unbelief, of the creature's self-enclosed defiance of God's constituting love, to a mere matter of finding no good uses for the small word 'God', whereas Anselm, who took serious things seriously, was interested in the unbelief that issued from the heart, not that which merely skimmed across the surface of the mind.

Anselm knew that only from the heart of faith's relationship with the mystery of God may we obtain, perhaps, some glimmer of understanding of that mystery. Hence Barth's respect for Anselm. And Barth knew that self-destructive 'foolishness', the creature's preposterous defiance of the ground of its creation, is a kind of absurd 'miracle'. However, unlike Barth (perhaps) and certainly unlike John Updike, I see no reason to suppose that Anselm did not also appreciate the absurdity of unbelief.

EXPERIENCE AND EXPERTISE

If we go back a hundred years before Karl Barth's first lectures on St Anselm, we come to the publication, in 1821, of the most influential and powerfully original work of Protestant theology produced during the nineteenth century: Schleiermacher's *Christian Faith*. On the title-page we find two brief quotations, both from Anselm.

The first quotation is from the opening chapter of the *Proslogion*: 'I do not seek to understand so that I may believe; but I believe so that I may understand'; 'credo ut intelligam'. (Karl Barth will later comment: 'It goes without saying that Anselm's *credo ut intelligam* is completely out of place on the title-page of Schleiermacher's *Glaubenslehre*.' But this is just a piece of mischievous polemic. For Schleiermacher, as for Barth, the Christian theologian seeks to make some sense of the experience of faith. For both men, theological investigation is, in a nice phrase of Richard Reinhold Niebuhr's – speaking, incidentally, of Schleiermacher – 'preaching-faith's descriptive science of itself'.)[8]

The other quotation on Schleiermacher's title-page comes from Anselm's *Letter on the Incarnation*: 'One who does not believe, will not experience; and whoever does not experience, will not understand.'[9] We often say of people who shoot their mouths off, on matters in which they lack experience or expertise, that they do not know what they are talking about. Or, as Anselm puts it, more succinctly: 'whoever does not experience, will not understand'. And, where the knowledge of God is concerned, it is discipleship which furnishes the necessary context of experience. I say 'discipleship', rather than 'believing', because we will not hear what Anselm is saying if we indulge our pernicious modern habit of *contracting* the sense of words like 'faith', 'hope' and 'love' until they refer to individual, private, psychic states or attitudes, rather than to shared and public patterns of conviction and behaviour. For Anselm, 'believing' is living the life of a disciple: a life of obedience to God's command, nourished (as he puts it) by the Scriptures in the way of wisdom.

In other words, the second of the sentences from Anselm set on Schleiermacher's title-page simply fills out the message of the first, of the 'credo ut intelligam', in order to make plain that it is the following of Christ which furnishes the context in which we may gain some understanding of the mystery of God.

[8] *Proslogion*, pp. 115, 114; Barth, *Fides Quaerens*, p. 26; Richard R. Niebuhr, *Schleiermacher on Christ and Religion* (London: SCM Press, 1965), p. 148.

[9] 'Nam qui non crediderit, non experietur; et qui expertus non fuerit, non cognoscet' (*S. Anselmi Cantuariensis archiepiscopi opera omnia*, I, (ed.) F. S. Schmitt, (Stuttgart: Friedrich Fromann Verlag, 1968)), p. 284; Schleiermacher has 'intelliget' for 'cognoscet': see Friedrich Schleiermacher, *Der Christliche Glaube* (Berlin: 1884). R. W. Southern translates this as: 'He who does not believe, cannot *experience;* and whoever does not *experience*, cannot understand' (R. W. Southern, *Saint Anselm. A Portrait in a Landscape* (Cambridge: Cambridge University Press, 1990, p. 178, his stress)).

MAKING SENSE OF THINGS

It is now necessary to change tack a little in order to pick up my second motto, which is to be found on another title-page: that of the second Part of the philosopher Hans-Georg Gadamer's massive and influential study *Truth and Method*, which appeared in 1960. This time, the quotation comes not from Anselm, but from Martin Luther: 'Qui non intelligit res, non potest ex verbis sensum elicere';[10] which I would translate as: 'The person who does not understand the subject-matter will not be able to make sense of the words.'

In saying this, Luther had the New Testament in mind. But what is the 'subject-matter' of the New Testament? One has only to ask the question to appreciate that it defines the territory of Christian faith's quest for understanding. In other words, the history of the answers that have been given to this question simply *is* the history of Christian theology.

Suppose, then, that we said (simply by way of illustration) that the subject-matter of the New Testament is the Gospel, the good news that God has made both Lord and Christ this Jesus who was crucified. Which of us would be so daft as to pretend that we had 'understood' these things? And yet, according to Luther, if we do not understand them, we cannot make sense of the words, cannot appropriately read a text worn smooth by dangerous familiarity.

But in what setting, against what kind of background, might we make some sense of the New Testament, get some glimpse of what may be entailed by the announcement that the glory of God's Word made flesh amongst us has been seen? The answer, surely, is that the appropriate setting would be that complex of memories and practices, arguments and aspirations, which first produced the texts and which still constitutes the continuing existence of a people dedicated to their interpretation in the following of Christ?

I am, in other words, suggesting that Luther, like St Anselm, took the practice of discipleship to be the context in which we

---

[10] See Hans-Georg Gadamer, *Truth and Method*, p. 151.

may gain some understanding of the mystery of God. Each of the two mottoes, Anselm's and Luther's, when well read, says much the same thing. (And, for what it is worth, Friedrich Schleiermacher and Karl Barth both understood this; which is why these two stout sons of the Reformation took their bearings by the programme of a medieval monk.)

Now, I am not suggesting that Barth and Schleiermacher were secret scholastics, crypto-medievalists. Nor am I insinuating that the abbey of Bec was, in the twelfth century, a nest of proto-Lutherans. The two points I have been trying to make are these. First, that notwithstanding the dizzying differences – in spirit and structure, economy and imagination – which separate the worlds of Anselm, Luther, Schleiermacher and Barth, they were, as Christian theologians, bound together in a common project: that of the quest, within the practice of discipleship, for some glimmer of understanding of the mystery of God.

The second point, however, is that this continuity of project has been obscured from view by propagation of the myth that the great achievement of the early modern world was the discovery that each of us must choose, on all occasions, between reliance on others – on 'authorities' – and thinking for ourselves; between the sleepy repetition of the past and alertness to the fresh requirements of the present; between blind faith and clear-eyed reason. And nowhere do these unreal dichotomies do greater damage than when they issue in instructions to us to choose our 'starting-point'. You *must begin* (or so the story goes) from either 'faith' or 'reason'. Now, please make up your mind!

We have already seen that there is a trace of this (at least on Updike's reading) even in Karl Barth's understanding of St Anselm. Hence all that talk about the 'gap' between belief and understanding. As this gap widens to unbridgeable abyss, each one of us must choose which way to jump – onto the safe but (as it now so often seems) dreary and unsatisfying ground of reason, or into the dangerous, irrational, security of faith. Or so the story goes.

A little earlier, presenting Luther as one who knew full well that it was only within the climate of belief that we might hope to make some sense of things, I set his programme for reading the New Testament under the sign of Anselm's motto, 'credo ut intelligam'. This is not, however, quite the way things seemed to orthodox eighteenth-century Lutherans. Thus, according to the historian Johann Georg Walch, writing in the 1720s, Luther's genius consisted in having greatly weakened the stranglehold of human authorities, especially Aristotle and the pope, thereby freeing the Christian for the right use of reason in the understanding of transmitted texts.[11]

There are questions touched on here too deep to be considered within the confines of one lecture. The most important of these would concern the doctrine that the Word of God, unlike all other words, is self-interpreting. This doctrine, unexceptionable as a theological principle, tragically became the ancestor of modern fundamentalisms because it was developed and expounded in a climate which tended, on the one hand, to collapse together the text of Scripture and God's eternal Word and, on the other, subjecting all authority to 'reason', to make 'right use of reason' the criterion of faith. Ironically, in other words, the early modern descendants of those who first sought to liberate theology from Aristotle and the pope did so in obedience to lessons learnt from such other human authorities as Descartes and Kant.

Leaving such deep and complex questions on one side, however, the point is that, when Luther's motto is read through spectacles designed by the Enlightenment, it may be invoked both by those who 'start from faith' and those who 'start from reason'. 'The person who does not understand the subject-matter will not be able to make sense of the words.' Read from the standpoint of 'faith', this will be taken to mean that Christian credenda are a closed book to all but the elect. Faith is a gift which you, my friend, appear to lack and, lacking it, you miss the point. Bad luck. Goodbye. Read from the stand-

---

[11] Gadamer, *Truth and Method*, p. 246; Gadamer gives his source as Walch's *Philosophisches Lexikon* (1726).

point of 'reason', on the other hand, the motto keeps at arm's length all but the priests of reason, those with doctorates and higher degrees, the experts – for they alone understand the subject-matter, know what is what.

In order to ward off misunderstanding, let me make it clear that I am not suggesting that Luther himself got bogged down in this morass. On the contrary, I earlier recommended that his motto be interpreted as keeping quite close company with Anselm's. The problems start when 'faith' and 'reason', heart and head, belief and understanding, are taken to be antithetical, mutually exclusive. We must each stand *somewhere* (so the story goes), find some firm ground beneath our feet, and we must choose where. And spokesmen for both 'faith' and 'reason' know full well that what the other party takes for granite rock is but shifting quicksand; hence the assurance, the missionary urgency, with which each party propagates its cause.

In such a climate, 'credo ut intelligam' rings out like a battle-cry of obscurantism and irrationality. First take the leap of faith and then you will understand; first close your eyes and then, at last, you will see! Even quite sensible and educated Christians may be affected by this nonsense. We have all taken part in conversations in which it seems to be assumed that those who think do not pray and in which those who would pray well are encouraged not to think too hard. To extricate us from this maze, I turn again to Anselm.

THINKING PRAYERFULLY

The *Proslogion* was produced eleven years after William of Normandy defeated Harold at Hastings (there's 'medieval' for you!). Here is the second paragraph of the opening chapter:

Come, then, Lord my God, teach my heart where and how to seek you, where and how to find you. Lord, if you are not present here, where, since you are absent, shall I look for you? On the other hand, if you are everywhere why then, since you are present, do I not see you? But surely you dwell in 'light inaccessible'. And where is this inaccessible light, or how can I approach the inaccessible light? Or who shall lead me and take me into it that I may see you in it?[12]

And, at the other end, here are the opening sentences of the final chapter, Chapter XXVI:

My God and my Lord, my hope and the joy of my heart, tell my soul if this is the joy of which you speak through your Son: 'Ask and you will receive, that your joy may be complete'. For I have discovered a joy that is complete and more than complete. Indeed, when the heart is filled with that joy, the mind is filled with it, the soul is filled with it, the whole man is filled with it, yet joy beyond measure will remain.[13]

But now, listen to Chapter III:

And certainly this being so truly exists that it cannot be even thought not to exist. For something can be thought to exist that cannot be thought not to exist, and this is greater than that which can be thought not to exist. Hence, if that-than-which-a-greater-cannot-be-thought can be thought not to exist, then that-than-which-a-greater-cannot-be-thought is not the same as that-than-which-a-greater-cannot-be-thought, which is absurd. Something-than-which-a-greater-cannot-be-thought exists so truly, then, that it cannot be even thought not to exist.[14]

And here is the next sentence: 'And you, Lord our God, are this being. You exist so truly, Lord my God, that you cannot even be thought not to exist.'[15]

It is extremely difficult to imagine someone moving as seamlessly, today, as Anselm did in the eleventh century, between what appear to us to be two such different registers of discourse. Is this philosophy, or is it prayer? What, exactly, is going on?

One thing is certain, and that is that the basic language of the text – the key, we might say (to take a musical analogy) in which the *Proslogion* is set – is that of Christian contemplation, of address to God in adoration. It is, as Anselm points out in the Preface, a '*pros*logion', which he translates into Latin as

---

[12] *Proslogion*, p. 111.   [13] *Proslogion*, p. 153.
[14] *Proslogion*, p. 119.   [15] *Proslogion*, p. 119.

'alloquium': an allocution, ad-locution, a 'speaking-*to*'.[16] To overlook this, and to isolate the logic from its context, as philosophers of religion often do, thereby presenting Anselm as doing 'natural theology' in the modern sense – as attempting, that is to say, to gain some measure of impersonal or purely theoretic purchase on the reality of God – is seriously to mistreat the text.

On the other hand, St Anselm, who was a most distinguished logician, clearly cared as much as any modern philosopher might do about the quality of the argument that he constructed. There is, therefore, a sense in which the logic of the argument does enjoy a kind of autonomy or independence in relation to the context of its use. There is, accordingly, a second way of mistreating the text, and that is to take it (as Karl Barth, in his little book, did show some tendency to do) as being simply concerned with the internal analysis of the discourse of Christian faith.

What Anselm sought to do, in a text set to the key of Christian worship, of faith's attentive, loving focus upon the mystery of God, was to establish with the use of two different 'figures', or linguistic melodies, what can be said of God with understanding.[17]

IN DANTE'S COMPANY

Anselm's world is not ours, nor can we make it so. Even if we could, we would not wish every feature of it to return. There is a great deal to be said for democracy, and dentistry, and modern drains. Nevertheless, as the world that we call 'modern' draws swiftly and dangerously to a close, some good things that have been hidden for a long time are beginning to be visible again. One of these, I have suggested, is the possibility of liberation from that obsessive search

[16] See *Proslogion*, pp. 104–5.
[17] See Richard Campbell, *From Belief to Understanding* (Canberra: Australian National University, 1976); G. R. Evans, *Anselm and a New Generation* (Oxford: Clarendon Press, 1980).

for solid starting-points which so preoccupied the modern mind.

When Anselm says, in Chapter 1 of the *Proslogion*, 'I do not seek to understand so that I may believe; but I believe so that I may understand' – 'Neque enim quaero intelligere ut credam, sed credo ut intelligam'[18] – he is not resolving a dispute as to whether faith or reason should serve as starting-point or intellectual foundation. Like St Augustine (from whom he had learnt much) Anselm is at ease in the ceaseless interplay of elements within the larger whole that is the Christian quest for wisdom in relation to the mystery of God. The relations between *credere* and *intelligere* are those between the context and one aspect of the goal.

Perhaps the deepest reason for surrendering the modern search for safe and solid starting-points is that none of us, in fact, ever begins at the beginning. Finding ourselves somewhere, we do our best to work out where we are and what to do about it, to make some sense of things, to find our way around. Instead of wasting time casting about in search of absolutes, of a kind of safety, a possessed security, of solid ground beneath our feet that simply is not offered to us – neither by science nor Scripture, not by popes or presidents, not by proofs or private revelations – we would do better to get on with the business of trying to help each other take our bearings on a dark and dangerous road.

Those who are in the habit of reading Heidegger, or Wittgenstein, or fashionable French philosophers may find the tone of these last remarks of mine somewhat 'postmodern' in flavour. In this respect, at least, postmodernism seems to be a matter of rediscovering that the starting-point, for all of us, the place at which we all begin, is, as another medieval master put it: 'Nel mezzo del cammin di nostra vita' – in the middle of the journey of our life.[19] Dante was writing in 1300, nearly two hundred years after Anselm's death. But Anselm would not, I think, have been at all surprised about the darkness of the

---

[18] *Proslogion*, p. 114. [19] Dante, *Inferno*, I.I.

wood in which the journey starts because the date, according to Dante, is Good Friday.

'Credo ut intelligam.' Today, as in St Anselm's day, Christian faith, discipleship – which furnishes the context of our quest for understanding – is lived out, enacted, undergone, close to Gethsemane and Calvary. For us, as for our guides who went before – for Barth and Schleiermacher, Luther and St Anselm – understanding lies, for the most part, far ahead, when we shall be brought out of darkness into the radiant daylight of 'L'amor che muove il sole e l'altre stelle' – the love that moves the sun and the other stars.[20]

---

[20] Dante, *Paradiso*, XXIII.145.

CHAPTER 9

Creation, courtesy and contemplation[1]

AN AGE OF UNREASON

On 5 October 1994, forty-eight members of an apocalyptic cult known as the Order of the Solar Temple died in Switzerland in horrifying circumstances. Twenty-three bodies were found in a burned-out farmhouse in Cheiry, near Fribourg, and a further twenty-five in 'two devastated chalets in Granges-sur-Salvan, on the Italian border'. There were empty champagne bottles lying on the floor of the farmhouse. Some of the dead seem to have been suffocated, some shot, and some 'were wearing red and black cloaks, reflecting an alternative name for the group, The Cross and the Rose'.[2]

The next day, the *Guardian* published an article, reflecting on the tragedy, by Maureen Freely, entitled: 'Mysterious power of the age of unreason'. The first sentence taught her by her father (a man whom she describes as having been 'cured of Catholicism by a doctorate in physics') was, she tells us, 'God does not exist.' The daughter learnt her lesson well, and is now simply baffled by the number of buildings full of apparently sane adults who 'bow their heads', confident that 'they are not speaking to themselves, but to a larger power'.[3]

---

[1] A lecture given in Trinity College, Dublin, on 3 November 1994, in a series of public lectures 'exploring the development and significance of Christian Mysticism for contemporary life'. I am greatly encouraged by the extent to which the drift of my argument in this lecture has since been given powerful support by Denys Turner's brilliant and learned study of *The Darkness of God: Negativity in Christian Mysticism* (Cambridge: Cambridge University Press, 1995).

[2] *Guardian*, 6 October 1994, 1.

[3] Maureen Freely, 'Mysterious power of the age of unreason', *Guardian*, 6 October 1994, 26.

However, as an honest woman, she admits that she herself takes part in 'many cults': 'Every time I make myself available for surgery', she says, 'or have a baby, or fasten my seat-belt on an aeroplane, I am giving myself over to a larger power.' It is quite clear, from the context, that she does not mean that when she does these things she prays, but that to put one's life in someone else's hands is to surrender to unreason. Ours is thus a world, it seems, in which intelligent and well-educated journalists can identify all trust with infantile behaviour and find all surrender of autonomy evidence of irrationality, of people 'wanting someone bigger and better to do their thinking for them'.[4]

Modern Western culture has, we are often told, been 'secularised'. And those who tell us this seem usually to suppose that the more secularised a society, the more irreligious it becomes. This I do not believe. In one of the largest bookshops in Cambridge, two shelves (hidden from view on the blind side of a counter) are devoted to a flea-bitten collection of Bibles and popular works of Christian theology. Behind them a magnificent display case, six or seven shelves high, is piled with a varied and colourful collection of works on yoga and astrology, on parapsychology and science fiction, on Tarot cards and oriental exercises, on spirituality and mysticism.

The dissociation between a disenchanted public order – the territory of what counts as 'rational behaviour', the world of calculation in which, increasingly, we do not trust – and anarchic private fantasy has seldom, if ever, been so deep-rooted or, perhaps, so dangerous. About one thing Maureen Freely seems quite right: ours is, in many ways, an 'age of unreason'. As someone who believes, with passion, that serious theological reflection begins and ends in prayer, I admit that, nevertheless, talk of 'mysticism' makes me nervous and I mistrust the widespread interest shown, these days, in 'spirituality'.

[4] Ibid.

'MYSTICISM' AND THE MYSTICAL

Few scholars in the English-speaking world have studied Christian mysticism more thoroughly, or with more good sense and even-handedness, than Professor Bernard McGinn of the University of Chicago. Nevertheless, having worked through the first volume of his massive history of Western Christian mysticism, I am left with a sense of something missing or not quite resolved: of a shadow hanging over the design.

At the outset, McGinn defines 'the mystical element in Christianity' as 'that part of its belief and practices that concerns the preparation for, the consciousness of, and the reaction to what can be described as the immediate or direct presence of God'.[5] This definition is then helpfully glossed with the remark that 'immediacy', in these matters, may be interpreted along the lines suggested by Bernard Lonergan's notion of 'mediated immediacy'.[6] (By way of illustration: a handshake is a medium of friendship, not a way of keeping friends apart!)

'Part' (in his definition) worries me. Are there, then, 'parts' of Christian belief that are not concerned with our acknowledgement of God's presence in the world? If so, what would they be? And if the mystical element is only *part* of Christian practice, what is it that we do, as Christians, that is *not* the work of grace, the immediate action of God's Holy Spirit in our hearts and minds?

But, you might say, we do not always *notice* this, advert to it, thus understand our Christian life or recognise that it is so. Agreed – however, when I am introducing students to Karl Rahner, I usually tell them that the most important clue to understanding his theology is his assertion that 'the possibility of experiencing grace and the possibility of experiencing grace *as* grace, are not the same thing'.[7]

---

[5] Bernard McGinn, *The Presence of God: A History of Western Christian Mysticism*, i, *The Foundations of Mysticism* (London: SCM Press, 1992), p. xvii.
[6] See note 17 to McGinn, *Foundations*, p. xx.
[7] See Karl Rahner, 'Concerning the relationship between nature and grace', *Theological Investigations*, i, (trans.) Cornelius Ernst (London: Darton, Longman and Todd, 1961) p. 300; this essay was first published in 1950.

McGinn insists that 'mysticism', as he understands it, is not to be confined to special experiences of God's presence, or to a kind of union with God which only a handful of individuals (if any) enjoy; and he admirably emphasises the extent to which, for the greater part of Christian history, mysticism was 'exegetical in character'.[8] 'Mystical theology', we might say, was Christian living shaped by Scripture taken seriously, attentively, contemplatively.

'No mystics', says McGinn, '(at least before the present century) believed in or practised "mysticism". They believed in and practised Christianity (or Judaism, or Islam, or Hinduism).' 'Augustine, like any thinker before the seventeenth century, would not have known what "mysticism" meant', for the very good reason that it was only in the seventeenth century that the substantive term 'mysticism' was invented.[9]

The word flared up, in circumstances that Michel de Certeau charted with such brilliance in *The Mystic Fable*,[10] flourished for little more than half a century,[11] then died away again until, in the late nineteenth century, it became the focus of intense discussion, especially in the English-speaking world; a discussion whose most striking feature (as was agreed by commentators as different as Dean Inge and Abbot Cuthbert Butler) was sloppy thought and poor theology.[12] But then, as that neglected giant of twentieth-century theology, Marie-Dominique Chenu, said in a remark which McGinn quotes with characteristic generosity (because he cannot bring himself wholeheartedly to endorse it): 'la vie mystique n'est autre, en son fond, que la vie chrétienne':[13] when all is

---

8 McGinn, *Foundations*, p. 64; see pp. 130, 171.
9 McGinn, *Foundations*, pp. xvi, 252.
10 Michel de Certeau, *The Mystic Fable*.
11 See de Certeau, *Mystic Fable*, pp. 16–17; 76–7.
12 'The early decades of this century abounded in . . . woolly accounts of what mysticism meant' (Rowan Williams, 'Butler's *Western Mysticism:* towards an assessment', *Downside Review*, 102 (1984), 199; see Nicholas Lash, *Easter in Ordinary*, p. 106).
13 M.-D. Chenu, OP, 'Une théologie de la vie mystique', *La vie spirituelle*, 50 (1937), 49; quoted McGinn, *Foundations*, p. 424, note 88.

said and done, the mystical life is really nothing other than the Christian life. Nevertheless, in view of the fact that the adjective 'mystical' has been around since Clement of Alexandria first used it in the second century CE,[14] am I not making heavy weather of the fact that the substantive, 'mysticism', is a concoction of the modern world? I think not.

Consider, first, the case of 'supernatural'. Until the seventeenth century this term, also, had only been used adjectively or adverbially, to indicate the difference that is made when someone is enabled to behave in ways above their ordinary station. You come across a rabbit playing Mozart? That rabbit is performing supernaturally, is the beneficiary of supernatural gifts. So also (things being the way they are since we were barred from paradise) is the human being whom one finds behaving generously, justly, truthfully. (And, of course, it is only *God* to whom the term 'supernatural' could *never* be applied: who graces God? Who elevates the nature of divinity?)

In the seventeenth century, for the first time, 'supernatural', the substantive, began to connote a realm of being, a territory of existence, 'outside' the world we know. With 'nature' now deemed single, homogeneous and self-contained, we labelled 'supernatural' that 'other' world inhabited (some said) by ghosts and poltergeists, by demons, angels and suchlike extraterrestrials – and by God.

It is, I think, almost impossible to overestimate the importance of the massive shift in language and imagination that took place, in Europe, in the seventeenth century; a shift for which de Certeau has two striking phrases: the 'dethroning of the verb', and the 'spatialisation of knowledge'.[15] One aspect of this shift was a transformation of the way in which relations with the Holy One, Creator and Redeemer of the world, were understood. For sixteen centuries, Christian discipleship had been understood as creaturely dependence transformed into friendship: from being subjects of the king of heaven we

---

[14] See McGinn, *Foundations*, p. 101; and it was the Pseudo-Denys who created the term 'mystical theology' (p. 158).
[15] De Certeau, *Mystic Fable*, pp. 125, 104.

became his kin. To 'know God' was to know oneself drawn by love outpoured in Christ towards the heart of that imponderable mystery of life and truth 'quod omnes dicunt deum' (as Aquinas put it): 'which everyone calls worshipful'. (My translation may seem eccentric: it is intended as a reminder that Aquinas' was still a world in which, firstly, the word 'god' was known not to be a proper name and in which, secondly, it was still understood that 'the idea of worship is inherent within the concept of God',[16] which is best understood not as the label of a 'nature' of some kind, but as freighted with acknowledgement of power. As the fifth-century Creed of Damasus put it: 'Deus est nomen potestatis non proprietatis'.)[17] By the end of the seventeenth century, 'believing in God', which, for Augustine and Aquinas, had been a matter of setting as our heart's desire the holy mystery disclosed in Christ towards whose blinding presence we walk in company on pilgrimage, had become a matter of supposing that there is, outside the world we know, a large and powerful entity called 'God'.

During this same period, a new ideal for the working of the human mind was born: namely, the production of a body of knowledge that has 'an unequivocal language with which it speaks and uniform objects of which it speaks'.[18] In this new world, people are expected to speak as plainly and straightforwardly of *God* as of any other object of investigation. In this new world, those Christians who most single-mindedly devote their time and energy to prayer (people known hitherto as 'contemplatives') begin to seem like 'experts' in an esoteric branch of knowledge. And, since they seem to have some difficulty in straightforwardly communicating quite what it is that they are on about, theirs appears to be a *secret* knowledge, a knowledge of extraordinary facts, obtained by people who enjoy unusual experiences. This new field of expertise deserves a name: let's call it 'la mystique' (or, as de Certeau's

---

16 Panikkar, *The Trinity and the Religious Experience*, p. 26.
17 See Denziger, 71 (text cited Panikkar, ibid., p. xiii).
18 Funkenstein, *Theology and the Scientific Imagination*, p. 41.

translator nicely coins it, 'mystics' – to set alongside 'ethics' and 'dogmatics'). And the experts who work in this field? We'll call them 'mystics'.

Just one more strand, before pulling the threads together. The last few years have seen a burgeoning interest (often on the part of people who would not dream of entering a church on Sunday) in what is nowadays known as 'negative theology'. And when it is discovered that Aquinas taught that people came to the knowledge of God through learning that they do not know what God is, the poor man is held up as some kind of marvellous exception to the rule.[19] It would, in fact, be nearer the mark, historically, to say (paradoxically) that it is what we might call the cataphatic cockiness of the seventeenth and eighteenth centuries that is unusual – a brief period interrupting two thousand years of wiser recognition that all language breaks, and fails, and crumbles, as we stammer out our praise and adoration of the mystery of God.

Why is it so difficult to speak sensibly of God? From the deist standpoint that defines and dominates the modern imagination, it seems obvious that the reason is that God is *so far away* from us. We cannot see him, taste him, touch him, and he inhabits (does he not?) another world.

But suppose we come at it from a different angle, from a Christian angle; from, that is to say, a standpoint shaped by recognition of God's uttered Word and outpoured Spirit. When some Romeo starts stammering, unable to find words that will do justice to his love, it is not because the beloved is *unknown* to him – he has not forgotten Juliet's name, address, or what she looks like – it is because she has become too *well* known for glib description to be possible. The closer we grow to one another in love, the more intimately we understand each other, the more impossible it becomes to circumscribe the one we love in speech.

God is not far from us. God's self-giving constitutes our very being, intimates each element and movement of our heart. It is not those who know not God who find God difficult to talk

[19] See above, Chapter Three, note 38.

about, but those who know God well. Moreover, this conviction – so constant and so central in Christian tradition – also finds expression, in different forms and figures, in Judaism and Hinduism, in at least some forms of Buddhism, and in Islam.

Chenu was surely right: the 'mystical life' is really nothing other than the Christian life lived to maximum intensity. If (to return to McGinn's own definition) the 'mystical element' in Christianity is a matter of preparing for, becoming conscious of and reacting to, the ever deeper sense and recognition of God's presence, then it is – in vastly varying degrees of actualisation – an element in *every* Christian life. Professor McGinn knows this much better than I do; the whole drift of his study points in this direction, and it is one of the reasons for his admiration of von Hügel.

Under the abiding influence of thought-forms established in the seventeenth and eighteenth centuries, however, many people still suppose that 'mysticism' is a matter of unusual experiences, enjoyed by a handful of unusual individuals known as 'mystics' – experiences of a God to whom the rest of us have, at best, precarious and inferential access through the thick filters of the world. When I referred, earlier, to what I called a shadow hanging over the design of Bernard McGinn's splendid book, what I had in mind was this: because linguistic habits first learnt in the early modern world are still shaped by their deistic origins, speaking of 'mysticism' and of 'mystics' risks perpetuating the quite unchristian misapprehension that 'experience of God' is, at best, something esoteric and, at worst, close cousin to the paranormal.

IN FAVOUR OF TRIANGLES

A few years ago, I wrote a book, entitled *Easter in Ordinary*, in which I tried to unscramble some of the confusion that there seems to be between 'religious experience', as understood by psychologists and sociologists of religion, and what might count, for Christians, as experience of God. In the first part of the book, I concentrated on the immensely influential work of William James and, later on, I enlisted the help of Baron

Friedrich von Hügel, who shared both my respect for James and my profound misgivings as to the direction in which *The Varieties of Religious Experience* pointed the discussion.

Von Hügel drew a distinction between what he called 'inclusive' and 'exclusive' mysticism. According to the latter, mysticism means the private psychic state of those individuals who enjoy apparent perceptions of something usually known (for vagueness' sake) as 'the transcendent' or 'a larger power'. In this direction, 'mysticism' soon becomes, he says, the name for 'an abnormal faculty for perceiving phenomena' that seem at present 'inexplicable by physical and [psychological] science'.[20] Taken to its logical conclusion, as it was in a study by Frits Staal, published in 1975, mysticism is then deemed not necessarily to be 'regarded as a part of religion at all',[21] but simply the name of a family of unusual psychological conditions whose exploration is the business, not of the theologian, but of the psychologist.

Taking the term 'mysticism' to refer, in general, to 'both the right and the wrong use of feeling in religion', von Hügel described *inclusive* mysticism as simply a matter of allowing, in both the practice and the theory of religion, 'the legitimate share of feeling in the constitution of the religious life'.[22] Hence the Baron's admirable preference for taking the term 'mysticism', *adjectivally*, to refer to one of three elements constitutive of all religious life.

In the last analysis, the strategies contrasted by von Hügel rest upon mutually incompatible accounts of what is meant by 'God', and of the relationship between the love of creatures and the love of God. Thus, for example, to suppose that there could be what he calls a 'specifically distinct . . . purely mystical mode of apprehending reality'[23] is to imagine that the

---

[20] Friedrich von Hügel, *The Mystical Element of Religion as Studied in Saint Catherine of Genoa and her Friends*, ii (London: Dent, 1923), p. 308; see Lash, *Easter in Ordinary*, pp. 76, 97, 163.

[21] Frits Staal, *Exploring Mysticism* (Harmondsworth: Penguin Books, 1975), p. 4; see Lash, *Easter in Ordinary*, p. 106.

[22] Von Hügel, *Mystical Element*, ii, p. 291.

[23] Von Hügel, p. 283.

distinction between the world and God may itself appear, within the world, as some kind of *feature* of the world. The God thus apprehended would thereby function as an object in the world, an idea, fact or thing alongside other ideas, facts and things, competing with them for space and interest and affection.

Von Hügel acknowledges that it is *easier* to think of God like this, as what he calls 'the First of Creatures', worthier than all other creatures of our love. But the fact is, as he puts it, that the love of God is 'the "form", the principle of order and harmony; our natural affections are the "matter" harmonized and set in order'.[24] It is God's love which sets in order all those other loves by which, if we love well, God is thereby loved. Discipleship is a matter of learning to display, in the school that we call Christianity, that courtesy to creatures in which reverence for the Creator finds expression.

The distinction between the world and God, which is not itself a fact about the world, only appears within the world as those changes in the condition of the world which (in Christian terminology) we call the world's redemption; changes effected by God's act in human acts and words, silences and suffering, patterned to the form of their creation. It follows that everything that human beings are and think and do and undergo either gives expression, in the world, to the reality of God or else, towards the world's destruction, fails to do so.

Each of the three 'elements' into which von Hügel differentiates religion – the 'mystical', the 'institutional' and the 'intellectual' – interacts, both singly and in conjunction, with the others. The pattern of their interplay, however vulnerable it may appear to be to our propensity for idolatry, our endlessly ingenious capacity for finding in some *one* fact or feature of the world the form or 'nature' of divinity, is, by God's grace, kept sacramental. That is to say: in this ceaseless, mutually corrective, interaction the eternal stillness of God's self-constitutive relations – in utterance of Word and outgiving of Spirit – finds some created shadow or transcription.

[24] Von Hügel, p. 353; see Lash, *Easter in Ordinary*, p. 165.

Von Hügel did not, of course, make all this up. He learnt it from Newman who learnt it from the Fathers of the Church. And if I have made it sound a little like the better part of Hegel, I had in mind Bishop Walter Kasper's claim that 'the history of modern thought' (by which he means the history of modern *German* thought!) is a history of attempts to 'reconstruct the doctrine of the Trinity'[25] – attempts made largely by philosophers, because the theologians, for the most part, were mesmerised by deism.

Thus it is, as I have tried to indicate, that, on the one hand, there are connections between such apparently dry and trivial matters as substantival uses of words like 'mysticism' and 'mystic', and the *isolation* of religion from the rest of modern life and thought and culture – an isolation rooted in the deist view of God as one amongst the items that make up the constitution of the world. Whereas, on the other hand, if we could learn again to live and think and pray and make connections according to the pattern and the 'rhythm' of God's Trinity, then we might discover that we no longer needed anxiously to set aside some special sector of our lives, to the exclusion of the others, as the place where we would hope to find the face of God.

ALLOCUTION AND SOLILOQUY

My mistrust, which I mentioned earlier, of contemporary interest in 'spirituality' arises from the suspicion that quite a lot of the material set out in bookstores under this description sells because it does not stretch the mind or challenge our behaviour. It tends to soothe rather than subvert our well-heeled complacency.

There is, of course, another side to the story. Works sold as 'spirituality' tend to be less technical in argument, less burdened by references to obscure learned journals, than those labelled as 'theology'. And it would be perverse to criticise a genre of literature for being intelligible! It is not

[25] Walter Kasper, *The God of Jesus Christ*, p. 264; see Lash, *Easter in Ordinary*, p. 132.

reader-friendliness alone, however, which helps 'spirituality' to sell better than 'theology', but also the suspicion that titles which deserve the latter label will be not merely erudite, but abstract; not merely technical, but products of pure reason – passionless and unimaginative.

Karl Barth thought it a mistake to suppose the ethos of 'enlightenment' to be rationalist. It was not 'pure reason' that marked the temper of the eighteenth century, but the *dissociation* of reason from imagination, of head from heart, of inference from imagination.[26] The fall-out from that period still clouds the air today, and, if (as I believe) Karl Barth is right, then we should not waste our time arguing the respective merits of 'spirituality' and 'theology', but should set to work healing the divorce between them.

Thus Karl Rahner, who shared my mistrust of spirituality dissociated from theology, emphasised, especially in his later writings, that all our theology must be 'mystagogic': 'The theology of the future will, in a more direct sense than hitherto, be a missionary and mystagogic theology, and no longer be so willing as has been the case in the past few centuries to consign this department of missionary mystagogy to the realm of personal practice or ascetic and mystical literature.'[27] His argument (if I may adapt it to a metaphor of my own) goes something like this. In a Christian culture, a culture in which scholarly attentiveness goes hand in hand with contemplation, a culture quite at ease with prayer, it is society as a whole that sings the song, that makes the music. In such a society, it is quite in order for the academic theologian simply to function as *technician* – as music critic, we might say, or as historian of musicology. However, in a culture such as

---

[26] Thus, siding with F. C. Baur and Ritschl, against Troeltsch and Hoffmann, Barth insisted that pietism and rationalism represent 'the two forms of the one essence, of Christianity as shaped by the spirit of the eighteenth century' (Karl Barth, *Protestant Theology in the Nineteenth Century. Its Background and History*, (trans.) Brian Cozens, John Bowden, et al. (London: SCM Press, 1972), p. 85).

[27] Karl Rahner, 'Possible courses for the theology of the future', *Theological Investigations*, XIII, (trans.) David Bourke (London: Darton, Longman and Todd, 1975), p. 40; a lecture first published in 1970.

ours (and, for this purpose, it matters not whether we call it 'secular' or 'pagan') – a culture lacking in contemplativity, finding prayerfulness a *problem* – in such a culture, *no* Christian can afford the luxury of sitting in the audience, but *all* are called to sing the song, to make the music of the Gospel. And this applies, not least, to theologians.

Rahner's plea was not that our theology should become less rigorous in argument, less critically meticulous in treatment of the evidence, but that – irrespective of the level of technicality or accessibility at which a work is pitched – it should spring from and contribute to the articulation of that Word whose utterance, as *Christian* theology, it serves.

But if, obliterating the disjunction between 'theology' and 'spirituality', we insist that all theological reflection be true to its vocation as a contribution to the proclamation of the Word, how might distinctions between 'theology' and 'philosophy' be most appropriately drawn? The practical importance of this question (its bearing on what goes on in education, for example) becomes clear if, in accordance with the custom that prevailed until the nineteenth century, we cast the connotations of 'philosophy' wide enough to cover the sweep of secular enquiry, from astronomy to anthropology, and from psychology to physics.

In the eleventh century (which seems as sensible a place to take our bearings from as any other!) Anselm, in his Preface to the *Proslogion*, drew the distinction as lying between soliloquy and allocution.[28] The philosopher (or, in our day, the scientist) conducts a monologue (hence, incidentally, the title which Anselm gave his previous work: the *Monologion*). The only voice heard in scientific discourse is that of the scientist. Theology, in contrast, is an attempt to say something sensible in the presence of God. The theologian speaks in response to the prior utterance of God's eternal Word. Theological discourse is allocutory: not monologue but address. But it can only be so, and remain so, in the measure that the theologian

[28] See *St Anselm's Proslogion*, (trans.) Charlesworth, p. 104.

(and, of course, *every* Christian is in some way a theologian) stays attentive to the silence of God's speech.

The cultural crisis of the seventeenth century was, in many ways, as comprehensive as our own. Old worlds had crumbled, new worlds not yet been quite born. De Certeau notes that, in a society which still started from the premise (learnt from Anselm) that 'the art of knowing was situated in the field of prayer', and that 'allocution was for knowledge its condition and beginning',[29] it was the newly problematic character of the *connection* between God's speech and ours, between what we *said* and what (it now began to seem) we could no longer *hear*, which preoccupied the builders of that new bridge across the silence known as 'mystics'.

The hiddenness of God has always been a central theme in Christian, as in Jewish, life and thought. God's ways are not our ways, nor God's thoughts ours. By *naming* things we put them in our power: there is no name that we might use to gain some leverage on God. That is the lesson of the burning bush. In early modern Europe, however, the figure of God's hiddenness underwent a subtle, but decisive, shift. This was a culture which set great store by plain, transparent speech, stripped bare of allegory or allusion, because the *hiddenness* of truth made people nervous. Masks are disguises; things hidden may be lost – perhaps beyond retrieval. The literature is thick with imagery of masks and veils, of objects sought and found. But all this imagery supposes truth to be *inert*. The only *voices* in the modern world are those of human beings, weeping in the stellar darkness that so terrified Pascal.[30]

To try to put one's finger on some *one* dilemma at the heart of our contemporary cultural malaise may seem a foolhardy, perhaps preposterous, thing to do. Nevertheless, I am increasingly convinced that – whether in science or politics, in ethics, art, or economics – *no* division now goes deeper than that between the expectation, on the one hand, that such sense as may be found in things is, in the last analysis, imposed by our

[29] De Certeau, *Mystic Fable*, p. 160.
[30] 'Le silence éternel de ces espaces infinis m'effraie' (Blaise Pascal, *Pensées*, 3.206).

soliloquies and, on the other, that, even in this disenchanted world, we may remain *attentive* with integrity, may *address* the dark, respond in wonder to the silence that surrounds us as the voice of God.

De Certeau quotes Angelus Silesius, writing in the later seventeenth century: 'Gott spricht nur immer Ja';[31] God says always only 'Ja', where this small syllable not only stands for 'Yes', but also abbreviates the non-name given to Moses at the burning bush. God's holy mystery transcribed within the world as 'Yes', as Christ's obedience and – by his grace – as ours, or else obliterate, leaving the dust upon the tombstone undisturbed.

FEAR OF THE DARK

The mystical element of Christianity, as Professor McGinn defines it, is a quest, a search, a preparation, for the recognition of God's presence. But what would the signals of such presence be? To what, in such a search, should we be looking forward?

In the tradition that von Hügel calls 'exclusive mysticism', the tradition which supposes there to be a special territory marked out for 'spiritual' affairs, a 'Sunday-place' kept separate from the mundane, exhausting, dangerous ambivalence of things, the dominant tendency has been to suppose that God is met as strength, benevolence and consolation; as friendliness and light and peace.

Von Hügel warns us, however, that 'Mysticism, as such, has ever tended to deny all positive character to Evil.'[32] Exclusive mysticism, or what he here calls 'mysticism as such', tends to be in flight from finitude's distortion, evasive of the thick web of toxic cause and consequence, of idolatry, unmeaning and injustice, that holds the world in thrall – evasive not only of the *fact* of this satanic tapestry but, more dangerously, of

---

[31] Angelus Silesius (Johannes Scheffler), *Der Cherubinische Wandersmann*, 2.4, quoted by de Certeau, *Mystic Fable*, p. 175.
[32] Von Hügel, *Mystical Element*, II, p. 293.

the extent to which we are ourselves participant in its construction.

According to Christian tradition, however, and notwithstanding much modern misunderstanding of monasticism, God is not found in flight. The search for God is not the search for comfort or tranquillity, but for truth, for justice, faithfulness, integrity: these, as the prophets tirelessly reiterated, are the forms of God's appearance in the world. Von Hügel insists, accordingly, that it is 'not the smoother, easier times and circumstances in the lives of individuals and of peoples, but, on the contrary, the harder and hardest trials of every conceivable kind, and the unshrinking, full acceptance of these, as part of the price of conscience and of its growing light, [that] have ever been the occasions of the deepest trust in and love of God to which man has attained'. This is neither stoicism nor sadism, but simply a reminder that the paradigm of God's appearance in the world is Christ's obedience in Gethsemane.[33]

Few people except civil servants and other professional administrators admit to being fond of institutions. In Christian company, it is quite common for something called the 'institutional Church' to be treated with irritation and disdain. Leaving on one side the fact that language is an 'institution', that all relationship and common life, routine and regularity, have institutional dimensions, and that distaste for institutions may be little more, in fact, than further evidence of the flight from finitude, I simply note that, on the whole, we tend to think of institutions as a burden on our backs, convention's weight inhibiting our freedom. The world of institutions is the *weekday* world, the world of work, from which we need, at weekends and on holiday, some 'spiritual' relief.

In his editorial Postscript to an issue of *Concilium* devoted to the theme of *Mysticism and the Institutional Crisis*, Christian Duquoc neatly set this stereotype upside-down. It is, he said, 'The mystical approach to God' that is hard work, the

---

[33] Von Hügel, pp. 291–2; see Lash, *Easter in Ordinary*, p. 163.

following of an 'arduous path'. It is a journey of 'persistent will', of an unswerving dedication that necessarily entails 'discarding the peripheral forms of desire . . . Joy bursts out in this place, but it is always a place of night.'[34] There are no weekends in Gethsemane.

We underestimate at our peril the seriousness with which we are required to take the metaphor of 'night'. Duquoc reports a vision of St Sylvanus in which the voice of Christ was heard instructing him to 'Remain in hell, but do not despair.' In so acute a form, this is not (except, it may be, intermittently) every Christian's vocation. 'Not everyone', Duquoc goes on, 'can "remain in hell" without despairing. Not everyone can live in the dark night without the risk of going mad.' If, therefore, we take seriously the extent to which the 'mystical element' is a constitutive dimension of *every* Christian life, of *all* discipleship, then the need for what he calls 'havens of rest and compassion' will come as no surprise. Unfortunately, in our 'concern for rigour', we too easily forget that the institutional Church exists to serve as a 'diversion'.[35]

Civil servants (ecclesiastical and other) may suppose that rules and regulations are the real thing. On the contrary, they are a kind of necessary pantomime, enabling the mediocre Christians that we are to totter on. Without this diversion, left naked before the full blast of reality, we would 'fall by the wayside out of weariness, anxiety or madness'.[36] Like all good ideas, Duquoc's suggestion can be misinterpreted, but it is, I think, worth pondering.

IN SEARCH OF A BODY

Few themes are more constant, in Christian contemplative literature, than the insistence that our heart's ache, our quest for God, finds in this life no final resting-place. ' "This isn't it",

---

[34] Christian Duquoc, 'Postscript: the institution and diversion' in Christian Duquoc and Gustavo Gutiérrez (eds.), *Mysticism and the Institutional Crisis. Concilium*, 1994/4, 101.

[35] Duquoc, pp. 101–3.   [36] Duquoc, p. 103.

"this isn't it", endlessly, till the end of one's strength'. This gesture, says de Certeau, 'is the mainspring of the mystic life'.[37] We are called, as Christians, to be members of a pilgrim people, people who 'cannot stop walking', people who know of every place and object that they pass along the way 'that it is *not that*'.[38]

As with the darkness of the night, however, it is of paramount importance not to *romanticise* our restlessness. It is no disparagement of God's good creation to acknowledge the destructive, wintry bleakness of the world that we have made. It is not, I think, surprising that, in solidarity with those in whom both hope and dignity are stifled and suppressed by destitution and neglect, we sometimes find that (as de Certeau put it) 'all that remains of "prayer" or "communication" is its negativity':[39] not this; not this.

During the last four hundred years, we have enriched our understanding and control of things beyond the wildest dreams of those who lived before the 'modern' age. There is no force more dangerous, however, for us and for the world of which we form a part, than knowledge and control untuned by wisdom. And as, in recent decades, we have begun painfully to discover this, we have, for all our ingenuity, become increasingly confused. We no longer know what to say or do or value, or how to realise the goals we seek. We are, like children in the forest, lost.

In the beginning, according to Luke's Gospel, a child got lost. His parents sought him, sorrowing, for 'three days' and, on the third day, found him amongst the learned people in the Temple.[40] Luke's first two chapters serve as a 'trailer', narrating in miniature the story as a whole. Thus (as I indicated when I used this image at the end of Chapter Three) this discovery happened on that same 'third day' on which Mary Magdalene 'stood weeping outside the tomb' because, she said, 'they have taken away my Lord, and I do not know

---

[37] De Certeau, *Mystic Fable*, p. 289.   [38] De Certeau, p. 299.
[39] De Certeau, p. 291.   [40] See Luke 2. 41–9.

where they have laid him'.[41] As readers of the gospel text, *we*
know that she was in the presence of the one whom she
thought lost; that what she knew as absence, deprivation, was
– in fact – the form and context of God's presence. But then, as
Rahner said, experience of grace, and experience of grace *as*
grace, are not the same thing.

---

[41] John 20.11, 13.

CHAPTER 10

Hollow centres and holy places[1]

THE ICARUS BAR

Perhaps the motto for our meeting might be Seamus Heaney's
direction for the uncoding of all landscapes of 'things founded
clean on their own shapes, / Water and ground in their
extremity'.[2] We are gathered, this weekend, at an extremity
of Europe, if not at the margin. But where would one find
Europe's centre? A politician might choose Brussels, but a
banker or a businessman would more likely opt for Frankfurt.
There is no parable more poignant of the predicament of
modern Europe than that provided, in the departure area at
Frankfurt airport, by what journalists call a watering-hole,
labelled in proud lights: 'Bar Ikarus'.

There are, of course, other candidates for Europe's centre.
It was from Rome, in 1991, that a hastily assembled Synod
summoned 'Europe' to make a 'choice for God'. No one seems
quite sure what this means but (at least in England) suspicion
of 'Maastricht' is, in part, bound up with half-formed fears
that ancient and imperial forces gather strength, that caesaro-
papal banners are somewhere being unfurled. Meanwhile,
in quite high places in the Catholic Church there seems
to be, as Jean-Louis Schlegel recently remarked, 'a marked

---

[1] A lecture delivered to a conference of the West of Ireland Research Association in
Galway, in 1993, the theme of which was 'Marginalised societies, the secular world,
and the Gospel'.

[2] Seamus Heaney, 'The peninsula', *Door into the Dark* (London: Faber and Faber,
1969), p. 21.

184   *Emerging from modernity*

ambivalence, not to say ominous confusion, over the notion of secularisation'.[3]

Brussels? Frankfurt? Rome? The list of candidates for Europe's centre might now be extended to include Budapest, or Cracow. After all, Western Europeans are already learning to rename as 'central Europe' the territories, between what was the Soviet Union and the West, which (until recently) we unhistorically and most misleadingly referred to as the 'Eastern bloc'. And while some Westerners suppose us to be generously extending eastwards the benefits of capitalism, democracy and free enquiry, there are those in Poland, and Slovakia, and Hungary, proud of the strength of spirit wrought through solidarity in suffering, who see Western Christianity as simply decadent, dissipated by collusion with the godlessness and materialism that are deemed to be defining features of a 'secular' society. Pride comes, they say, before a fall and, as seen from parts of Poland, the wax is melting rapidly from the wings of Icarus.

CRUMBLING AND COAGULATION

In April 1992 I was in Stuttgart for the first Congress of the European Society for Catholic Theology.[4] One of my English colleagues at the Congress offered the best description of what went on. We were, he said, like Pierre at the Battle of Borodino, stumbling around good-naturedly, fumbling for our spectacles, thrown into the centre of some world-historical event quite beyond our comprehension. I still feel like that, which is why I have little more to offer in this paper than a kind of meditation on our predicament in the light of the twin themes of our meeting. And if I concentrate on Europe, I do so partly because that is where we are, and partly because it is

---

[3] Jean-Louis Schlegel, 'The strategies of reconquest in the new Europe and the impossibility of getting past secularization' in Claude Geffré and Jean-Pierre Jossua (eds.), *The Debate on Modernity. Concilium*, 1992/6, 101.

[4] For some reflections on the Congress, see Nicholas Lash, 'Theology on the way to Stuttgart', *America* (4 April 1992), 266–8; 'The broken mirror', *America* (16 May 1992), 432–4; 'In search of the prodigal', *America* (6–13 June 1992), 506–8.

still the 'secular' societies of Europe and North America which are the most efficient generating centres of other people's marginalisation.

The guiding thread of my remarks will be the conviction that Catholic Christianity has still untapped resources which could contribute to, if not the resolution, then at least the clarification of a question near the heart of all our futures: namely, what makes for 'peopleness' and what, if anything, might make for peopleness in peace? Moreover, a Research Association such as yours (I shall suggest) is excellently placed to contribute to this urgent exploration.

'Peopleness' is not a pretty word, but perhaps its very awkwardness may serve to point towards a kind of vacuum in our social and political typology. Thus, for example, as old frontiers diminish in significance, and the economic, political and cultural autonomy of the nation-state is eroded with bewildering rapidity, Europe appears to be simultaneously crumbling and congealing. On the one hand, it moves – economically and logistically – ever nearer to becoming a single mass, the weight and wealth of which are concentrated in Germany, while the outlook at the margins grows increasingly bleak. On the other hand, fissures and fractures everywhere appear, as older fears and memories, ancient dreams and loyalties and nightmares, exert their pressure, releasing fresh destruction. We speak of 'nations' and of 'races', of 'communal' and 'sectarian' violence, of 'civil' war and 'ethnic' cleansing. All these are 'people' words, evocative of what it is that furnishes, sustains and threatens our sense (whoever 'we' may be) of who we are and how things go with us. But categories of political analysis shaped by the assumptions of early modern secularity cannot easily handle what is happening. As a result, there is too much loose talk about 'religious' conflict, 'sects' and 'fundamentalism'.

Later in the paper, I shall make one or two suggestions as to the part that might be played by theological reflection in making sense of what is happening. For the time being, I simply register the conviction that, until the mythical components of the secular imagination have been (to use the fashionable jargon) deconstructed, and until we learn effectively to display what might be called a 'preferential option for extremities', we shall neither understand what makes for peopleness nor foster its appropriate appearance.

CENTRES AND SYSTEMS

A system without centres would, of course, also be a system that lacked margins and extremities. One theme that kept recurring at the Stuttgart Congress concerned our need to learn how to render habitable a Europe (and a world) *without* stable and enduring centres of power and privilege and understanding. And yet, while powerful centres will tend disastrously to disadvantage the people, places and ideas which they consign to the periphery, we should perhaps remember that, without their centres, wheels would fall apart. There simply is no evading the ambivalence of the symbols that we use to shape our social discourse and imagination.

The fashionable talk, these days, is all of pluralism and dispersal, of myriad playgrounds of particular and private preference: each his own centre in a world which knows no overarching story or design. The more clear-sighted versions of such fantasies are those in which bright postmodernist exuberance is overshadowed by the terrifying shapeless form, implacable machinery, of that dark god alluded to by Lyotard, for example, simply as 'the system'.[5]

Postmodernists acknowledge that, beyond our diverse private chatterings, there are still energies and powers at work, forces and structures of production, distribution and exchange, but these are now said to have become autonomous, mechanical, beyond mere human understanding and control. According to Gregory Baum, Lyotard's 'brilliant caricature... cannot account for ... the deadly irrationalities capitalism is

---

[5] See, e.g. Jean-François Lyotard, *The Postmodern Condition: A Report on Knowledge*, (trans.) Geoff Bennington and Brian Masumi, Foreword by Frederic Jameson (Manchester: Manchester University Press, 1984), p. 66. Lyotard defines postmodernism as 'incredulity towards metanarratives' (p. xxiv).

producing in the human community, not least among them the multiplication of the poor, the homeless and the hungry'.[6] But, as I read Lyotard, there is no question of *accounting for* the dark god's deeds: the most that we can do is to postpone their consequences for a little while, evading nemesis by playfulness. Though one might never guess it from some American celebrations of 'pluralism', there often lurks (I am suggesting) beneath the surface of postmodernism what might be called a 'negative idolatry', a palpably religious veneration of implacability. In bright new temples, very ancient gods are being worshipped.

There are, of course, more upbeat versions of the story, mostly produced in North America, in which the religious character of late capitalist culture is explicitly acknowledged. Thus Michael Novak, according to whom God's Trinity finds symbolic expression in the structures of democratic capitalism, tells us that 'The point of Incarnation is to respect the world as it is . . . and to disbelieve any promises that the world is now or ever will be transformed into the City of God.' With redemption thus excised from the purposes of incarnation, it is not too surprising that, devoutly respecting 'the world as it is', Novak should upbraid Gregory Baum for foolishly supposing there to be connections between the wealth of some and the poverty of others. 'The theory', says Novak, 'of the "centre" and the "periphery" is merely a clever restatement of the proposition that the poverty of the poor is explained by the wealth of the wealthy. For this there is not a shred of evidence.'[7] Later on, I shall consider the strange temple, with its empty shrine, which Novak sees at the centre of capitalist America. But, before doing so, there are one or two elementary observations to be made concerning 'secularisation'.

---

[6] Gregory Baum, 'Modernity: a sociological perspective' in Geffré and Jossua (eds.), *The Debate on Modernity*, p. 9.
[7] Michael Novak, *The Spirit of Democratic Capitalism* (London: IEA Health and Welfare Unit, 1991), pp. 341 (on the Trinity, see pp. 337–8), 285. Novak's study was first published in 1982.

SECULARITY AND GODLESSNESS

The *Oxford English Dictionary* (even in its 1976 Supplement) knows no sense of 'marginalise' other than that of making marginal notes upon a page. The metaphorical extension of the word, its social use, describing the process whereby the weak and vulnerable are extruded to the 'edge' of things, is therefore very recent. 'Secularisation', by contrast, has been with us well over three hundred years, its original, legal sense of the procedures whereby ecclesiastical property was transferred to 'worldly' ownership or use gradually evolving into the idea of 'the process whereby religious institutions become less powerful in a society and religious beliefs less easily accepted'.[8]

In the vast literature examining, deploring, celebrating the story of modern Western culture as an irreversible process of secularisation, it still seems too little understood that the modern invention of the 'secular' carried with it concomitant *re*definitions of 'religion'. Something of this was understood by those who launched the project of 'enlightenment'. Hence the care with which they sought newly to distinguish 'natural' religion, the religion of a secular society – 'universal in embrace, rational in character, and benign in its consequences'[9] – from what they saw as the dangerously divisive, irrational, priest-ridden and intolerant particularities of 'positive' religion. It was not in irreligion that the great project of 'rationality' was born and its cool, machine-like marketplace, the parliament of secularity, constructed. Rather than suggest that, in the process of secularisation, religion became privatised, it would be more accurate to say that, as the bones of 'natural religion' faded in the public square, bleached by 'rationalisation', what, increasingly, was privatised was the role of religion as a medium of truth.[10]

And if liberal enthusiasts for secularisation contributed to

---

[8] David Martin, *A General Theory of Secularization* (Oxford: Basil Blackwell, 1978), p. 12.
[9] John Clayton, 'Thomas Jefferson', p. 8.   [10] See Chapter One, p. 16.

the confusion, so too did those, especially in ecclesiastical high places, who construed their own diminishing social clout and dignity as evidence of disbelief in God. But secularisation and the spread of irreligion do not straightforwardly go hand in hand. Indeed, if we take into consideration the situation in even the most 'modernised' parts of Africa and South-East Asia, it would seem that David Martin's definition needs to be reworked: the declining social power of religious institutions by no means necessarily leads to or fosters the erosion of religious beliefs and devotional practices.

At this point, I take up the thread of a suggestion I made earlier: namely, that the invention of the secular carries with it concomitant redefinitions of religion. The territory of the objects of traditional religious faith and worship, it is often said, was the territory of the 'supernatural' or the 'metaphysical'. We too easily forget, however, that, during the seventeenth century, all the maps were comprehensively redrawn. During this period, the old belief in one world in which creatures might act supernaturally (you might find human beings being kind and honest, for example), and in which only God could *not*, was replaced by a belief in two worlds – one natural, the other supernatural – in the second of which the most important occupant was an entity called 'God'.

Even David Martin's definition of secularisation seems to suppose that the concept of 'religion' refers, in a secularised society, to the same objects as it did before the process of secularisation got under way. But this cannot be so. In inventing the 'secular' – the territory of 'rational' behaviour, in which the component of 'natural' religion gradually modulated into 'civil' religion, 'public philosophy', class or national ideology – we invented, alongside it, a new world of private feelings, hermetic practices, individual and tribal fantasies, which was first called 'positive' religion and then, in due course, tended to be referred to simply as 'religion', *tout court*.

The drift of these remarks becomes, I hope, quite clear: it would be an exceedingly dangerous illusion to suppose that the only gods worshipped in our society were those whose temples are located in the culturally marginal territory which we still label as 'religious'.

We could come at it from a different angle. Suppose we follow Durkheim's lead and define religion as 'the system of symbols by means of which society becomes conscious of itself'. We would then construe 'religion' as the 'totality of [social] practices concerned with sacred things',[11] concerned, that is to say, with practices, beliefs and institutions which prove too hot to handle, too dangerous to touch. Practices protective, for example, of 'the system', or the market, or the male character of priesthood, or professorial self-esteem. The possibility would then emerge, as John Milbank has powerfully argued, that the narratives of secularisation merely serve to render ideologically invisible the religious character of many of our most powerful institutions and foundationally entrenched beliefs.[12]

According to the myth of secularity, what happens in the public realm is 'rational'. At the centre of this realm, there are no wayward human agents, only calculable and impersonal forces which we seek to understand and, so far as possible, to control. Through the operation of these forces, some lose, some win. That's life. Learning, therefore, 'to respect the world as it is', we learn to take no credit and accept no blame.

But let us, for a moment, entertain the possibility that banks, bureaucracies and stock exchanges are not, after all, machines, but *temples* in the liturgies of which all power and honour, agency and possibility, are ascribed *non nobis, Domine, non nobis*, but to 'the system'. If this were so, we might, with a little elementary demythologising, begin to understand that, in the last analysis, it was just us, just human beings, who were

---

[11] Emile Durkheim, *Suicide: A Study in Sociology*, (trans.) John A. Spaulding and George Simpson (London: Routledge and Kegan Paul, 1970), p. 312; 'Concerning the definition of religious phenomena' in W. S. F. Pickering (ed.), *Durkheim on Religion: A Selection of Readings and Bibliographies* (London: Routledge and Kegan Paul, 1975), p. 88.

[12] See John Milbank, *Theology and Social Theory*. Amongst the extensive discussion which this study has provoked, see the special issues devoted to it of *Modern Theology*, 8, 4 (October 1992) and *New Blackfriars*, 73 (June 1992).

performing these rituals, producing these results. In which case, the destitution, squalor and starvation of the marginalised would not be the fate of those less fortunate but the condition of the victims whom we sacrifice upon our altars. It is time, perhaps, more closely to examine Michael Novak's empty shrine.

THE EMPTY SHRINE

All cultures, all societies, express, elaborate and search for patterns and narratives of plausibility. Giving, as they do, identity and purpose, these overarching structures of significance are to be approached with awe, treated in fear and trembling. These canopies, as Peter Berger said, are sacred. 'In a genuinely pluralistic society', however, according to Michael Novak, there is, deliberately and of set purpose, 'no one sacred canopy'. At the 'spiritual core' of such a society,

there is an empty shrine. That shrine is left empty in the knowledge that no one word, image, or symbol is worthy of what all seek there. Its emptiness, therefore, represents the transcendence which is approached by free consciences from a virtually infinite number of directions . . . Believer and unbeliever, selfless and selfish . . . all participate in an order whose *centre* is not socially imposed.[13]

This may not, of course, be quite the way things seem when viewed from the bleak battlegrounds of Los Angeles, Detroit, or the south side of Chicago. Moreover, does not each dollar bill proclaim: 'In God we trust'? Novak fearlessly confronts the problem:

Is not God at the centre? For those who so experience reality, yes. For atheists, no. Official religious expressions . . . have a pluralistic content. No institution, group, or person in the United States is entitled to define for others the content signified by words like 'God', 'the Almighty', and 'Creator'. These words are like pointers, which each person must define for himself . . . Such symbols are not quite

---

13 Peter Berger, *The Sacred Canopy: Elements of a Sociological Theory of Religion* (Garden City, New York: Doubleday, 1967); Novak, *Spirit of Democratic Capitalism*, p. 53 (his stress).

blank; one may not fill them in with any content at all. They point beyond worldly power. Doing so, they guard the human openness to transcendence . . . It is in the light of such transcendence that progress is inspired and reforms are called for.[14]

It matters not what each one trusts in, provided that the currency is kept in circulation and no one mentions their ambition to anybody else.

Novak is no utopian. If anything, his vision is closer to a kind of nihilism: 'The "wasteland" at the heart of democratic capitalism is like a field of battle, on which individuals wander alone, in some confusion, amid many casualties. Nonetheless, like the dark night of the soul in the inner journey of the mystics, this desert has an indispensable purpose . . . It is swept clean out of reverence for the sphere of the transcendent.'[15] (Those kept outside the centres of the world that we call 'first' may well wonder whether there is much to choose between the ineluctable *système* of European postmodernism and this ascetic explanation as to why the urban deserts of America must be kept the way they are, 'swept clean' of all particular conviction, all shared narratives of human hope, 'out of reverence' for transcendence.)

It is worth noticing how closely Novak keeps within the framework set down at the Enlightenment. Thus, whereas Berger's description of the 'sacred canopy' is general and formal, applicable to societies at whatever level of complexity and scale, Novak contracts it to the territory of the 'positive', of small, inward-looking 'enclaves' (his word) of likemindedness, in which all 'make similar moral and aesthetic judgements, laugh at the same jokes'.[16] Correlatively, of course, the 'empty shrine' of pluralism is a direct descendant of eighteenth-century 'natural' religion.

Metaphysics may not be fashionable, but the transcendence reverently acknowledged on the dollar bill is, apparently, alive and well. I call Novak's vision nihilist because, by depriving 'words like "God"' of any content other than that of pointing to

---

[14] Novak, *Spirit of Democratic Capitalism*, p. 54.
[15] Novak, pp. 54–5.   [16] Novak, p. 53.

unspecifiable transcendence, such words mean simply 'more' of whatever each individual decides to set their heart on, seek and struggle for. 'In God we trust' may, therefore, mean: in property or power, in sex or simply self-importance, provided only that my devices and desires may not find fulfilment except beyond the present limits of imaginable satisfaction or, as Novak puts it, 'beyond worldly power'. Meanwhile, between here and there, lie only battlefields and wastelands of the spirit.

One of the structuring myths of modern secularism is that public facts are cool and neutral, calculable, mathematical, and that the only place for poems and stories is the private hearth. Grown-ups, human beings come of age, on weekdays only count and tap computer keyboards, reserving story-telling for carpet-slippered gatherings in enclaves at weekends.

But, of course, this myth is itself a story, a questionable piece of fiction protective of the interests of those in power. Thus, if one were to wonder why (in Novak's story) 'democratic capitalism . . . permits individuals to experience alienation, anomie, loneliness, and nothingness' (I like 'permits'), the answer according to the same story is that democratic capitalism is 'constantly renewed by such radical experiences of human liberty'.[17] In plainer English, suffering keeps the system going.

'Democratic capitalism', in other words, like 'secular-isation' and the 'empty shrine', are narrative inventions, fictional conceits. Moreover, the tales in which they figure are, like all metanarratives, metaphysical and, more specifically, theological in character. Novak's shrine *looks* empty only because one consequence of secularisation, and its concomi-tant privatisation of the symbol-systems and the stories that most people now think of as 'religious', has been to obscure from view the images of other gods. Democratic capitalism, as interpreted by Novak, is undoubtedly (on Durkheimian criteria) a religion, a set of practices concerned with sacred things. That is its danger, and its power.

A friend of mine, a bishop of the Church of England, said

<hr>

17 Novak, p. 56.

recently that the prospect of a vast agglomeration of economic, military and political power without publicly expressed moral principle is truly awful. To which a mutual friend replied that vast agglomerations which claim high moral justification, and, even worse, religious benediction, may be even more dangerous. Christian doctrine, I have often said, functions, or should function, as a set of protocols against idolatry.[18] It has, in these postmodern times, become a little easier to win a hearing for the suggestion that *Ideologiekritik* is always, in the last analysis, critique of idolatry.

HERE, THERE AND EVERYWHERE

Europe, I said earlier, seems simultaneously to be crumbling and congealing. But the larger context in which this is occurring is the outstanding *novum* of our time: namely, the discernible extent to which the whole system or structure of the world is forming – culturally, politically, economically – one large complex fact, one artefact, one single outcome of human energy and ingenuity. And, of course, the boundaries of this one fact, one world, may not be drawn round human culture. Our working of the world, fuelled by the restless energy and ambition of the will to power – the will to be, and have, yet 'more' – squanders non-renewable resources, daily destroys whole species, strips off the topsoil, threatens the sustaining envelope we breathe.

Notwithstanding the supposed fragmentation of intellectual practices, it is clearly no coincidence that sociological preoccupation with social structures as global networks of communication should coincide with a strategic shift (to put it crudely) from correspondence to coherence in philosophy and literary theory while, in the physical sciences, the (happily misnamed) buzzword now is 'chaos'. To adapt the well-known slogan: when a butterfly flaps its wings in Tokyo, a baby dies in Mozambique.

In this *one* world of which we form a part, a world in which

---

[18] See, e.g., Lash, *Easter in Ordinary*, p. 261.

each force and feature, each territory, enterprise or aspect, is interdependent with all others, power is gathered into fewer and fewer centres or structures of monopoly while yet becoming, at the same time, ever more dispersed, invisible, evasive of discernment and control. Moreover, this seems true, not only of what we still think of as political power, but also of economic structures such as the interwoven webs that trace the ownership of banks and pension funds, airlines and arms sales and – not least through advertising – of design and music, clothing, chemicals and soft drinks. (My son once tried to buy a can of Coca-Cola at the United States pavilion, sponsored by Coca-Cola, at the Epcot Center in Orlando, Florida; they were out of stock, but he obtained one from the Japanese pavilion next door.)

It is, increasingly, one world, and yet those whose lives are lived furthest from its centres of control and influence (however dispersed and indiscernible these now seem to be) exist not so much at the margins of a global culture as in its carefully constructed underworld, an underworld so dark as to render them invisible, thereby enabling Michael Novak to observe with an apparently straight face that 'under democratic capitalism, the individual is freer than under any other political economy ever experienced by the human race'.[19]

Surrounded, carried, shaped and driven, as we are, by this vast, ambivalent, indecipherable, apparently quite uncontrollable 'system' we have made, it is not surprising that despair, the worship of necessity, should be among the more widespread manifestations of religion. But, like all religions, it performs a narrative, enacts a tale. In other words: that all events and institutions, things and people, forces and processes within the world are but expressions of imperious necessity (whose name, in some accounts, is 'freedom') is not itself a further fact about the world. It is one way of telling a most sophisticated story which, while not self-evidently true, is not, by any means, self-evidently false.[20]

---

[19] Novak, *Spirit of Democratic Capitalism*, p. 339.
[20] See Lash, *Believing Three Ways in One God*, pp. 106–11.

We learn such stories, and discern their truth or adequacy, by being participants in cultural contexts which endorse them and embody them in social practices and institutions. But, on the other hand, we *un*learn such stories, discern their untruth and inadequacy, only by learning in some other school, embodying, in some other set of practices, another tale. For Christians, this other story, which they read in Scripture, finds distilled or nuclear expression in the creed. Thus, to the critical or negative responsibilities of Christian theology, as critique of idolatry, there corresponds the duty to establish, through the performance of the Gospel, that eucharistic counter-culture of the virtues, that 'peopleness', responsive to the mystery of God, which is what the Church is meant to be.

'Peoples' *are* the stories that they tell, perform, and celebrate; the narratives that they indwell. And the most powerful (and, hence, most dangerous) people-constituting narratives are those that take the words and images which render their particular identity to refer, in principle, to everyone. Something of this *pars pro toto*, 'sacramental' function of the narrative is common, in very different ways, to Judaism and to Christianity, to Islam, 'manifest destiny', the myth of 'science as salvation', 'socialist realism' and 'democratic capitalism'. In all these cases, the particular story that is told is told as somehow telling the story of the *world*. And, for better and for worse, sometimes through conflict and devastating suffering, sometimes through growth in mutual understanding and the interweaving of interpretations, the interaction of such stories *is* the story of the world.

PILGRIMAGE AND HOLY GROUND

The Christian story of the world declares, requires and promises the primacy of peace beyond all violence, of utterance beyond response, of gift beyond possession. And, as I have tried to indicate elsewhere, 'the ceaseless, self-corrective character of good uses of the Creed protects the forms of faith in God from ... freezing to idolatry by mistaking some form of our relationship with God for an object of our worship'.[21] (It is, moreover, beginning to be noticed that there are affinities between such uses of the creed and postmodern emphasis upon 'deferral' of meaning. But that would be another story.)

'It is simply *not* self-evident', says Milbank, 'that every game of truth is but a local ritual.'[22] But, if some 'games' are more than this – if they play, celebrate, sacramentally display, God's promise, presence, gift – they only do so *as* a gift, to everyone, from some particular time and place. The metanarratives which postmodernists like Lyotard rightly find incredible are those that speak of everywhere from nowhere in particular. But, between such dead, destructive, universals, on the one hand and, on the other, the night battle of innumerable merely private, tribal tales and pastimes (each of which, some-one will say, is true 'for me'), there remains the sacramental possibility: the possibility of sense, and life, and peace, and friendship, instantiated and offered and received.

But (to repeat) only from some particular place, in some particular configuration, shaped by particular experience and memory, can such comprehensive possibility be glimpsed, and born. Incarnation is particular; Bethlehem's world-birth took place then, and there. Without such reference, such rootedness, all large talk, all grand designs, are not merely abstract but destructive, hegemonic, riding roughshod over other stories, other places, other people.

Hence the immense importance, pregnant possibility, it seems to me, of the kind of Centre that your West of Ireland Theology Research Association seeks to be. Moreover, its location at an edge, a margin, an extremity, may help it to become the kind of home, or hearth, or holy ground, that centres of good pilgrimage should be.

In saying this, I have one final image in mind, that of the margin as horizon, limit of our visibility. Listen to the voice of

[21] Lash, *Believing Three Ways*, p. 94.
[22] John Milbank, 'The end of enlightenment: post-modern or post-secular?' in Geffré and Jossua (eds.), *The Debate on Modernity*, 42.

Ulysses (not Joyce's, I'm afraid, nor even Homer's, but Lord Tennyson's):

> I am a part of all that I have met;
> Yet all experience is an arch wherethro'
> Gleams that untravell'd world whose margin fades
> For ever and for ever when I move.[23]

Of this exhausted pilgrim's voice Matthew Arnold, in what Christopher Ricks has called 'one of the most penetrating remarks ever made about Tennyson', said: 'It is no blame to their rhythm . . . that these three lines by themselves take up nearly as much time as a whole book of the Iliad.'[24]

The ever-fading margin of Tennyson's world-weary exile is in striking contrast to the horizon Seamus Heaney sees in Ireland:

> We have no prairies
> To slice a big sun at evening –
> Everywhere the eye concedes to
> Encroaching horizon,
> Is wooed into the cyclop's eye
> Of a tarn.[25]

Thus wooed, the traveller's gaze can come to rest, can focus on 'things founded clean on their own shapes', edged, particular, incarnate; 'Water and ground in their extremity', which may sketch God.

---

[23] Alfred Lord Tennyson, 'Ulysses', 18–21; from *Tennyson's Poetry*, selected and edited Robert W. Hill, Jr (New York: W. W. Norton and Company, 1971), p. 53.
[24] Christopher Ricks, *Tennyson* (London: Macmillan, 1989), p. 116; Ricks quotes Matthew Arnold from *On Translating Homer* (1861).
[25] Seamus Heaney, 'Bogland', *Door into the Dark*, p. 55.

CHAPTER 11

Hoping against hope, or
Abraham's dilemma[1]

THE END OF THE WORLD – AND THE
THEOLOGIAN'S DIFFICULTIES

I have discovered that, while it is in order for educated people to contemplate the end of history, it is less acceptable to mention the end of the world (notwithstanding the extent to which these notions may be interchangeable). Thus, in September 1992, the London *Observer* carried an article, entitled 'End of the world', which began like this: 'The end of the world is one of those features peculiar to primitive religions, e.g., Norse mythology and fundamentalist Christianity.'[2] When religious symbols are situated, as they tend to be these days, somewhere between the primitive and the private, it becomes difficult to see what useful contribution theology might make to the reinvention of our common future.

Some world *is* ending now: whether its death-knell was sounded with the demolition of the Berlin Wall, with Auschwitz or Hiroshima or Vietnam, or even with the outbreak of the First World War. And one name we have given to the world now ending is the 'modern' world – hence all the talk these days, whether in celebration or contempt, about 'postmodernism'.

The centre of the modern world, the world invented in the

---

[1] A lecture given in 1993 in a series sponsored by the Global Security Programme of the University of Cambridge. The theme of the series was: 'Reinventing the Future: Dangers, Dreams and Prospects'.

[2] Keith Boot, 'End of the world', *Observer* (27 September 1992), 45.

seventeenth and eighteenth centuries, was the cool and reasonable market-place, the democratic parliament of 'secularity'. In this space governed (so it was supposed) by argument and calculation and not by power or passion, religion's sole admission was as divine endorsement of the empire or the nation-state. Durkheim understood this, defining religion as 'the system of symbols by means of which society becomes conscious of itself'.[3]

There is, by now, a wealth of literature assisting our re-reading ('reinvention', if you will, since *invenio* comes out, in English, as both 'find' and 'fashion') of the early modern world. It is, however, far too little understood that the modern invention of the 'secular' carried with it concomitant *re*definitions of 'religion'.

Thus, David Martin once defined secularisation as 'the process whereby religious institutions become less powerful in a society and religious beliefs less easily accepted'.[4] But suppose we were to follow Durkheim's lead, and construe as 'religious' the 'totality of [social] practices concerned with sacred things':[5] concerned, in other words, with practices, beliefs and institutions which prove too hot to handle, too dangerous to touch. The possibility would then emerge, as I suggested in the previous chapter, that the narratives of secularisation merely serve to render ideologically invisible the religious character of many of our most powerful institutions and passionate beliefs. In this twilight of the twentieth century, we need urgently to understand how little the destructiveness of gods and demons is diminished by denying their existence or by clothing them in 'secular' and hence (supposedly) more innocuous descriptions.

'Religion', Fergus Kerr has said, 'has to do with something deep and sinister in *us*',[6] in human beings, the power of which is ended neither by refutations of arguments for the existence

---

[3] Emile Durkheim, *Suicide*, p. 312.
[4] David Martin, *A General Theory of Secularization*, p. 12.
[5] Emile Durkheim, 'Concerning the definition of religious phenomena' in W. S. F. Pickering (ed.), *Durkheim on Religion*, p. 88.
[6] Fergus Kerr, *Theology after Wittgenstein* (Oxford: Basil Blackwell, 1986), p. 162.

of a deity, nor by the use of easy slogans such as 'sect' and 'fundamentalist', nor by futile attempts to confine its sphere of operation to private recesses of individual imagination. (In this respect, at least, religion is like sex.)

Consider the vocabulary that we use, today, to name the symbol-systems by which societies sustain their consciousness of who they are: we speak of 'nations' and of 'races', of 'communal' and 'sectarian' violence, of 'civil' war and 'ethnic' cleansing. All these are 'people' words, evocative of what it is that furnishes, sustains and threatens our sense (whoever 'we' may be) of who we are and how things go with us. Whatever else is happening in the ending of the modern world – which ending is a deconstruction of key features of the project of 'enlightenment' – some fresh sense of what it is that makes for 'peopleness' seems urgently to be required.[7] And these preliminary remarks of mine amount to little more than the reminder that this twofold task is, in part, theological in character, for theologians seek to understand the stories that their people tell, and to bring the fruits of their interpretation into critical correlation with other stories told by other people.

By the stories that we tell – and make our own – we take our bearings, work out where we stand and what we ought to do, construct some sense of how things hang together. And if, in some societies, it has seemed as if all things could be gathered, more or less straightforwardly, into some single overarching system or description, some single plotted narrative with a beginning, a middle and an end – then this is not how things now seem to most of us. We have become increasingly aware not merely of how fragmentary is our sense of things, how shaped by time and place and circumstance, how misshaped by fear and prejudice and power, but also of how different different peoples are: their memories, their dreams, their sufferings; the symbol-systems which they use to make some sense of things.

---

[7] 'Peopleness' is not a pretty word, but perhaps its awkwardness can stand as a reminder of a vacuum at the heart of our vocabulary of the social order.

And yet, notwithstanding the fragmentation and diversity of the stories that we hear, and tell, and dramatise, we are also shaped ('narrated', if you will) by metanarratives, world-stories, tales of how all things go – from their beginning to their end. Such stories, such self-contained narrations of the world, within which and according to whose rhythms people live their lives, execute their projects, sustain the ambition and the terror of their dreams, have sometimes been called 'myths'. That label will do well enough, provided we construe the pejorative overtone it carries as implying, not that such stories are not true, but rather that they stand continually in need of critical, corrective, purificatory attention and restraint.[8] There are, as I remarked in Chapter Ten, some people-constituting myths that take the words and images which render their particular identity to refer, in principle, to everyone, thereby purporting to say something of the story of the *world*.[9]

At the mid-point of this century, the clash of two such meta-narratives threatened the survival of the world. Who then foresaw that, by 1993, Europe would seem less threatened by 'great-power' hegemony than by fragmentation through the conflict of much smaller-scale people-constituting myths? A particular challenge (I shall argue, in due course) to European Christianity concerns the extent to which it can communicate 'transpopular' values in the future as effectively as, in the past, it has often contributed to the formation of 'national' identities.

'Reinventing the future: dangers, dreams and prospects.' Not being an economist or a political scientist, a psychologist or an international lawyer, I am less well equipped than such specialists may be to offer expert comment on some one particular apocalyptic beast or horseman of disaster darkening our road towards the future. But then, in fact, we all rely on other people to help us form our estimates of the threat from 'sword' and 'famine', 'pestilence' and 'wild beasts'.[10]

---

[8] See Lash, *Believing Three Ways in One God*, p. 6.
[9] See Chapter Ten, p. 196.   [10] See Revelation 6.8.

(These, as you will recognise, are categories from the Book of Revelation, than which no part of Christian Scripture will be more used and misused in the closing years of the millennium.)

So far as 'dreams' about the future are concerned, we would, I think, be well-advised to discipline our dreaming. In saying this, I am not recommending that we should rein in our imagination. On the contrary, 'Where there is no vision', says the Book of Proverbs, 'the people perish.' (But take all proffered vision with a pinch of salt: according to one more up-to-date translation, that verse should read, 'With no one in authority, the people throw off all restraint'!)[11] My general point, however, is that there is simply far too much that needs, with urgency, to be both done and understood for us to waste our time either, on the one hand, day-dreaming of how wonderful the world would be if everything were different or, on the other, allowing ourselves to be mesmerised and paralysed by nightmare.

Therefore, in quest of what I deem realism (though to some it may seem utopian and, to others, nearer to a glimpse of hell), I propose to sketch a threefold Christian 'prospect' of our plight. Keeping close to classical accounts of those dispositions of the mind and heart by which human beings grow in relation with each other and the mystery of God, dispositions traditionally known as 'theological virtues', I shall say something of a way of seeing, a way of trusting and a way of relating, and of the blindness, despair and egotism that are, respectively, the refusals of these ways.

In the winter of 1270–1, three years before his death, Thomas Aquinas began to write the massive study of particular virtues which was the second half of his most original contribution to Christian theology, the 'Secunda pars' of the *Summa theologiae*. In the Prologue, he remarked that, in moral matters, general statements are of minimal utility, because actions are

---

[11] Proverbs 29.18 (in the Authorised Version and the Revised English Bible).

particular.[12] With that warning in mind, being very conscious of the level of abstract generalisation that seems unavoidable in covering so large a canvas in a single lecture, I decided to earth or counterpoint the argument with reference to the memoir which Nadezhda Mandelstam wrote of the last four years before her husband's final exile to and death in a camp near Vladivostok, in December 1938.

The title of that memoir is, in English, *Hope against Hope*. In his Introduction, Clarence Brown remarks: she

often mentioned her English governesses in letters to me . . . and she savors the slightly fusty Victorianism of some of her idioms. 'Hope against hope' is one of these, which I count so often as I read back through her letters that it has practically become her slogan in my mind . . . It doesn't make a bad title for her book, which has none in Russian.

And he reminds us that, in Russian, 'Nadezhda' means 'Hope'.[13]

Nadezhda Mandelstam herself asks:

Why, at the dawn of the new era, at the very beginning of the fratricidal twentieth century, was I given the name Nadezhda? All I now heard from our acquaintances was: 'Not a hope!' [It is April 1937; nearly three years since their first exile started.] Not a hope that anybody would help us, or give us work, or read letters from us, or shake us by the hand. By now everybody was too used to thinking of us as doomed. But one cannot live without hope.[14]

Abraham will make an entrance later on; at this point, I would just remind you that both Osip and Nadezhda Mandelstam were Jews.

---

[12] 'Sermones enim morales universales minus sunt utiles, eo quod actiones in particularibus sunt' (Thomas Aquinas, *Summa theologiae*, IIa IIæ, Prologue). For the assessment of the 'Secunda pars' see James A. Weisheipl, OP, *Friar Thomas D'Aquino. His Life, Thought and Works* (Oxford: Basil Blackwell, 1975), pp. 256, 361.

[13] Clarence Brown in Nadezhda Mandelstam, *Hope against Hope. A Memoir*, (trans.) Max Hayward, introduction by Clarence Brown (London: London Collins Harvill, 1989) p. vii. I am grateful to Professor David Ford for suggesting Mrs Mandelstam's memoir to me.

[14] Mandelstam, *Hope against Hope*, p. 211.

A WAY OF SEEING

A way of seeing everything – and God

'For now we see through a glass, darkly; but then face to face: now I know in part; but then shall I know even as I am known.'[15] From St Paul to Plato's allegory of the cave, eyesight is so deeply rooted and pervasive a source of metaphors of knowledge and understanding that we easily lose sight (!) of the fact that, when we say we 'see' this, that, or the other, what, in fact, we usually mean is that we 'see the point', that something has been understood.

For example, God is sometimes said to be 'invisible'. This is not, however, quite so straightforward an assertion as, at first sight (!), it may seem to be. After all, God is not said, at least in Judaism and Christianity, to be 'inaudible'. On the contrary, the Christian and the Jew know themselves set to a lifelong discipline of attentiveness: to the unending task of trying, in every circumstance, more truthfully, more accurately, to 'hear' God's silent Word.

That God is invisible says something about us rather than about God. It acknowledges the depth of darkness in which we find ourselves; in which we know ourselves incapable of seeing the point. There is nothing that is 'obviously' the case, concerning God, whether for affirmation or denial. But then, something similar is true of words like peace, and truth, and love, and justice, and integrity. Glibness is deeply decadent – and is no less so in its irreligious than in its pious forms.

God is invisible. We cannot see the point of everything and, beyond all things, of God. But, if this is the first thing to be said, it is not the last. As with our hearing, so also with our sight: Christians and Jews know themselves set to lifelong discipline of learning to see in the dark. That disposition of the mind and heart which we call faith is thus a matter of learning to keep one's eyes open – against two kinds of closure, two forms of blindness: on the one hand, the credulity which

[15] 1 Corinthians 13.12.

invents and rests in fancies that have not, in fact, been seen
and, on the other hand, the scepticism which lacks courage to
acknowledge the visibility of something, whatever it may be,
that *has*, in fact, been seen.

The past is unforgettable

Thinking back upon her life, Nadezhda Mandelstam said:
'People who were silent or closed their eyes to what was
happening also try to make excuses for the past', but 'The past
weighs heavily on us and we still have to make sense of it.'
Thus, there was Kazarnovski, 'the first more or less authentic
emissary' who brought news of her husband's last days in
Vladivostok. She sheltered him for three months from the
police, while she slowly drew his story from him. 'Whether
inside or outside the camps', she says, 'we had all lost our
memories . . . Of course those witnesses who have kept a clear
memory of the past are few in number, but their very survival
is the best proof that good, not evil, will prevail in the end.'[16]

In other words, in order to keep our eyes open for the future,
it is essential that we do not close them to the past. Amnesia,
forgetfulness, is a kind of blindness, a form of unbelief. And
this is so for two reasons.

In the first place, it is as true of cultures and societies, of
languages and institutions, as it is of individuals that we are
formed and fashioned, made to be the way we are, by the past.
It may weigh heavily upon us, but its burden is not lessened by
forgetfulness. 'The past', as Leszek Kolakowski has said, 'can
be cursed but never cancelled.'[17] The future does not yet exist,
and what we call the present slips into the past even as we
mention it. The first reason why we must not forget the past,
why we must continually attempt to see it better, make better
sense of it, is simply because there is, in fact, nothing else for
us to see, make sense of, understand.

[16] Mandelstam, *Hope against Hope*, pp. 289, 379.
[17] Leszek Kolakowski, 'A calamitous accident', *Times Literary Supplement*, (6 November
1992), 5.

But the second reason why keeping our eyes open means keeping memory alive is that, even if we could, we have not the right to close our eyes to what has happened. 'There remains', says Jürgen Habermas, 'a stain on the idea of a justice that is bought with the irrevocable injustice perpetrated on earlier generations. This stain cannot be washed away: it can at most be forgotten. But this forgetting would have to leave behind traces of the repressed.'[18] All utopian fantasies, all simply sunlit futures forgetful of the past, are disallowed, subverted, by the silent witness of shed blood.

One image with which Christianity has tried to hold this almost intolerable paradox has been that of one man once crucified, God's own appearance in the world, the 'Lamb' of God, standing, even in heaven's glory, 'as though it had been slain'.[19] There are scars, it seems, in heaven.

The future is unknown

The future does not yet exist. And that is one good reason why consideration of our future prospects is always a matter of seeing in the dark. But, of course, there is more to it than that. Our experience, these last few years, in Europe should have reminded us how unexpected are the forms the future takes when it becomes the present and the past. Whether for better or for worse, immense surprises lie in store for us. The fact that we are better placed than previous generations to issue a variety of well-warranted extrapolations – concerning the exhaustion of non-renewable resources, for example, or the sink limits of the ecosystem – may foster the illusion that we know just what is going to happen. We do not.

In one sense, of course, we do. Each of us will die and,

---

[18] Jürgen Habermas, 'A reply to my critics' in John B. Thompson and David Held (eds.), *Habermas: Critical Debates* (London: Macmillan, 1982), pp. 246–7. For some discussion of this passage and issues that it raises, see Nicholas Lash, 'Conversation in Gethsemane' in Werner G. Jeanrond and Jennifer L. Rike (eds.), *Radical Pluralism and Truth: David Tracy and the Hermeneutics of Religion* (New York: Crossroad, 1991), pp. 51–61.
[19] Revelation 5.6.

notwithstanding the columnist in the *Observer* and the loonier kinds of prophecy offered by some scientists, so will the planet and the human race. But, on the whole and in the medium term, foreseeing is a kind of seeing in the dark. The future is unknown because the end is not in sight.

'Ends', however, are not only *termini* but purposes. To speak of our existence before God as an apprenticeship in seeing in the dark is to refuse the nihilistic closure which insists that there is simply nothing to be seen, no purpose to discern, no sense to make of things, no 'readings' of the world that are not merely arbitrary playthings of despair.

I said earlier that religion 'has to do with something deep and sinister in *us*'. In contemporary culture, attitudes towards religion sometimes seem divided between those who, noticing the violence, energy and passion unleashed by adoration, deplore the dangerous thing and, on the other hand, those who suppose religious beliefs and practices to function like an infant's comforter, affording some small solace or warm shelter from the storm outside. What both these attitudes quite overlook is the central place allotted, in all the great traditions of the world, to discipline, *ascesis*, the taming of the violence of the human heart, lifelong education into patterns of attentiveness, and peacefulness, and trust. Humanity, we might almost say, does not come naturally to us.

It is very frightening to gaze, without illusion, on the prospects for the world: to be attentive to the sound of alienated, frightened self-contempt emanating from our cities; to listen to the cries of those, especially the old and very young, the causes of whose destitution are, in fact, not 'natural' disaster, but political and economic choices enacted elsewhere, by other people, at another time; to remember that the resources for nuclear catastrophe are controlled by people, like ourselves, of dubious and fragile prudence. The prospects, not only for the human race, but for the whole system of the world which we so signally mismanage, are terrifying.

The quite new thing, moreover, in our day is the discernible extent to which the system or structure of the world now forms one single outcome of human ingenuity. And, against this juggernaut, clear-sightedness demands that we admit that, as things at present stand, there seems no chance at all of bringing off, within the time-scale that would be required, the necessary comprehensive transformations of heart, and will, and institution. There are, admittedly, more optimistic estimates around but, in my experience, they usually seem either to have in mind merely the prospects for the majority of people in the economically more 'developed' regions of the world, or else to be little more than wishful thinking dressed up as what 'in principle' is possible, as in: we could now, in principle, breed pigs with wings.

Yet, if the prospects are so bleak, why stay awake, remain alert, keep watchful? One not inappropriate context for consideration of such questions would be Gethsemane, at night, in which dark garden the disciples closed their eyes and slept (Luke says, 'for sorrow').[20] And yet, according to the story, it is the one who stayed awake whose watchfulness worked the transformation of the world. Moreover, Jesus' watchfulness, his way of seeing in the dark, is not portrayed as stoic heroism, stiff upper-lipped, but as a kind of trusting – which found expression in a kind of prayer. Which brings me to the second aspect of the threefold disposition that I am considering.

A WAY OF TRUSTING

Hoping against hope

This time, we can begin with Abraham, whose story sets the contours to Jewish, Christian and Islamic narratives of human hope. An elderly and childless couple (Abraham is seventy-five) set out into the unknown, trusting the promise's fulfilment: 'Go from your country and your kindred and your father's house to the land that I will show you. And I will make of you a great nation, and I will bless you . . . and by you all the families of the earth shall bless themselves.' The Book of

---

[20] See Luke 22.45.

Genesis thus sets nothing less than the entirety of human flourishing within the framework of the promise made to this prototypical patriarch – whose story hovers on the boundary between prehistory and myth. 'Abraham', according to the Qur'an, 'was neither Jew nor Christian. He was an upright man, one who surrendered himself to God.' Or, as Paul had put it, in the letter to the Romans: 'In hope he believed against hope, that he should become the father of many nations.'[21]

Since the Enlightenment, we have come to set such high value on autonomy as to suspect all talk of trust, surrender, vulnerability and dependence as, at best, soft-headed and, at worst, slavery. It is, of course, possible for trust to be misplaced, unwarranted, betrayed. And yet, as Mary Midgley has said, not only do we not deem admirable systematically mistrustful people, but some degree of what she calls 'social courage . . . is an essential cognitive tool',[22] without which nothing worthwhile gets discovered, thought out, done.

I am, however, primarily concerned here not with the forms of trust appropriate in our political, domestic, cultural or scientific relations with each other and with the world we work but, more fundamentally, with that basic trust (which finds expression in these forms) the religious name for which is hope in God.

Against impossibility

Thomas Aquinas, who made good use of Paul's slogan 'Hoping against hope', put the point succinctly: 'The difference between hope and despair is the difference between possibility and impossibility.'[23] It is, in other words, a great mistake to confuse hope with optimism. The optimist looks on the bright side, expects a happy ending. Hope, on the other hand, simply

---

[21] Genesis 12.1–3; Qur'an 3:60; Romans 4.18.
[22] Midgley, *Science as Salvation*, p. 110.
[23] 'Spes differt a desperatione secundum differentiam possibilis et impossibilis' (Thomas Aquinas, *Summa theologiae*, IIa IIæ, 40, 1 ad 3; cf. 41. 3. 3; 102.5.1).

refuses the foreclosure of despair, resists the absoluteness of impossibility.

Let me bring in, once more, Nadezhda Mandelstam: 'Expect nothing and be ready for anything – that was the key to sanity.' And again: 'In the face of doom, even fear disappears. Fear is a gleam of hope, the will to live . . . Losing hope, we lose fear as well.' Consider in that light, perhaps, the cry attributed to Jesus, dying: 'My God, my God, why have you forsaken me?' It is the first line of a psalm which ends: 'Posterity' will 'proclaim [the Lord's] deliverance to a people yet unborn.'[24] Even that Calvary cry, in other words, remains within the framework of the promise made to Abraham.

Hope and desire

'Fear is a gleam of hope.' We tend to think of prayer and politics as operating in quite different territories tenuously connected, if at all, by the irritating habit, in our liturgies, of reminding God of crises of which he is, presumably, already well aware. But the fundamental form of prayer, without which politics is reduced to mere administration, is the silent cry resistant to impossibility, the unquenched yearning of the human heart for nothing less than everything. Politics may be said to be the art of the impossible, and hope finds first expression as desire.

Desire, of course, is just as dangerous and, often, as destructive as are the surrogates of sight in glibness and illusion. Hence, once again, the need for pedagogies of discrimination, cultures of *ascesis*. One often hears it said that the great traditions (and, in this respect, perhaps especially Buddhism) aim at the abandonment or overcoming of desire. But this is most misleading: it is not the cancellation, suppression, or abolition of desire that is required but, on the contrary, the cleansing of its constructive energy through conquest of possessiveness, released attachment, surrender of predation. 'Private property', as Marx said in one of his wiser moments,

---

[24] Mandelstam, *Hope against Hope*, pp. 62, 42; Mark 15.34; Psalm 22.1, 30–1.

'has made us so stupid and one-sided that an object is only *ours* when we have it.' And Eliot knew what he was doing when, having quoted the Lady Julian, 'And all shall be well and / All manner of thing shall be well', he indicated the direction necessary: 'By the purification of the motive / In the ground of our beseeching.'[25]

But if, as I indicated earlier, it is only in sustained beseeching, fundamental trust, that we could find the courage to keep our eyes open in the dark, what (in turn) could ground the possibility of such trust? Nadezhda Mandelstam provides a clue: 'The loss of mutual trust is the first sign of the atomization of society.'[26] In other words, only a moral culture in which individuals are nurtured into friendship by the relationships which constitute them could sustain such trust. Which brings me to the third and final strand of the threefold disposition by which (at least according to Christian accounts of these things) human beings grow into relationship with each other, with the world and with the mystery of God.

A WAY OF FRIENDSHIP

Who are 'we'?

In the beginning, I emphasised how urgent is the need for a fresh sense of what it is that makes for 'peopleness' and what, if anything, might make for peopleness in peace. Where the relationships that bind human beings to each other – through common memory and shared experience, by contract and association, through work and suffering, belief and need – where these relationships are forged in mutual respect, donation and responsibility, there we speak of friendship.

If I had to find some single phrase by means of which to indicate the heart and centre of the relationship between the

[25] Karl Marx, 'Economic and philosophical manuscripts' in *Early Writings*, introduced by Lucio Colletti, (trans.) Rodney Livingstone and Gregor Benton (Harmondsworth: Penguin Books, 1975), p. 351; T. S. Eliot, 'Little Gidding'.
[26] Mandelstam, *Hope against Hope*, p. 95.

world and God, according to the Christian story, I might well settle for the statement that we have been made capable of friendship. Capable, that is to say, of effectively resisting the degradation of relationship into bonds of ownership and exploitation, dominance and violence and unconcern.

We have been made capable of friendship. Let me at once puncture the dangerous abstractness of the statement by suggesting that, whenever the word 'we' is thus being waved around, three questions are in order: whom do those waving it have in mind? Whom do they suppose themselves to have in mind? Whom should they have in mind? (This triple test is worth applying to the opening phrases of the American Declaration of Independence.)

In his 1990 Reith Lectures, *The Persistence of Faith*, the Chief Rabbi of the United Kingdom said that 'we each have to be bilingual. There is a first and public language of citizenship ... And there is a variety of second languages which connect us to our local framework of relationships.' Between the individual and the state, he argued, there is the neglected element of community, or, rather, of a 'community of communities ... the local communities where we discover identity, and the national community where we conduct our conversation about the common good'.[27]

Reviewing these lectures, Alasdair MacIntyre wondered how Dr Sacks made the move from his bleakly accurate description of our present plight to a surprisingly upbeat assessment of the prospects for the future. 'Is there in the background', asked MacIntyre, 'some prophetic understanding of human possibility never made explicit in the lectures themselves?'[28] The answer, I think, is: 'Yes, and quite properly so'. Nevertheless, I share MacIntyre's worry that possibility is too easily asserted. And it is too easily asserted because Dr Sacks confines the reference of who 'we' are to

[27] Jonathan Sacks, *The Persistence of Faith* (London: Weidenfeld and Nicolson, 1991), pp. 66, 90.
[28] Alasdair MacIntyre, review of *The Persistence of Faith*, in *The Tablet*, 245 (23 February 1991), 242.

'local framework[s]', on the one hand and, on the other, to the nation-state.

But this restriction of reference simply will no longer do. It is not bilingual that we need to be, but polyglot. I indicated earlier the importance of the recognition that the whole system of the world has, quite recently and irreversibly, become one single fact, one context, workplace, market, home or burial-ground. And we first *saw* this, some thirty years ago, in the astonishing beauty of those first pictures of the planet photographed from outer space. Amongst the languages we need to learn are those for which the range of reference of 'we' and 'us' is simply unrestricted.

'We have been made capable of friendship.' To say this, seriously, against our actual background of brutality and devastation, of ancient and deep-rooted group and individual egotism, of terror, isolation and exhausted disbelief, is to say something either very foolish or, if sensible, then very dark and strange indeed. And yet, I have been taught by that particular people which identifies me more deeply than does my British nationality – namely, by Catholic Christianity – that I must try to learn to place my fundamental loyalty with no people, no possibility of friendship, more restricted than the human race.

Parables of paradise

Jews, Christians and Muslims have different ways of drama-tising – in parable, and act, and imagery – such seemingly impossible yet absolutely necessary comprehensive friend-ship. And, in all three traditions, the images of friendship are those of food and drink, of common meals and hospitality. Not only the golden images of paradise regained, 'gardens of delight' in which God's servants feast on fruit, gardens at the heart of which is set 'the tree of life with its twelve kinds of fruit' and leaves 'for the healing of the nations', but, in the times between, travellers' food, eaten in haste, bread broken, bitter herbs and times of fasting.[29]

[29] See Qur'an 37:41; Revelation 22.2.

In 'Fourth prose', which he wrote in 1929, Osip Mandelstam affirmed that he was 'proud' to bear 'the honourable title of Jew'. Moreover, since 1911, he had also borne the title Christian, having in that year been baptised in the Methodist church in Vyborg. In 1920, in a short poem more redolent, perhaps, of Eastern Orthodoxy than of Methodism, he speaks of the Eucharist as 'a gold sun . . . an instant of splendour . . . the whole world held in the hands like a plain apple'.[30] (We might set that image against the picture of the world as seen from space.) And yet, as I said earlier, as things at present stand there seems no chance of bringing off, within the time-scale that would be required, the necessary transformations towards friendship. It seems quite likely that the burden of the world, held in our hands, will prove too heavy. Set in such thick darkness, it is not then surprising that, to many people, instants of sunlit splendour seem mere dreams or interludes of unreality.

'We were all the same', says Nadezhda Mandelstam, 'either sheep who went willingly to the slaughter, or respectful assistants to the executioners . . . It was not, indeed, a question of fear. It was something quite different; a paralyzing sense of one's own helplessness to which we were all prey . . . Crushed by the system each one of us had in some way or other helped to build.'[31] Despair stays paralysed, deadened by impotence and guilt. Optimism, on the other hand, pretends – at varying levels of dishonesty and ignorance – that the situation really is not all that serious and that we can muddle on, indefinitely, more or less as we are.

And hope? Beyond the permanent requirement to bind up wounds, to do whatever can be done for friendship, *hic et nunc*, hope continues to enact, construct and dramatise, even in the dark, parables or metaphors of friendship's absolute

[30] Osip Mandelstam, 'Fourth prose', in *The Noise of Time and other Prose Pieces*, collected, translated and introduced by Clarence Brown (London: Quartet Books, 1988), p. 186; see Clarence Brown, 'A note on Fourth Prose and Journey to Armenia', ibid., p. 172; Osip Mandelstam, *Selected Poems*, (trans.) Clarence Brown and W. S. Mervin (London: Penguin, 1977), no 117, p. 55.
[31] Mandelstam, *Hope against Hope*, p. 369.

fulfilment. Nothing *less* is asked of us than this, since it seems every day more evident that any less ambitious programme, any more moderate or 'sensible' requirement, would amount to little more than brief postponement of the planet's doom.

Moreover, if, as I said earlier, fatalism is ruled out because the future is unknown to us, because there are surprises still in store, then what MacIntyre called 'prophetic understanding of human possibility' perhaps demands some fresh imaginative effort in suggesting prospects that might, even now, be opened up. In conclusion, for one small intimation of the ways such work might go, I return to Abraham.

Medieval Toledo and the children of Abraham

Any serious consideration of the prospects for Europe and the Middle East is bound to take into account the part that might be played by Judaism, Christianity and Islam.

In referring, in my title, to 'Abraham's dilemma', I had in mind the intrepidity required of him as, taking a deep breath, he weighed up what was at issue in leaving home and the familiar world behind and setting out into the unknown, trusting God's obscure promise that the apparently impossible was, indeed, his destiny. And off he goes, seventy-five years old and childless, hoping against hope that 'all the families of the earth' will find blessing through his progeny.[32]

Moses, Jesus, Muhammad: three individuals who stand, in very different ways, at the particular beginnings of the stories of Judaism, Christianity and Islam. Behind all three of them stands Abraham. This is an image of the sense in which the promise on which Jews, and Christians, and Muslims set their hopes is not – on any of their three accounts – a promise made to them alone. It is a promise that their obedience has a part to play in bringing blessing, in extending friendship, to all the families of the earth. It follows that the duty to work for structures and narratives of common human friendship, the duty to foster what I earlier called 'transpopular' values and

32 Genesis 12.3.

responsibilities, is already inscribed in the catalogue of particular responsibilities that makes a Jew a Jew, a Christian a Christian, and a Muslim a Muslim. And since this is a duty that is common to all Abraham's children, it is a duty which they should perform in common.

It is, in other words, a matter of some urgency that Jews, Christians and Muslims should rediscover a sense of shared responsibility for 'all the families of the earth', and should set up whatever processes and institutions of mutual education and collaboration seem best suited to enable this duty to be appropriately discharged. I do not underestimate the extent to which the bloodstained darkness of our common past renders this proposal most implausible. I do not put it forward as the obvious or the easy thing to do, but simply as our duty. (Not, indeed, our duty alone – my argument has no imperialist or exclusionist implications – but ours, *as* ours, at least.)

We need an image or an emblem for this enterprise and, for this, I suggest we turn to thirteenth-century Castile, which was 'a special mix of Muslim, Christian, and Jew'; to the Toledo of the 'Emperor of Culture', King Alfonso X.[33]

It would be easy to romanticise that world, just as it has been too easily asserted that Christian, Muslim and Jewish cultures 'mingled freely' in the Sicily of Frederick II.[34] Nevertheless, in these Mediterranean cultures of the Middle Ages there were achievements of collaboration and mutual enrichment between the children of Abraham which might astonish many Jews, Christians and Muslims today.

Thus, for example, Dante's *Divina commedia* was influenced

[33] Robert I. Burns, SJ, '*Stupor Mundi*: Alfonso X of Castile, the Learned' in Burns (ed.), *Emperor of Culture: Alfonso X the Learned of Castile and his Thirteenth Century Renaissance* (Philadelphia: University of Pennsylvania Press, 1990), p. 12. I am most grateful to Dr David Abulafia for pointing me towards Toledo. 'The Kingdom of Valencia by the end of the thirteenth century held 50,000 Christians, 140,000 Muslims, and 10,000 Jews' (Robert I. Burns, *Muslims, Christians and Jews in the Crusader Kingdom of Valencia* (Cambridge: Cambridge University Press, 1984), p. 171).

[34] See Weisheipl, *Friar Thomas D'Aquino*, p. 15. Weisheipl was relying on C. H. Haskins, *Studies in the History of Medieval Science* (Cambridge, MA: Harvard University Press, 1924), pp. 242–71.

by a Muslim text (based on Sura 70 of the Qur'an, 'The ladders') which was translated in 1263 by Abraham Ibn Waqar, a member of an 'eminent family of Jewish diplomats' who was court physician to Alfonso X. Toledo is still 'a city of mosques, synagogues and church buildings', and might be an appropriate place in which to establish a centre in which could be explored the common duty which the children of Abraham bear to all the families of the earth.[35] It is my impression that Osip and Nadezhda Mandelstam might have approved.

[35] Norman Roth, 'Jewish collaboration in Alfonso's scientific work' in Burns (ed.), *Emperor of Culture*, p. 71; Julia Bolton Holloway, 'The Road through Roncesvalles: Alfonsine formation of Brunetto Latini and Dante – diplomacy and literature' in *Emperor of Culture*, p. 113.

CHAPTER 12

Eagles and sheep: Christianity and the public order beyond modernity[1]

The world we had got used to is crumbling before our very eyes. Because this world was, to a significant extent, construct in terror, the disappearance of familiar, threatening landmarks has, understandably and quite properly, given rise to rejoicing. There are, I think, no precedents for such swift collapse, almost without bloodshed, of vast sprawling networks of oppression. And there could hardly be deeper cause for gratitude than the fading of the fear of nuclear war.

Nevertheless, celebration would be premature. We do not yet know what new world will now be made, nor what confused mixtures of dark and light, of friendship and inhumanity, it will contain. The world now ending is the 'modern' world: a world which came to birth with Locke and Newton, Jefferson and Descartes; a world of which (at its contemporary edge) communism and capitalism were variant expressions.

If ever there were a *kairos*, a moment of opportunity, an occasion for coming to our senses, for understanding something, a unique and unrepeatable occasion for that repentance which Jews call *teshuvah* and Christians 'conversion', it is surely now. Our first response to what is happening, I acknowledged, should be of gratitude and rejoicing. But our second should be to call into question, to subject to relentless critical examination, the narratives and thought-forms which made the modern world, which made (that is to say) ourselves.

One central role in those narratives has been played by

---

[1] A lecture given at several universities in the United States during the academical year 1991–2.

Reason: 'pure' reason, autonomous and disinterested, driven (so the story went) only by the passion to explain and understand. A not ignoble tale. But listen to Wendy Steiner, Professor of Humanities at the University of Pennsylvania. The 'great scandal of our time', she tells us, has been 'reason's inability to offer an acceptable answer to the pain that everywhere surrounds us'.[2] Dear God! What kind of madness is it which supposes pain to call for 'answers'? Agony seeks healing, not riposte. We read our situation best by setting its context as Gethsemane. There are no 'answers' there. There is only obedience, a kind of patience, and what we now know to be the hope of Easter. Professor Steiner asks too much of reason. The great scandal of our times is not the inability of reason to perform that healing which would be the world's redemption. It is, if anything, our elevation of such creatures as 'reason', 'freedom' and 'necessity' into attributes of God.

My aims in this chapter are rather more modest than its subtitle might indicate. I want to do three things. First, to draw upon John Milbank's work in order to suggest that there are affinities between the challenge that we face and that to which Augustine sought to respond in *The City of God*. Do we, as Christians, agree to be defined by, and to come to some accommodation with, the dominant narratives of our culture, or do we – as our strategy of resistance – seek rather to 'out-tell' them with a better tale? (Under this heading, it will be necessary to make some remarks concerning the 'public' character of Christian discourse.) In the second place, I shall suggest not only that time is running out, but that the background against which we take our human and Christian decisions is ineluctably tragic: there are no grounds for optimism, nor is it the Church's business to pretend otherwise. Finally, I shall indicate what form – in word and deed and institution – a Christianity might take which understood its faith and hope and duty in these terms.

For those who are puzzled by the zoological allusions, here is

2 Wendy Steiner, reviewing Andrea Dworkin's novel *Mercy* in the *New York Times Book Review* (15 September 1991), 11.

a passage from the First Essay in Nietzsche's *On the Genealogy of Morals*:

That lambs dislike great birds of prey does not seem strange: only it gives no ground for reproaching these birds of prey for bearing off little lambs. And if the lambs say among themselves: 'these birds of prey are evil; and whoever is least like a bird of prey, but rather its opposite, a lamb – would he not be good?' there is no reason to find fault with this institution of an ideal, except perhaps that the birds of prey might view it a little ironically and say: '*we* don't dislike them at all, these good little lambs; we even love them: nothing is more tasty than a tender lamb'. To demand of strength that it should *not* express itself as strength, that it should *not* be a desire to overcome, a desire to throw down, a desire to become master, a thirst for enemies and resistances and triumphs, is just as absurd as to demand of weakness that it should express itself as strength.[3]

THE EAGLE AND THE PUBLIC SQUARE

In January 1990, I found myself among eight hundred delegates to a very grand affair in Moscow, a 'Global Forum' of what the organisers called scientific, parliamentary and spiritual leaders. Our concerns were not trivial: the survival of the planet and of the human race. The long list of important persons who addressed us included the Secretaries-General of the United Nations and Unesco, Carl Sagan, Elie Wiesel and President Gorbachev. It was a most interesting occasion but, for a Christian theologian, somewhat dispiriting. It became increasingly evident that the organising narrative went something like this: it is the duty of scientists to find out what is going on, of parliamentarians to develop public policy in the light of the scientists' conclusions, and of spiritual leaders to persuade people so to modify their values and preferences as to facilitate the smooth implementation of policies designed by the politicians at the scientists' behest.

Not the least galling feature of this exercise in scientistic

---

[3] Friedrich Nietzsche, *On the Genealogy of Morals*, (trans.) Walter Kaufman and R. J. Hollingdale, (ed.) Walter Kaufman, 'First essay', Section 13 (New York: Vintage Books, 1989), pp. 44–5.

hubris was the way it was presented as encouraging evidence of 'science's' new estimation of and desire to co-operate with 'religion'. When a group of us – a splendidly ungrateful confederation of Catholics, Protestants, Jews, Muslims, Buddhists and Hindus – protested that, in our understanding, the narratives of religion also laid claim to truth, it was agreed (with great reluctance) that this bizarre opinion should be entered in the record.

I offer this as a parable of attitudes and assumptions at the very heart of the imaginative projects of the 'modern' world. The theme, of course, has been played with many variations, according to most of which, however, what is called 'religion', though it may serve public purposes, has more to do with private feeling than with public truth.

Thus, for example, by the end of the nineteenth century, Western religious thought found itself trapped by the dominant narratives into an uncomfortable dilemma: either, on the one hand, adopt discredited and outdated particularities of worship, association and belief ('sect', 'ghetto' and 'dogma' not being labels of approbation); or, on the other, embrace that diffuse religiosity of discourse which suffuses national identity, ambition and public control with a warm glow of transcendent benediction, giving currency (sometimes quite literally!) to the sentiment 'In God we trust.'

In a paper read to the Catholic Theological Society of America in 1986, the historian David O'Brien expressed the fear that American Catholics, 'reacting against the uncritical celebration of the American political economy, worried sick about abortion, the arms race, military and diplomatic unilateralism and the suppression of the aspirations of the world's poor', might be tempted to withdraw into the ghetto, turn back upon themselves, 'fleeing to caves or church basements'. The Catholic Church, in other words, having at last made it into the public square, owes it to itself and to the nation at large to stay there. The argument is similar to Richard John Neuhaus' contention that, if religion is banished (or goes voluntarily into exile) from the public square, leaving the individual and the state as the only actors in it, then there is nothing left to check the secular state's propensity to turn totalitarian.[4]

The state undoubtedly does have such propensity, although religion is surely just as likely to reinforce as to constrain the violence of public power. Nevertheless, Neuhaus correctly challenges the myth that 'secularity' is cool and neutral, reasonable, friend alike of rich and poor, while religion, shaped by particular passions, memories and hopes, is narrow, irrational, arbitrary and wild. The voice of the secular, of course, is science. And science, according to the myth, is neutral, lacks particular interest, simply tells it as it is. Theology, accordingly, must accept either to be shaped by science, informed by its findings and obedient to its drift, or else must stand convicted, at worst, of arbitrary fantasy and superstition and, at best, of private poetry for the lonely heart.

But suppose that, however innocent science or scientists in themselves may be, 'scientism', the metaphysics of the secular, should turn out to be just another mask for predatory violence, the eagle's beak, what then? What if it were not alone 'the state' that threatened the safety of the public square but the very foundations on which, at the beginning of modernity, that square was built?

Let me come at that question from another angle. Most of us are interested in getting to the heart of the matter, finding out what is *really* going on behind the myths and illusions that complicate our world. Some people call this interest common sense. Philosophers call it 'ontology': the consideration of what there 'really is'. The modern world, a world in which it is commonly deemed the duty of science, and of science alone, to find out what is going on, is a world the ultimate constituents of which are numbers and calculations. Its 'laws' are mathematical and its 'lawyers' calculators or, as we say,

---

[4] David J. O'Brien, 'The historical context of North American theology: the US story' in George Kilcourse (ed.), *Catholic Theology in the North American Context* (*Current Issues in Theology*, 1, CTSA, 1987), pp. 9, 14–15. See Richard John Neuhaus, *The Naked Public Square. Religion and Democracy in America* (Grand Rapids: Eerdmans, 1984).

scientists. That, at least, is how it often seems and, seeming so, it gives rise to boundless optimism and to deep despair – for though the achievements of technology are breathtaking, the vision of innumerable particles wheeling coldly in the void seems hardly to be a glimpse of paradise.

But suppose we took this cool and neutral world, this secular theatre of modernity, and especially the accounts that are given there of human institutions and behaviour, and subjected them to a dose of what it is now fashionable to call 'deconstruction'. This is what John Milbank has recently attempted in a difficult and most ambitious book, entitled *Theology and Social Theory: Beyond Secular Reason*. The work is divided into 'four sub-treatises, corresponding to four distinct variants of secular reason': one on the 'liberalism' of Locke, Hume and Adam Smith; one on the 'positivist' traditions which run, concurrently, from Malebranche to Durkheim and from Kant to Weber; a third on the 'dialectical' tradition centring on Marx and Hegel and, finally, one on engagement with postmodern philosophies of 'difference'.[5] (This fourth sub-treatise includes a chapter subverting scientific 'realism' on behalf of a resolutely instrumentalist account of natural science.)

Central to Milbank's project is the contention that 'secularity' – the systematic exclusion of theological or meta-physical considerations from the structure of social explanation – is, in all these versions, illusory and self-defeating. Secular theory sought to render worship manageable, to *tame* it, either by relegating it to the private sphere, or by showing that, when properly explained, its objects were familiar and friendly features of the world: like you, or me, or America, or beautiful ideas. According to Milbank, however, it can be shown that 'secular' social theories are, in fact, 'theologies or anti-theologies in disguise'. Purporting to be scientific explanations of the social world (including, therefore, of Christianity), in fact they tell stories which, from the stand-

---

[5] John Milbank, *Theology and Social Theory*, p. 3.

point of a Christian narrative of the world's creation, are either deviant or false, heretical or neopagan.[6]

Milbank is particularly scornful of those theologies which say: 'where once we took our concepts and techniques of inference from philosophy, today we learn our lessons, find out what is going on, from social science'. The point is, of course, that a Christian theology built on the groundwork of social theories which are themselves questionable though concealed theologies could hardly hope to stay faithful to its own original identity, character and concerns. And the irony is that, at the very time when theologians have at last ceased fighting the rearguard actions of the nineteenth century (all those exhausting skirmishes, for instance, between religion and science) and have learnt to acknowledge the due autonomy of the secular, postmodernist thought has (with Nietzsche's help) come to suspect all forms of secularity, all sweet voices of 'pure reason', to be really not much more than masks and disguises of passion and the will to power.

John Milbank takes Nietzsche very seriously indeed. Throughout the book, until the final chapters, two very different voices sound and, often quite confusingly, seem to mingle with each other. The first voice is not unlike that of Alasdair MacIntyre, to whom Milbank is enormously indebted. This voice opposes the modern control or management of power in the name of classical and medieval Christian virtue. The other voice is relentlessly Nietzschean, pressing the case for nihilism, 'seeking to show that every supposedly objective reasoning simply promotes its own difference, and disguises the power which is its sole support'. It is this voice which, when all other possibilities seem to be exhausted, utters the dark and terrifying cry: 'is there [then] anything *but* power? Is violence the master of us all?'[7]

Summon up quietly, with such clear-sighted courage as you can, the cumulative evidence – from the depths of each one's psyche to the centre of our politics; from the arbitrary and

---

[6] Milbank, *Theology and Social Theory*, p. 3; see pp. 23, 27.
[7] Milbank, *Theology and Social Theory*, pp. 5, 276.

sporadic barbarism of our wars and cities to the well-oiled
structures of rapacity and greed we call world trade – which
suggests that the answer to the question is: 'there is, indeed,
only power; and violence *is* master of us all'. To make this
answer one's own is to surrender to despair. And yet, until
we feel its force, take the full weight of it as possibility, we
have not touched the heart of things nor entered yet into
Gethsemane.

'Is there anything *but* power? Is violence the master of us
all?'. What kind of question is this ? How does one deal with it?
Not by words and arguments alone, that much is for sure.
Nothing less than complete gentleness stronger than all force,
absolute peacefulness transforming violence, the healing –
beyond imagination – of all spilt blood, could bring from this
dark night some dawn.

But this is to move too fast. Of course we need far more than
words, yet words and images are where we start. At this point,
I intend to take it as a question, not about the future – shall we
one day make peace, learn one day to be honest, or less self-
centred? – but rather about ontology, about the structure of
the world, the way things 'really' are which, being so, have
brought us to this plight.

Myths – whether Jewish, Christian, or pagan – talk ontology
in tales of how things are 'in the beginning'. And, in the beginning, according to Nietzsche, there is violence: the exaction,
by the strong, of obligations laid upon the weak. The beginnings of ethics, in exacted obligation, were, he says, 'like the
beginnings of everything great on earth, soaked in blood
thoroughly and for a long time'. Something, however, did get
done this way and, indeed, still does: what Nietzsche calls the
'beast of prey . . . prowling about avidly in search of spoil
and victory', still prowls our boardrooms, playing-fields and
schools, constructs our wealth and takes us to the moon. The
bitterness at the heart of Nietzsche's nihilism arises (as I
read him) from the recognition that the great work which
we call civilisation, by taming – at least to some extent
and intermittently – the predatory violence of the will to
power, has drained our energy, dulled our dreams, leaving us

weary.[8] In the beginning, then, for Nietzsche, there is violence; in the end, despair.

I mentioned earlier that Milbank mingles Nietzsche's voice with one which sounds like MacIntyre. In his final chapters, he sorts the voices out and makes his own position clear. He stands quite close to MacIntyre, with two important differences. In the first place, he is 'more critical of antique virtue than MacIntyre allows', finding the will to power, the eagle's strut, alive and well in the ethics of ancient Greece.[9] As a result, he puts more weight than MacIntyre does on a distinctively Christian account of where we come from and how we are to go.

In the second place, MacIntyre's perspective is somewhat more academic, supposing it to be our Christian duty to win through by force of better argument. Milbank does not despise good argument (his own is rather good!) but he believes that the case for 'secularity' – whether in its ancient, or liberal, or dialectical, or postmodern, Nietzschean, nihilist form – cannot be refuted. This is not because, as theory, it is flawless, but because it draws its strength from sources lying much deeper than the roots of theory: from myth, a comprehensive, self-contained *narration* of the world within which and according to whose rhythms people live their lives, execute their projects, sustain the ambition and the terror of their dreams.

If, then, there is another way of acting out the world, another way of being human, than as the agent or the victim of the will to power, than as the eagle or its prey, it will be shown, enacted, in the performance of a better myth, a more persuasive tale.[10]

All the passages that I used earlier from Nietzsche were taken from his three essays *On the Genealogy of Morals*. These essays, says Milbank, are, as it were, Augustine's *City of God* 'written back to front'.[11] In the beginning, according to

---

[8] Nietzsche, *Genealogy*, II, 6 (p. 65); I, 11 (pp. 40–1); see I, 11, 12 (pp. 42, 44); II, 6, 11 (pp. 66, 76).
[9] Milbank, *Theology and Social Theory*, p. 5.
[10] See Milbank, *Theology and Social Theory*, pp. 319, 330, 344–5, 375, 432.
[11] Milbank, *Theology and Social Theory*, p. 389; cf. pp. 285–6.

Nietzsche, there is violence, the struggle for mastery, the will to power. In the beginning, according to Augustine, is pure peacefulness, gift given 'out of nothing' for the possibility of all things' healing into peace. What we call Christianity is the enactment of this possibility, the announcement of this peace. Nietzsche's antagonism to Christianity arose from his percipient recognition that it represents 'the total inversion of any heroic identity of virtue with strength, achievement or conquest'.[12] Christianity celebrates dependence, mutuality. Its emblem is neither lion nor eagle, but the sheep.

What the prospects are for so vulnerable and improbable a project, and why on earth we should suppose it to be more viable in the present than it has been in the past, and (even if it were) quite what its tasks and duties in the public realm might be; these are questions some of which I shall consider in due course. Before doing so, however, I want once more briefly to emphasise quite how desperate is the predicament in which, at the end of the millennium, we find ourselves.

THE SIGN OF THE CROSS

Quite how desperate may be gauged from our tendency to suppose that our situation is really not so serious after all. Thus, for example, Richard Bernstein, commenting in the *New York Times* on the collapse of Soviet Communism, observed that debates among 'scholars and political analysts' will no longer 'be about such grand questions as the way to organise society'. Oh? What, then, will they discuss? Already, says Bernstein, the debate between liberals and conservatives is 'showing signs of focussing . . . on smaller, more personal, domestic issues like poverty, crime, race'! And Professor Martin Seligman of the University of Pennsylvania, explaining in an interview the importance of training Americans in the art of optimism, acknowledged that 'In spite of all its

---

[12] Milbank, *Theology and Social Theory*, pp. 285–6.

advantages . . . optimism has a cost, and that is that pessimists see reality better.'[13]

Actually, as I have often argued, the weighing of the odds between pessimism and optimism is not a game that Christians ought to play.[14] Others may argue for stoicism or suicide, on the one hand, or, on the other, for variations on the speculative cheerfulness which is so concerned with feeling good about itself that it does not even hear the cries of those it tramples underfoot on its march towards Utopia. Our business, however, is with hope. Where optimism sees sunlight, and pessimism is resigned to Stygian gloom, hope stays watchful, attentive, even at the dead of night, even in Gethsemane. It is less eloquent than either optimism or despair (both of which, knowing the outcome, confidently complete the story). Sometimes in silence, sometimes in more articulate agony or Job-like anger, the mood of the discourse of Christian hope is less that of assertion than request: its form is prayer.

Professor Seligman had, of course, a point. The rhetoric of optimism, of boundless possibility, today (as in the later nineteenth century) at some level *knows* itself sung to tunes of desperation. That is why we are so afraid of silence, so afraid of rendering audible our own despair, so fearful of the sounds of worthlessness and self-contempt emanating from our cities; afraid of the weeping of refugees and those bereaved by warfare; frightened by the cries of those, especially the old and very young, the causes of whose vulnerability and destitution we know to be, in fact, not 'natural' disaster, but political and economic policy freely entered into elsewhere, at some other time.

Even on today's appalling scale, human suffering is, of course, no new phenomenon in human history. What *is* new,

---

[13] Richard Bernstein, 'New issues born from communism's death knell', *New York Times* (31 August 1991), 1; Martin E. Seligman, interviewed by John Roderick in *Life Today* (September 1991), 12.

[14] See, for example, Nicholas Lash, *A Matter of Hope: A Theologian's Reflections on the Thought of Karl Marx* (London: Darton, Longman and Todd, 1981), pp. 231–80; Lash, 'All shall be well: Christian and Marxist hope' in *Theology on the Way to Emmaus*, pp. 202–15.

however, is the discernible extent to which the whole system or structure of the world forms one large complex fact, one single outcome of human energy and ingenuity. And Nietzsche was not obviously wrong in identifying, as the motor driving this vast enterprise, the unquiet individualism which sustains the will to power. (We usually prefer, in Western culture, to speak of 'freedom' but Nietzsche was – again – not obviously wrong in identifying freedom, when construed as my control over my space, my things, my actions, with the will to power, the eagle's flight, the predator's autonomy.)[15]

The boundaries of this one large single fact, one world, may not, of course, be simply drawn round human culture. Our working of the world, fuelled by the restless energy and ambition of the will to power, squanders non-renewable resources, daily destroys whole species, threatens the sustaining envelope we breathe. Catastrophe, of course, is no more novel in the history of the planet than suffering. All the dinosaurs are dead. What is new is the engineering of catastrophe by creatures rightly proud of their unique capacity to make other plans, to do things differently.

Optimism knows that things will turn out well. Despair acknowledges necessity, the dire, inevitable outcome: nothing different can now be done. And hope? Hope, as I see it, is first required clear-sightedly to recognise the terrifying scale and complex, interlocking singleness of the catastrophe we face. Second, hope is required quite calmly to admit that, as things stand, there seems no chance at all of bringing off, within the time-scale that would be required, the kind of comprehensive transformation of narrative and imagination, of ontology and myth, of structure and performance and ambition, of lifestyle and of terminology, which might alleviate the suffering that we inflict upon each other and contribute more effectively (in Barbara Ward's fine phrase) to 'the care and maintenance of a small planet'.[16]

---

[15] See Nietzsche, *Genealogy*, II, 18 (p. 87).
[16] Barbara Ward and René Dubos, *Only One Earth. The Care and Maintenance of a Small Planet* (New York: Penguin, 1972).

My argument is not that the times we live in are uniquely doomed. I do not know that this is so, nor do I believe comparative morbidity to be a fruitful exercise. My claim is that, the way things are, the way things go at present, we are doomed but that, nevertheless, the crumbling of 'modernity', though pregnant with chaos, makes it possible for us not merely to *notice* our predicament, to set our face against 'necessity', refusing despair's embrace of the inevitability of doom, but also, perhaps, to do something about it.

THE SIGN OF THE SHEEP

The first thing we can learn to do is watch our language, be careful what we say. To Nietzsche, as to Darwin, it seemed evident that the struggle for survival lay in the nature of things. By 1950, however, scientists no longer spoke of 'struggle': they now saw survival, more bureaucratically, as the attainment of 'advantages in differential reproduction' and, by 1986, Professor Lynn Margulis could assure us that science had progressed once more and now saw evolutionary process as a matter of 'continual cooperation . . . and mutual dependence among life forms'.[17]

Scientists can be astonishingly naïve. Less innocent souls might wonder whether it was quite complete coincidence that, in each of these three cases, the fashionable politics of the day was refracted in the scientists' description of what they simply 'saw'. The point is: there is something of our creative ingenuity, our narrative preference, our selection and decision, in all the images we use to characterise the structure of the world, the 'nature' of things, including, of course, our own.

Nietzsche denied this, insisting that some people were, simply 'by nature, "master"'. He said of these 'blond beasts of prey' that 'their work is an instinctive creation and imposition

---

[17] Lynn Margulis and Dorion Sagan, *Microcosmos. Four Billion Years of Evolution from our Microbial Ancestors* (New York: Allen and Unwin, 1986), pp. 14–15. For other references, see Nicholas Lash, 'Production and prospect: reflections on Christian hope and original sin' in Ernan McMullin (ed.), *Evolution and Creation* (Notre Dame: University of Notre Dame Press, 1985), pp. 278–9.

of forms; they are the most involuntary artists' that there are. Again: 'just as the popular mind separates the lightning from its flash and takes the latter for an *action*, for the operation of a subject called lightning, so popular morality also separates strength from expressions of strength, as if there were a neutral substratum behind the strong man, which was *free* to express strength or not to do so. But there is no such substratum.'[18] Neither lions nor eagles select their species, opt for predatory violence.

Quite true, but we, originally, are neither lions nor eagles. If that is what we choose to be, our choice is neither involuntary nor instinctive. 'The behaviour of the strong man', says Milbank, 'is never spontaneous, it is always imitative of a cultural paradigm of strength.' We play the game of being eagle-like and, in doing so, acquire the skill to soar and strike. Therefore, continues Milbank,

Given the dedication of the strong to a narrative which invents their strength, it is possible for the weak to refuse the necessity of this strength by telling a different story, posing different roles for human beings to inhabit. This might, indeed, be a questionable metaphysical story about a disembodied, characterless soul always free to choose, but it could also be a story which simply changed the metaphors: which, for example, proposed a humanity become sheep-like, pastoral.[19]

In the beginning, according to Nietzsche, there is violence, the struggle for mastery, the will to power. Christianity announces and enacts another tale, according to which in the beginning, and in the end, is peace, pure donated peacefulness which, in the times between, makes its appearance in the endless uphill labour of transfigurative harmony. That, at any rate, is my account of what it ought to be and do. Before deciding whether the proposal is mere wishful thinking, a kind of day-dream to distract us from the suffering and violence of the world, we need to consider what, in fact, the options are that lie to hand.

---

[18] Nietzsche, *Genealogy*, ii, 17 (p. 86); i, 13 (p. 45).
[19] Milbank, *Theology and Social Theory*, p. 283.

It is, of course, important, at the outset, to insist that Christianity is, like Judaism, a fundamentally political affair. To be a Christian is to inhabit and enact a social narrative, a story of humankind called from nowhere, *ex nihilo*, towards its proper place, its promised *polis*, the new Jerusalem. As early as Origen, the structure or (as we might say) the life-style of Christianity is referred to as a 'polity', a *politeia*.[20]

The question is: what is the proper relationship between the 'polity' of Christian discipleship and the enterprises that people usually have in mind when they speak of 'politics'? From the bewildering variety of answers that have been given to this question, during two thousand years of Christian history, I mention only four.

First, there are those which, seeing Caesar's realm as firstfruits of the new Jerusalem, look to the Church for benediction and endorsement of the state. Even Augustine saw in the earthly city a 'symbolic presentation of the heavenly'.[21] But few have recognised more clearly than he did that the *mode* of symbolic presentation tends to be that of hideously distorting caricature – from the banners of Constantine's armies to the more recent spectacle of priests sprinkling with holy water submarines armed with thermonuclear warheads.

It is thus not surprising that a second tradition should have seen the Church's task not as endorsement of the dominant structures, practices and institutions, but rather as their strenuous subversion. The promise of the kingdom now serves as stimulus and incentive to the struggles of those enslaved within, or exiled from, the earthly city's walls. (We might call this the Spartacan Tradition.)

Whatever may be the abstract arguments in favour of the appropriateness of either of these strategies in this or that particular respect, in this or that particular context or occasion, they both inexorably tend, in fact, to grant too much to Nietzschean ontology. Wittingly or unwittingly, they concede the primacy of violence, seeing in 'politics' its containment or appropriate use.

[20] See, e.g., Origen, *Contra Celsum*, VII, 26. [21] Augustine, *City of God*, Bk. XV, Ch. 2.

Accordingly, there is a third tradition which, insisting that we come not from violence but from nothing, in pure peaceful gift, refuses all continuity between, all intermingling of, the politics of this world and the polity of Christ's disciples, of his sheep-like people. Again and again, from early monasticism to Amish and similar communities in the United States, expressions of this tradition have sustained the Christian narrative, exhibited its fundamental features, in circumstances which tended to obliterate it. And a similar, though not quite explicitly theological, conviction found expression in MacIntyre's recommendation, at the end of *After Virtue*, to build 'new forms of community within which the moral life could be sustained so that both morality and civility might survive the coming age of barbarism and darkness'.[22]

Suppose we recast the ancient distinction between 'precepts' and 'counsels', between what is required of all Christians in every circumstance and what is required of some people in some situations, as a distinction between strategy and tactics. What we may call the 'monastic' option – a policy of withdrawal from the confusion and compromise, the rhetoric and warfare, of the public square – bears witness, when well lived, to the uncompromising requirement, the absolute character, of the gift and promise of God's peace. As tactic, it has an ancient and honourable place in the performance of the Christian story. There are, nevertheless, at least three reasons for ruling out this third tradition, also, as a strategically appropriate option for the politics, the public style, of Christian discipleship.

I earlier described Christianity as the enactment of the possibility of *all* things healing into peace, into that pure peacefulness which, even now, appears in the endless uphill labour of transfigurative harmony. Withdrawal, as strategy, would be too close to stoicism, even to despair. We are, indeed, in exile, 'longing for a better homeland',[23] but we now have

---

[22] Alasdair MacIntyre, *After Virtue. A Study in Moral Virtue* (Notre Dame: University of Notre Dame Press, 1981), p. 263.
[23] Hebrews 11.16.

more important things to do than sit mourning by the river-
side. We are, as followers of Christ, the shepherd king, already
exiles heading homewards, along the way prepared for us, the
way of the Cross. That is the first point.

The second is that the story which we labour to enact is not
our private, tribal tale. We tell it as the tale of every people and
of all the world. Therefore, sustained engagement with the
destructive forces threatening to overwhelm the world and
humankind, an engagement required and rendered possible
by the outpouring of God's peacefulness, demands the
construction of the kind of *culture* which can embody, sustain
and communicate the tale.

The third reason for judging the monastic option strategically inappropriate concerns the ambivalence of 'power'. The
Nietzschean narrative tends to take all power as domination
and, at least implicitly, as violence. But rejection of the myth
of primal violence also entails rejection of the view that power,
as *such*, is tainted and to be eschewed. Unfortunately, those
who come close to recommending the monastic option as
Christian strategy too often fall into the trap of supposing that
refusal of the myth demands that we say 'No' to power.
Remember Milbank's question: 'Is there anything *but* power?
Is violence the master of us all?'[24] But these should be treated
as two questions and not one, for not all power is violence:
gentleness requires the greatest strength of all. Power is
ability, strength, skill, access to resources. We speak, quite
properly, of the power of speech. Nor is control necessarily
domination; good gardeners do not dominate: 'orchestrate'
might be a better word.

'It is recorded of Cain', says St Augustine, 'that he built a
city, but Abel, being a sojourner, built none.'[25] Abel, of course,
looked after sheep. Having ruled out, as strategically inappropriate patterns of Christian polity, the Constantinian,
Spartacan and monastic options, we might do worse than take
Abel as our patron. There is, of course, a twist. According to

24 Milbank, *Theology and Social Theory*, p. 276.
25 Augustine, *City of God*, Bk. xv, Ch. 1.

Genesis, Cain built his city long after Abel's death. Today, however, it is within that city's strife and suffering that we are required – politically, economically, educationally – to dramatise, enact, display, the possibility of 'humanity becoming sheep-like'. We shall, of course, look silly. Sheep always do. But, more than that, we shall be found subversive – and far more dangerously so, in fact, than if we contended, on its own terms and with its own devices, with the will to power.

I have, in this chapter, done nothing more than try to indicate something of the shape or character of the politics implied by our confession of faith in God the Creator, mystery of originating peace; in God the Spirit, gift-breathed bearer of that peace's promise; in God the Word, whose passion, death and resurrection tell what form peacemaking takes within a violent world.

We tend, these days, to treat the Christian story as if it were only of significance for those whose private preferences run to an interest in something called 'religion'. We leave the story on one side when we discuss, evaluate and make plans for action in the ordinary, public world. But, if the 'secularity' of that world is, in fact, as I have argued, a dangerous illusion; if that which we assert when we confess the creed is *true*, then it is powerful and public truth, the antidote to all the violence which defines and shapes our world. And, if this is so, if what the creed asserts is true, then we have no alternative but so to act and speak, although the likely consequences are that we be held to ridicule or put to death.

CHAPTER 13

Incarnation and determinate freedom

FROM DIGNITY TO PLIGHT

The obsession with freedom is a defining feature of the modern Western mind. Even though freedom has not always been the keynote of political action and moral argument, men and women everywhere have sought and celebrated such freedom as lay within their vision and their reach.

It is the correlation between our freedom and the being and action of God which especially interests me. And, on this topic, the dominant ethos in modern Western thought has undergone a series of most interesting modulations.[1] From the locus of our likeness to God, freedom became, first, the goal of our struggle against all absolutes, then the celebration of autonomy won and power displayed, then, gradually, under the pressure of much suffering and disillusionment, something much more modest, more stoical. Finally, in terror, freedom becomes our plight.[2]

In the beginning of modernity was the will. 'It is a supreme perfection in man that he acts voluntarily, that is, freely; this makes him in a special way the author of his actions and deserving of praise for what he does.' Thus Descartes, for whom the nature of the will and its freedom is the point

---

[1] 'Dominant ethos' is, actually, too strong, not least because, in the cacophony which currently stands substitute for moral conversation, there is no *one* account which sets the tone.
[2] Edward Craig, *The Mind of God and the Works of Man*.

of our *resemblance* to God. As constituted by God we are, like God, the authors of our acts. Freedom is our godlike dignity.[3]

That was 1644. Move on two hundred years, through the Enlightenment and the bourgeois revolutions, to the Paris Manuscripts of 1844: 'A *being sees* himself as independent only when he stands on his own feet, and he only stands on his own feet when he owes his *existence* to himself. A man who lives by the grace of another regards himself as a dependent being.' Human freedom, no longer our likeness to God, is now the principle of our antagonism to divine sovereignty. As Marx had put it the previous year, the question as to whether sovereignty resided in the people or in the monarch was liable to obscure the fact that we are here dealing with 'two *wholly opposed conceptions of sovereignty*, of which one can come into being only in the *monarch* and the other only in the *people*. It is analogous to the question, whether God or man is sovereign. One of the two must be false.'[4]

By the end of the century, the battle was over. Prometheus stood lord and master of his world, unchallenged and unchecked. But already the hubris is set in counterpoint to darker tones. To be unchallenged is, after all, to be alone. Here is William James in 1904:

From the fact that finite experiences must draw support from one another, philosophers pass to the notion that experience *überhaupt* must need an absolute support. The denial of such a notion by humanism lies probably at the root of most of the dislike which it incurs. But is this not the globe, the elephant, and the tortoise all over again? Must not something end by supporting itself? Humanism is willing to let finite experience be self-supporting. Somewhere being must immediately breast nonentity. Why may not the advancing front of experience, carrying its immanent satisfactions

---

[3] René Descartes, 'Principles of philosophy' (37) in *The Philosophical Writings of Descartes*, I, (trans.) John Cottingham, Robert Stoofhoff and Dugald Murdoch (Cambridge: Cambridge University Press, 1985), p. 205. On the significance of the theological overtones to this description, see Craig, *Mind of God*, p. 25.

[4] Karl Marx, *Early Writings*, pp. 256, 86; see Nicholas Lash, *A Matter of Hope*, p. 178.

and dissatisfactions, cut against the black inane as the luminous orb of the moon cuts the cerulean abyss?[5]

James' imagery, of ship prow and moonlight, suggests that solitude be borne in courage and tranquillity. And yet, as Craig remarks, for many this imagery will invoke 'as terrifying a feeling of the trackless void surrounding human life as anything ever produced by any purveyor of existentialist *Angst*'. Hence the slogan which Craig proposes for the twentieth-century *Weltbild* of freedom as predicament is that of the 'Agent in the Void'.[6]

In James, the terror is latent. Ever the patrician, he whistles stoically in the dark. In Sartre, however, as in many subsequent writers, the implications of the radically self-constitutive character of human freedom have been thought through without ambiguity: 'For human reality, to be is to *choose oneself*; nothing comes to it either from the outside or from within which it can *receive or accept*. Without any help whatsoever, it is entirely abandoned to the intolerable necessity of making itself be – down to the slightest detail.'[7]

'Intolerable necessity' – one need not be an existentialist to feel the cold wind that blows across the consequences of the choices we have made, across the wilderness of wartime Poland, Ethiopia, Japan and the differently devastated forests of Brazil and Vietnam.

Here is one more voice:

Mankind loses religion as it moves through history, but the loss leaves its mark behind. Part of the drives and desires which religious belief preserved and kept alive are detached from the inhibiting religious form and become productive forces in social practice. In the process even the immoderation characteristic of shattered illusions acquires a positive form and is truly transformed. In a really free mind the concept of infinity is preserved in an awareness of the

---

[5] William James, *Pragmatism and the Meaning of Truth*, introduction by A. J. Ayer, (eds.) Frederick Burkhardt, Fredson Bowers and Ignas K. Skrupskelis (Cambridge, MA: Harvard University Press, 1978), pp. 221–2.

[6] Craig, *Mind of God*, pp. 271, 282.

[7] Jean-Paul Sartre, *Being and Nothingness*, (trans.) Hazel E. Barnes (London: Methuen, 1958), pp. 440–1, cited in Craig, *Mind of God*, p. 304.

finality of human life and of the unalterable aloneness of men, and it keeps society from indulging in a thoughtless optimism, an inflation of its own knowledge into a new religion.[8]

Max Horkheimer detested 'the fetishist handling of categories' in *Being and Nothingness*, in consequence of which 'the dialectical finesse and complexity of thought has been turned into a glittering machinery of metal. Words like *l'être en soi* and *l'être pour soi* function as kinds of pistons.'[9] This may be overstating it, but the asceticism of his own account of freedom as protective, in acknowledgement of finitude and aloneness, of the echoes of infinity, is in sober contrast to the destructive, self-indulgent exuberance of both Promethean optimism and Sartrean despair.

The modern moods of freedom do not fall into any simple chronological pattern, for two reasons. First, even the darkest accents of freedom as predicament were already sounded by Nietzsche. Secondly, as new moods emerge from changing circumstances old ones seldom simply fade away. There are 'contemporaries' alive today not only of Sartre and Horkheimer, but also of James, and Marx, and even Descartes.

THE DISAPPEARANCE OF GOD

Read as a straightforward description of our circumstances, Sartre's characterisation of human reality seems simply false. We can and do receive and accept all manner of things from outside our individual selves: things such as language and identity, shelter and suffering, pain and delight, gratitude and disease. The self-constituting individual is a fiction of the modern imagination.

---

[8] Max Horkheimer, 'Thoughts on religion' in *Critical Theory*, (trans.) M. O'Connell et al. (New York: Continuum, 1972), p. 131. McLellan's comment on this passage is: 'The legacy of religion was the idea of perfect justice which, while it might be impossible of realisation in this world, yet served as a constant basis of opposition to the powers that were' (David McLellan, *Marxism and Religion* (London: MacMillan, 1987), p. 125).

[9] Max Horkheimer, letter to Lowenthal of August 1946, cited in Martin Jay, *The Dialectical Imagination: A History of the Frankfurt School and the Institute of Social Research 1923–1950* (London: Heinemann, 1973), p. 274.

Not that the fiction lacks sense. False as empirical description, it may with hideous accuracy portray our moral
condition. 'What this man lacked', says Stanley Cavell of
Othello, 'was not certainty. He knew everything, but he could
not yield to what he knew, be commanded by it.'[10] To yield, to
be commanded, to receive, to accept: fragile and fraught with
danger, pregnant with slavery and betrayal though concession,
obedience, reception and acceptance may be, they are yet the
hallmarks of both infancy and adulthood. Between them
comes adolescence, the age of autonomy. Like infancy,
adolescence has its time and place and its own defining freedom. But, if they endure, their times and tasks outlived, each
of these first forms of freedom enslaves with iron bands.
Whether 'Sartrean man' is mad or damned we do not need to
know. On either diagnosis he requires redemption; he needs
to be set free.

'The necessity of the task [of adulthood] is the choice of
finitude, which for us (even after God) means the acknowledgement of the existence of finite others, which is to say, the
choice of community, of autonomous moral existence.'[11]
These are sensible sentiments, but how did that little
parenthesis 'even after God' get in? The presupposition is
clearly similar to that in Horkheimer's claim that 'mankind
loses religion as it moves through history', but we perhaps
need to distinguish between the loss of religion and the
disappearance of God.

In its simplest form, the story of 'secularisation', as told
until recently, went something like this. Descartes could take
human freedom to be the form of our likeness to God because
he, very early modern that he was, had not yet observed the
antinomy on which Marx (following Feuerbach) put his finger.
But once the 'contradictions of theology' were unmasked, it
could only be a matter of time before the 'true or anthropological essence of religion' was plain to view; and this
essence, in turn, its errors and illusions banished and
dispelled, might leave at least such traces as Horkheimer's

[10] Stanley Cavell, *The Claim of Reason*, p. 496.   [11] Cavell, p. 464.

memory of the thirst for perfect justice setting constraints to tyranny.[12]

One difficulty with this story, of course, is that in fact, from the Pentagon to Tehran, from the hills of Peru to the corridors of the Vatican, from India to Bosnia, the world is *awash* with religion. The loss of religion did not, after all, occur. It is as easy, at present, to imagine a militant atheist being elected President of the United States as it is realistic to suppose that the next ruler of Iran will be a Roman Catholic.

This all makes the theologian's task not easier but much more difficult. The practical falsification of at least the more simplistic versions of the secularisation thesis has not been accompanied by any significant reconsideration of a key element in its theory. Religion may, for better and for worse, flourish on every side, but God, it seems, is dead. 'Getting rid of theology as part of the intellectual life of the West', says Richard Rorty, 'was not the achievement of one book nor one man, nor one generation, nor one century.'[13] Nevertheless, he has not the slightest doubt that the job has now been done.

One effect of this Olympian arrogance is to make all mention of God within its ambience *trivial*. In the mainstream traditions of both Judaism and Christianity, it is a defining feature of serious theological enquiry that finding proper uses for the word 'God' is known to be dauntingly difficult, to demand the most extended efforts of our minds and hearts, our logic, integrity and imagination. It must be so, for to talk lightly of the Holy One is to talk of something else. There is, as it were, a sense of fragility, of risk, of excitement and temerity in all serious theological speech, and it is just these qualities which disappear when the question of God loses its urgency and interest for believers and nonbelievers alike.

Nietzsche saw this coming: the unconcern of those who had

---

[12] See, in George Eliot's translation of Feuerbach's *The Essence of Christianity*, the chapter headings to the second part and the title of the first.

[13] Richard Rorty, *Consequences of Pragmatism* (Minneapolis: University of Minnesota Press, 1982), p. 34.

killed God convinced the Madman in *The Gay Science* that they did not understand what their knives had done.[14] The resultant juxtaposition in our culture (which Nietzsche surely did not foresee) of religious exuberance and theological paralysis is both unprecedented and very dangerous. Religion undisciplined by wisdom is as destructive as sexual activity unconstrained by love.

My aims in this chapter are much more modest than these large comments might suggest. It is widely supposed, by believers and nonbelievers alike, that faith in God takes the pressure off our finitude, rescues us from 'aloneness'; that it sets us free from the constraints of finitude by setting us in relation to a (real or imaginary) reassuring 'absolute'. Thus, for example, when Kai Nielsen denies that 'all reflective atheists are tortured souls despairingly longing for the absolute',[15] he clearly supposes that it is 'the absolute' which is the object of religious faith. Against the grain of this widespread deep assumption, I want to indicate what it might mean to say (adapting Cavell's description of our duty 'after God') that the necessity of the task of adulthood is the choice of finitude before God. Adulthood, thus construed, would be a matter of discovering that it is possible, without diminution of dignity, abdication of rationality, or loss of freedom, to yield to what we know and be commanded by it. Such discovery would, nevertheless, be both dark and painful, for its pattern was set in the garden of Gethsemane.

[14] See Michael J. Buckley, *At the Origins of Modern Atheism*, pp. 28–30. Not the least of the good reasons for resisting Rorty's claim that theology has been disposed of is that, as Buckley insists, it remains important to ask *what* god died beneath those knives.

It is a pity that Rorty would be unlikely to have the patience to work through the section on 'Bonhoeffer's contribution to the return of "Death of God" talk to theology' in Eberhard Jüngel, *God as the Mystery of the World: On the Foundation of the Theology of the Crucified One in the Dispute between Theism and Atheism*, (trans.) Darrell L. Guder (Edinburgh: T. & T. Clark, 1983), pp. 57–63.

[15] Kai Nielsen, 'God and coherence: on the epistemological foundations of religious belief' in Leroy S. Rouner (ed.), *Knowing Religiously* (Notre Dame: University of Notre Dame Press, 1985), p. 101.

TRANSCENDING AUTONOMY

Nobody familiar with Hegel's *Phenomenology* could sensibly suppose that 'absolute' freedom might be a proper goal of ethical and political activity. Freedom, in order to set us free, requires determinants, forms, shapes, configurations. Freedom is not a substance, a force, an entity. The functions of 'free' are adjectival: it qualifies our account of actions, arrangements, patterns of relationship, and does not of itself furnish us with materials for their description. Freedom is always particular, finite, contestable and vulnerable. It is not the name of our home or the description of our destiny but, at best, how we are at home and, at worst, how we may be at sea.

The point is so obvious and elementary that it would not need making were it not for the fact that the characteristically modern notion of freedom as autonomy, a notion first forged in resistance against absolutism, has itself again and again been absolutised and thus proved pregnant with fresh forms of tyranny and inhumanity. One corrective to this tendency might be the insistence that freedom, for its flourishing, demands articulation with other values such as truth and justice. Then, instead of setting any one single value on an imperial throne, we might get on with the more modest, practical, and demanding business of seeking and struggling for particular, finite configurations and achievements of justice and truth – and freedom. We have done damage enough with the worship of absolutes. It is surely time to learn the discipline of adulthood, the transcending of autonomy in community and finitude.

Such things are easily said, but where might such discipline be learned? And what would be the manner of its pedagogy? The ethics and the politics of such questions are not my present concern. I confine myself, instead, to some comments on their implications for religion and theology.

Religious maturity, I suggest, is a matter of learning to worship while yet not worshipping oneself or any other thing. Christianity and Judaism, when true to their common structuring convictions, have always been iconoclastic, and their iconoclasm has been rooted in suspicion of idolatry. Idolatry is the divinising, the taking as absolute and over-riding, of any value, fact, nation, dream, project, person, possession, or idea. It matters not what being I take as god and set my heart upon, whether it be freedom or efficiency, yesterday or tomorrow, America or me; to make of some being, of *any* being, an 'absolute', an object of worship, is idolatry.

But, if the worship of oneself or any other thing is to be contested and deplored, is it not then time, gently and without regret, simply to set an end to worshipping? Once we have learned the lesson that there is no thing, in heaven above or earth below, or in the waters under the earth, which is or could be the proper object of our worship, then what reasons are there left for worshipping? What would the point of worship be?

I do not want to say there is no point to worship, or that we worship for no reason. To do so would suggest that worship is irrational and arbitrary. I do not, as a matter of fact, believe mature and tested human hope to be more arbitrary or irrational than stoicism or despair. Whatever our funda-mental stance toward the meaning or unmeaning of the world, we can give reasons for it. And yet, whatever that stance, whatever the response that we enact to the question of the point or 'followability' of the world, in the last analysis we neither despair nor hope *'because . . .'*[16]

In order to render the notion of appropriate worship a little less obscure, consider it in the twofold light of the critique of 'foundationalism' and the doctrine of grace. To take the latter angle first: it is a commonplace of Christian doctrine to insist upon the utter, free ungroundedness of God's relation to the world and on that answering ungroundedness or *gratuité*, that unconstrained acceptance and response, in which we find our freedom. 'Christianity', Karl Rahner once remarked, 'would cease to exist if it no longer had the courage to speak of the

---

[16] On the relationship between faith and 'followability' (a concept borrowed by Frank Kermode from W. B. Gallie), see Nicholas Lash, 'How do we know where we are?' in *Theology on the Way to Emmaus*, pp. 62–74.

blessed uselessness of love for God: absolutely useless, since it would not be itself if man were to seek in it his own advantage . . . his own fulfilment.'[17]

My reference to appropriate worship was thus intended to paraphrase the notion of love of God 'for God's own sake'. But both expressions are unsatisfactory, mine because it makes no mention of God, and the classical formula because its anthropomorphism arouses all the familiar suspicions.

After four centuries of modern theism and its antitheses, four centuries of apologetic argument as to why it is that we 'need' God to explain the world, it is still too early to know what effect the ending of this episode will have upon the problem of the 'naming' of God. It is quite certain, notwithstanding the prejudices of the cultured despisers, that the attempt to make proper mention of God not only will but must continue, because we are always in need of some set of protocols against idolatry. It is idolatry, not faith, which corrupts humanity and frustrates freedom.

Feuerbach, in a most amazing sentence, once announced: 'The theory that God cannot be defined, and consequently cannot be known by man, is . . . the offspring of recent times, a product of modern unbelief.'[18] The opposite would be nearer the mark. Drawing upon both its Jewish inheritance (in which the impossibility of depicting or naming the Holy One was centrally inscribed) and on Neoplatonism, Christianity – both Eastern and Western – insisted, for more than a millennium and a half, that whatever we say of God is uttered against the silence of a deeper and more fundamental nescience. Whether in the writings of the mystics, or with the grammatical austerity of medieval scholasticism, the anthropomorphism of our symbols and our narratives was counterpointed and purified by insistence on unknowing.

In the early modern period this dialectic of narrative and

---

[17] Karl Rahner, 'The inexhaustible transcendence of God and our concern for the future' in *Theological Investigations*, xx, (trans.) Edward Quinn (London: Darton, Longman and Todd, 1981), p. 180.

[18] Ludwig Feuerbach, *The Essence of Christianity*, p. 14.

nescience, of anthropomorphism and agnosticism, underwent a series of displacements. In the hands of its most influential seventeenth- and eighteenth-century practitioners, Christian theology abandoned its traditional responsibility for the interpretation of Scripture and took for its task and territory the explanation of the natural world. This was a shift not merely of subject-matter but of discourse: a shift from formal to material objects or, as we might say, from 'grammatical' to 'empirical' procedures and concerns. And so, as philosophy developed into 'natural philosophy', which, in turn, took the form of Newtonian mechanics, the question of God became an empirical affair; and then the hunt was on to prove that somewhere, beyond the particular constituents and movements of the world, a thing, a being, might be found to serve as firm foundation of its existence and explanation of its design.[19] It is, I suggest, the theory that 'God' is the name of an object which can not only be defined but located and coordinated with other facts and objects in the world, and known as they are known (namely, by gazing at them); it is this theory which is 'the offspring of recent times, the product of modern unbelief'. And it is a theory which, in spite of the best efforts of Kant and Hegel (who admirably insisted that 'God does not offer himself for observation'),[20] is still alive and well in departments of the philosophy of religion.

It is, I think, just possible that the ending of modernity, and, with it, the setting to rest of the theisms and a-theisms which were so central to its concerns, may make it *easier* for Christian theology to return to its proper task: the consideration of our identity, our duty and responsibility, in relation to an eternal Word once uttered in a particular time and place.

What may have seemed a somewhat lengthy detour from my theme was, I think, necessary in order to indicate the proper background to the suggestion that we do not have nor do we

---

[19] See above, Chapters Four and Seven.

[20] G. W. F. Hegel, *Lectures on the Philosophy of Religion*, 1, *Introduction and the Concept of Religion*, (ed.) Peter C. Hodgson (Berkeley: University of California Press, 1984), p. 313.

need any idea or image of God except that furnished by the form and flesh of God's appearing. It is not our business, as Christians, to be continually attempting to peer or speculate 'beyond' the world in which we live, but rather, *in* that world to find and fashion our human finitude in the form of discipleship. The truth which, according to the Fourth Gospel, shall make us free is truth enfleshed, enacted, made finite and particular, arrested, tried, crucified; not truth sought elsewhere or somehow found in flight from the circumstances and predicaments and responsibilities and darkness of the world.

ON NOT TAKING FLIGHT

I have spoken of our need to transcend autonomy, to move toward adulthood in learning how to yield, in freedom, to what we know and are commanded by. But, if it is indeed adulthood at which we aim, then the transcendence of autonomy, experienced as dignity or as predicament, is a matter not of the transcendence of finitude, but, on the contrary, of finitude's acceptance.

The longing for unrestricted incorporeal freedom lies deep, if not in human nature, then certainly in the culture to which we belong. The craving to burst out of the bounds of body and of time may well be exactly what it takes to free animals of our kind into the space of culture and history; but it is an ambivalent gift. If we never learn to own our finitude we remain tormented by a powerful inability ever to be satisfied by *anything*.[21]

This place, this time, this flesh, these facts, these people: are we in place here? Or are we out of place, in exile, nostalgically restless, 'just visiting'? Central to the Jewish and Christian doctrines of creation, and specifically to their refinement in the doctrine of creation *ex nihilo*, is the conviction that this body, this finite fact, is our place and may, in God's graciousness, be made our home.[22]

---

[21] Fergus Kerr, *Theology after Wittgenstein*, p. 45.
[22] See Edward Schillebeeckx's analysis of the doctrine of creation in *God among Us: The Gospel Proclaimed* (London: SCM Press, 1983), discussed by Kerr in *Theology after*

Lacking the courage, the tranquillity, the self-knowledge to find our freedom here, we flee. Our flight takes one of two forms.[23] The first is the flight into feeling, on the run from darkness, inhumanity and impending chaos, in the cultivation of oases of private satisfaction. Whatever we make of William James' claim that drunkenness stands, 'to the poor and unlettered . . . in the place of symphony concerts and of literature'[24] (a claim which bites both ways), it would be difficult to deny that the upsurge of 'religiousness' in Western culture, of piety peddled as balm for frightened and alienated subjectivity, suggests that narcotic uses of religion are still as widespread and as influential as they were in Marx's day. All forms of the flight into feeling, however, are evasive of finitude, doomed attempts to find our freedom elsewhere than in the particular, public, fleshly facts, relationships, responsibilities and requirements that determine our existence in the world.

Our other favourite form of flight is the flight into thought, the quest for reassuringly comprehensive explanations of the world. It makes little difference whether the explanatory schemes that we devise do or do not include some use or mention of the word 'God', because all such schemes leave the bleakness of the facts around us more or less unchanged. Pushing back the frontiers of knowledge may increase our power but does not necessarily contribute to the transmutation of fate into freedom. And neither metaphysics nor cosmology feeds the hungry or sets the captives free.

To these two forms of flight there correspond, in Christianity, on the one hand, the range of pietisms and rebirths which castigate as infidelity all critical scholarship and strenuous engagement of the mind and, on the other, the rationalisms which, impatient of darkness and unknowing,

Wittgenstein, pp. 184–5; see also Richard J. Clifford, 'The Hebrew scriptures and the theology of creation', *Theological Studies*, 46 (1985), 507–23.
23 See Lash, *Easter in Ordinary*, pp. 280–5.
24 William James, *The Varieties of Religious Experience*, p. 30.

construct remarkably detailed positive descriptions of the nature and attributes of God. However widespread and influential these two forms of flight have been, they happily do not exhaust the diversity of Christianity. According to Matthew's Gospel, at the moment of Jesus' arrest by the authorities 'all the disciples forsook him and fled'.[25] And yet there have always been some brought back to the place and task of Calvary: the reconstruction, in reconciled relationship and the making of community, of what John Milbank calls a 'counter-history of peace'.[26] This counter-history happens through that occurrence of community which both expresses and makes possible the worship 'in Spirit' of the unknown God.[27]

We do not find our freedom in escaping from the flesh, in attempting to set our sights beyond the condition of our finitude, upon some glimpse of an absolute we might call God. As I put it earlier: we do not have nor do we need any idea or image of God except that furnished in the form and flesh of God's appearing.

This is not, of course, an original suggestion of my own. However forgetful of it modern discussions of theism may often have become, it has been, in fact, a central theme in Christian theology at least since the time of the writing of the Fourth Gospel: 'Philip said to him, "Lord, show us the Father, and we shall be satisfied", Jesus said to him "Have I been with you so long, and yet you do not know me, Philip? He who has seen me has seen the Father; how can you say, 'Show me the Father'"?'[28] I would therefore like to close by quoting a remarkable passage from the fourteenth-century English mystic Julian of Norwich. 'At this time', she says,

---

[25] Matthew 26.56.

[26] John Milbank, 'The second difference: for a trinitarianism without reserve', *Modern Theology*, 2 (1986), 227.

[27] For an account of the character and possibility of such community slightly less bleak than that offered by Alasdair MacIntyre in *After Virtue*, see Nicholas Lash, 'The Church's responsibility for the future of humanity' in *Theology on the Way to Emmaus*, pp. 186–201.

[28] John 14.8–9.

I wanted to look away from the cross, but I did not dare, for I knew well that whilst I contemplated the cross I was secure and safe . . . Then there came a suggestion, seemingly said in friendly manner, to my reason: Look up to heaven to his Father . . . Here I must look up or else answer. I answered inwardly with all the power of my soul, and said: No, I cannot, for you are my heaven. I said this because I did not want to look up . . . For I knew well that he who had bound me so fast would unbind me when it was his will. So was I taught to choose Jesus for my heaven, whom I saw only in pain at that time . . . And that has taught me that I should always do so, to choose only Jesus to be my heaven, in well-being and in woe.[29]

Notwithstanding the seemingly friendly manner in which the suggestion was recommended to her reason, the Lady Julian resisted, and would not look beyond the Crucified, to heaven, to find the Father. Her discipline displays the recognition that, in that figure, freedom is best determined and discerned. The poem of the Cross requires to be twice read: first as the form of God's freedom for the world, and then as the form of the human freedom to be found in God. There is, I think, a fascinating affinity between the Lady Julian's restraint and that exhibited in Max Horkheimer's refusal to indulge in 'thoughtless optimism'. There is also, of course, a difference which is no less profound. For Horkheimer, the concept of infinity was to be preserved in memory as ground and basis for resistance against tyranny. In Lady Julian's reading, the concept also serves to point toward a future: to indicate the unknown substance of our human hope.

---

[29] Julian of Norwich, *Showings*, (trans. and intro.) Edmund Colledge and James Walsh (New York: Paulist Press, 1978), pp. 211–21.

CHAPTER 14

Beyond the end
of history?

CONSIDERING WHAT LIES AHEAD

'Where there is no escape, people ultimately no longer want to think about it. This eschatological ecofatalism allows the pendulum of private and political moods to swing in *any* direction. The risk society shifts from hysteria to indifference and vice versa.'[1] Not all the voices that we hear, of course, are variants of fatalism, aspects of despair. There are still many people whose imaginations are tuned to some kind of optimism by the mythical conviction that modern industrial society, with 'its thinking in categories of economic growth, its understanding of science and technology and its forms of democracy', represents a 'pinnacle' of human achievement 'which it scarcely makes sense even to consider surpassing. This myth has many forms of expression. Among the most effective is the mad joke of the *end of history*.'[2]

Defending his original thesis, Francis Fukuyama insisted that 'What I had suggested had come to an end was not the occurrence of events, even large and grave events, but History: that is, history understood as a single, coherent, evolutionary process, when taking into account the experience of all peoples in all times.'[3] By this, Fukuyama might have meant that this long century's suffering had cured us of the illusion that 'History' had ever happened; that we (*whoever* 'we' may be)

---

[1] Ulrich Beck, *Risk Society. Towards New Modernity* (London: Sage, 1992), p. 37.
[2] Beck, p. 11.
[3] Francis Fukuyama, *The End of History and the Last Man* (London: Hamish Hamilton, 1992), p. xii.

might ever reasonably deem all other societies, past and present, inferior to our own. Unfortunately, notwithstanding his wistful recognition that 'The end of history will be a very sad time', with little left for human beings (or, perhaps, white American males?) to do except be caretakers of 'the museum of history', Fukuyama still supposes there to be no thinkable alternative to a historicist understanding of history as a tale of 'progress', an 'evolution from primitive to modern'.[4]

Writing at the end of the Second World War, Karl Popper recognised that the impulses of historicism were, in part, theological in character. 'It is', he said, 'often considered a part of the Christian dogma that God reveals Himself in history; that history has meaning; and that its meaning is the purpose of God ... I contend that this view is pure idolatry and superstition.'[5] Fukuyama would, I suspect, find this provocative fulmination unintelligible: for him, as for many inmates of supposedly 'secular' societies, the business of religion is, like the provision of cold beer, a matter of satisfying particular consumer preferences. Hence his belief that, except in territories influenced by Islam, 'religious impulses' have been 'successfully satisfied within the sphere of personal [i.e. private] life that is permitted in liberal societies'.[6]

As the collapse of Communism coincides with rapidly diminishing confidence in the ideals and visions of 'enlightenment', and the construction of a single global system of production, information and exchange goes hand in hand with recognition of the irreversibility of damage inflicted on the ecosystem of which we form a part, consideration of the way ahead has rarely seemed so urgent, so uncertain, or so difficult to undertake. When economists and social theorists, political scientists and experts in international relations gather to discuss these things, they usually do not invite theologians to take part in the conversation. It is not simple prejudice which

---

[4] Fukuyama, 'The end of history?', *The National Interest*, 16 (1989), 18; 'A reply to my critics', *The National Interest*, 18 (1989–90), 23.

[5] Karl Popper, *The Open Society and its Enemies*, II, *The High Tide of Prophecy: Hegel, Marx, and the Aftermath* (London: Routledge and Kegan Paul, 1966), p. 271.

[6] Fukuyama, 'The end of history?', p. 14.

leads to this omission so much as the characteristically
modern belief that the subject-matter of theology is religion,
and that the business of religion is with the private heart
rather than the public world.

Theologians will, of course, if they are wise, nevertheless
insist on joining in the conversation, on the grounds that the
subject-matter of theology is *not* 'religion', but rather 'all
things' – from their first beginning to their final end –
considered in relation to the mystery of God: *sub ratione
Dei*.[7]

We shall, in due course, consider why it is as misleading to
imagine that our 'end' lies simply in some distant future as it
would be to suppose that our 'beginning' now lies far behind.
The Omega of our existence is its Alpha, God's eternal Word
once uttered, the Crucified and Risen One, 'who is and who
was and who is to come'.[8] Nevertheless, the forms of Christian
reflection on, and planning for, the future of the world are,
naturally and properly, shaped by eschatology: by expectations of the end.

According to Carl Braaten, 'Christianity today stands at the
crossroads between two diametrically opposed interpretations
of eschatology': on the one hand, consideration of events
irrupting from another world in some near or distant future
and, on the other, the dramatisation of social-ethical objec-
tives sought within this world.[9] While acknowledging that such
dichotomies are false, he seems uncertain as to how they
might most truthfully be overcome. As in much contemporary
theology, this uncertainty is rooted in a tendency to treat the
issues in dangerous abstraction from the actual contexts in
which they arise. Thus, for example, the principal reasons that
Braaten advances for 'the emphasis on eschatology in today's
theology' are 'the general philosophical discovery of the
phenomenon of hope in human existence' and 'the historical

---

[7] See Thomas Aquinas, *Summa theologiae*, 1a, 1.7.
[8] Revelation 1.8.
[9] Carl E. Braaten, 'The kingdom of God and the life everlasting' in Peter C. Hodgson
and Robert H. King (eds.) *Christian Theology. An Introduction to its Traditions and Tasks*
(Philadelphia: Fortress, 1982), p. 293.

rediscovery of the eschatological core of the message of Jesus'.[10] Nothing here about the grounds of these discoveries in the collapse of nineteenth-century Europe's dreams of endlessly expanding power and wealth; no mention of Passchendaele and Auschwitz, nor of the impact of the recognition that the web of life on this small planet is not only finite but already damaged beyond repair by our bizarre performance.

Joseph Ratzinger, on the other hand, while strenuously resisting 'the transformation of eschatology into political messianism',[11] by no means underestimates the social and, indeed, cosmic implications of Christian hope. And a dispassionate observer might suppose there would be scope for fruitful conversation between his principle that 'The Kingdom of God is not a *political* norm of the political, but it is a *moral* norm of the political' and this suggestion from Jürgen Moltmann: 'Political theology is the internal critique of the modern world. Liberation theology is the external critique of the modern world. Is it not time for the critical theology of the First World and the Liberation Theology of the Third World to enter into some sort of alliance?'[12] When all is said and done, moral critiques of politics are ineluctably political in connotation.

We do not live, nor can we see, beyond the end of history. It is in time alone, the time that God has given us, that we are born and live, make plans, build cities, cherish or destroy the world, find hope or else despair, and die. In the remaining sections of this chapter, I shall briefly comment, under three heads, on the contribution that theology might make to the consideration of our common future. The hope that Christianity deems 'theologal' (that is, expressive of the relations with the mystery of God that human beings may, by

---

[10] Braaten, p. 275.
[11] Aidan Nichols, *The Theology of Joseph Ratzinger* (Edinburgh: T. & T. Clark, 1988), p. 167.
[12] Joseph Ratzinger, *Eschatologie. Tod und Ewiges Leben* (Regensburg: Pustet, 1977), p. 59; Jürgen Moltmann, 'Political theology and liberation theology', *Union Seminary Quarterly Review*, 45 (1991), 217.

God's grace, enjoy) first, in lifting us from despair, takes us also beyond optimism; secondly, takes us beyond the fantasy of science fiction to a more sober vision of the future of the world; and, thirdly, in liberating us from determinism, enables us to live beyond control.

BEYOND OPTIMISM

It is very frightening to gaze upon the prospects for the world: to tune in to the despair generated by urban and industrial disintegration; to listen to the cries of children starving in consequence of political and economic choices enacted, far from their place of destitution, by other people at another time; to take seriously the imperviousness to transformation of the structures of the global market; to bear in mind that 'ecological disaster and atomic fallout ignore the borders of nations. Even the rich and powerful are not safe from them.'[13] Clear-sightedness demands that we admit that, as things at present stand, there seems no chance of bringing off, within the necessary time-scale, those comprehensive transformations of heart, and will, and institution, that the healing of the world requires.

And yet, in my experience, discussions amongst 'experts' of what the future holds in store usually conclude with unwarranted expressions of optimism. The seldom quite explicit dialogue goes like this: 'We will make out.' 'How so?' 'Because the alternative is quite unthinkable.' Optimism is, in other words, often little more than a stoically courageous whistling against despair. Thus, for example, the international lawyer Philip Allott, in a most intelligent and original study, while admitting that 'it may be too late to stop, still less to undo, the havoc caused by international unculture',[14] nevertheless affirms that 'It is a purpose of the present study to suggest that society is, indeed, naturally capable of being

---

[13] Beck, *Risk Society*, p. 23.
[14] Philip Allott, *Eunomia. New Order for a New World* (Oxford: Oxford University Press, 1990), p. 385.

progressive, able to achieve its survival and prospering by the appropriate willing and acting of human beings.'[15]

One reason why secular narratives of optimism are so unconvincing is that, *as* narratives, they lack coherence. Still trapped in the 'modern' predilection for explaining things from no particular standpoint, they oscillate between impersonal abstraction and arbitrary personal testimony. Hence the importance of the increasing recognition that all theories are abbreviated forms of *someone's* story; that each of us is accountable for the stories that we tell, and that all our stories are ungrounded in the sense that they make tacit metaphysical appeals.[16]

Many people imagine that Christian theologians suppose themselves to possess all sorts of information about the future which other people lack. The fact of the matter is, however, that sensible Christians know themselves nescient: set to lifelong discipline of learning to see in the dark. To hope in God, in Christian terms, is to know that God's creation has, in God's love, its future; it is not to know the forms that future takes. Hence Karl Rahner's insistence that 'eschatological assertions' are not to be read as 'previews of future events', and that '*Docta ignorantia futuri* is from the outset the theme that is proper to the theologian.'[17]

Telling the story of the world within that world's continuing history demands a kind of reticence. Concerning the details of the outcome of the world, in God, we have no information now that Jesus lacked in Gethsemane.[18] What we do have, in the gift of the Spirit of the risen Christ, is the ability to 'keep awake and pray'. It is the characteristic weakness of both optimism and despair that, lacking the discipline of hope, they

---

[15] Allott, p. 105. Much hangs, admittedly, on how 'naturally' is construed.

[16] On the importance of accountability, see Alasdair MacIntyre, *Three Rival Versions of Moral Enquiry*, p. 201; on 'the critical non-avoidability of the theological and metaphysical', see John Milbank, *Theology and Social Theory*, p. 3.

[17] Karl Rahner, 'The hermeneutics of eschatological assertions' in *Theological Investigations*, IV, (trans.) Kevin Smyth (London: Darton, Longman and Todd, 1966), p. 328; 'The question of the future' in *Theological Investigations*, XII, (trans.) David Bourke (London: Darton, Longman and Todd, 1974), p. 181.

[18] See Lash, *Believing Three Ways in One God*, p. 120.

take it upon themselves to furnish the story with the ending which it has not yet achieved. Both optimism and despair claim to 'have the answer' to the question of the future, whereas Christian hope, knowing that the answer lies in God, rests in the nescience of prayer: 'Thy kingdom come.'[19]

And, in the meantime, within the bounds of time, our task – in ethics and in politics, domestically and ecologically – is healing (which is what *salus* or 'salvation' means). And, as every doctor knows, the work of healing is not made less urgent, less specific, less demanding, by the mere fact that the bodies and the minds we are required to heal are finite.

BEYOND SCIENCE FICTION

Salus means healing. But what is it that needs healing, that (according to God's promise) is to be made whole, complete, secure? Amongst the many answers given to such questions, I shall mention two: 'us' and 'everything'.

First, consider 'us'. Who are 'we'? I propose a rule for reading sentences that contain this little word. Whenever the word 'we' is being used, ask three questions: whom do those using it have in mind? Whom do they suppose that they have in mind? Whom should they have in mind?

As Christians considering 'salvation' we *should* have in mind no group more restricted than the human race. Where the future is concerned, even considerations of self-interest now alert us to this need: 'The potential for self-endangering developed by civilization in the modernization process' makes 'the utopia of a world society a little more real or at least more urgent.'[20]

The range of reference of the 'we' we use, as Christians, must, however, be as comprehensive in memory as in hope. All evolutionary accounts of human history, accounts that look

[19] Matthew 6.10; 26.41. For an attempt to explore the contrast between the *praxis* of Christian hope as a form of the tragic vision and Marx's endemic optimism, see Lash, *A Matter of Hope*, esp. pp. 248–72.

[20] Beck, *Risk Society*, p. 47.

only forwards from where the speaker stands, all utopian fantasies, all sunlit futures forgetful of the past, are disallowed, subverted by the silent witness of shed blood. 'We' are all those corpses shaded by the arms outstretched on Calvary.[21]

Among the more important lessons being learnt at the present time is that even 'all of humankind' is too small an answer to the question: 'What does God's love heal, make safe, bring to fulfilment in his peace?' 'Everything' would be a better answer. Out of nothing, God makes everything, and what God's love makes that same love heals. We may be better placed to understand this than our predecessors were, because the whole system of the world has irreversibly become one single fact, increasingly becomes one artefact, one context, workplace, market, home or burial-ground.

It is sometimes suggested that the 'universalism' which is so striking a feature of twentieth-century theology has arbitrarily ignored or set aside the traditional doctrine of hell. On the one hand, however, the rejection, in the tradition, of *apocatastasis* was not an affirmation that hell was well populated but a denial of the possibility of conversion after death.[22] On the other hand, to exclude the possibility that the screws of self-obsession can be turned so tightly as to render us impregnable to God's transforming generosity would be too easily to set aside the evidence of destructive arrogance and cruelty which makes the world, throughout its history, a kind of Golgotha, a place of skulls.

The stories told by scientists play a larger part in shaping the imagination of the modern world than tales told by theologians. There are, moreover, influential scientists who endorse the physicist Paul Davies' claim that 'science offers a surer path to God than religion'. But, from Stephen Hawking to John Barrow and Frank Tipler, the God thus sought seems

---

[21] See, for example, Johann-Baptist Metz's discussion of 'the future in the memory of suffering', in *Faith in History and Society* (London: Burns and Oates, 1980), pp. 100–18.

[22] See Karl Rahner and Herbert Vorgrimler, *Concise Theological Dictionary* (London: Burns and Oates, 1965), pp. 30–1.

little more than an idea or explanation: at most, a distant, still intelligence.[23]

There is, in the writings of some most distinguished scientists, much irresponsible speculation of the kind that, when indulged in by philosophers and theologians, gives 'metaphysics' a deservedly bad name.[24] Moreover, just as some scientists presume the physics of the world's beginning to supersede doctrines of creation, so others presume their speculation about the future to supersede Christian eschatology. Thus Barrow and Tipler classify their efforts as 'physical eschatology', defined as 'the study of the survival and behaviour of life in the far future'.[25]

Christian eschatology is, however, no more about the distant future than the doctrine of creation is about the distant past. Just as Christian confession of all things' createdness *ex nihilo* makes no empirical claims concerning the initial conditions of the system of the world, but simply acknowledges the absolute dependence of everything there is upon the mystery which we call God, so also Christian confession that, in the end, all things are with God warrants no speculation as to the way that things will be, but simply celebrates the world's fulfilment in God's peace.

The purely speculative character of the scientists' myths is, however, their least harmful feature. By appeal to principles such as 'Anything that cannot be read and understood as a christological assertion is not a genuine eschatological assertion',[26] Christian eschatology is anchored to particularity, its business being with the *sense* of finitude, the Emmanuel-value of the flesh. Undisciplined to such sobriety, some scientists give vent to dangerous fantasies of disembodied and infinite power. These come in different versions, but they have

[23] Paul Davies, *God and the New Physics* (London: Dent, 1983), p. ix; see Stephen Hawking, *A Brief History of Time*, pp. 136, 169, 175; John D. Barrow and Frank J. Tipler, *The Anthropic Cosmological Principle* (Oxford: Clarendon Press, 1986), p. 677.

[24] The most thorough study of this material, to which I am much indebted in what follows, is Mary Midgley's Gifford Lectures for 1990: *Science as Salvation*.

[25] Barrow and Tipler, p. 658.

[26] Rahner, 'The hermeneutics of eschatological assertions', p. 343.

in common an overestimation of the purity and the power of 'pure' intelligence, a disdain for the flesh, a terror of mortality.

'Complete knowledge', we are told, 'is just within our grasp. Comprehension is moving across the face of the earth, like a sunrise.' In case we had not noticed the Promethean overtones, a molecular biologist adds: 'What comprehension and powers over nature Omega Man will command can only be suggested by man's image of the supernatural.' (He apparently has not heard that man's best image of the super-natural is a dead Jew swinging on a Roman gibbet.) On the road to Omega, 'It is conceivable that in another 10^{10} years, life could evolve *away from flesh and blood*' until, with 'the advantage of containing no organic material at all', we shall find 'freedom from the biological ball and chain'.[27]

The notion that these writings convey, 'that our natural, earthly life can be despised is not just meaningless; it is disastrous . . . It promotes, here and now, a distorted idea of what a human being essentially is.'[28] And yet, in my experience, this material is too seldom subjected to the philosophical and theological criticism that it deserves.

BEYOND CONTROL

The belief that 'History' has ended implies that, at least from now on, it would be a mistake to imagine that any particular event could make a fundamental difference to the way things went. Here, Fukuyama's Hegelianism joins hands in disillusion with at least some versions of postmodern nihilism, dismally chorusing that 'there is nothing new under the sun'.[29]

---

[27] Peter Atkins, *The Creation* (Oxford: Freeman, 1987), p. 127; William Day, *Genesis on Planet Earth: The Search for Life's Beginning* (East Lansing: House of Talos, 1979), p. 392; Freeman Dyson 'Time without end: physics and biology in an open universe', *Review of Modern Physics*, 51 (1979), 454, my italics; J. D. Bernal, *The World, the Flesh and The Devil* (London, 1929), p. 35; Keith Oatley, *Brain Mechanisms and Mind* (London: Thames and Hudson, 1972); for these passages, see Midgley, *Science as Salvation*.

[28] Midgley, *Science as Salvation*, p. 223.

[29] Ecclesiastes 1.9.

It is incumbent upon Christians, confronting such exhaustion, and the unconcern and cynicism which it breeds, 'to resist the drift into a state of mind which regards all that passes before it as a kind of play, run for its interpretation, empty in itself of deep and drastic significance, except that significance be one which, in the mood of our generation, we impose upon it'.[30] It is, however, no less imperative to avoid falling into the trap of supposing that, *because* something of absolute significance is acknowledged to occur, in this or that particular place, on this or that particular occasion, *therefore* the new age which this event initiates must be protected, and its memory kept pure, through structures and institutions of control.

Lenin knew where he was going, knew in which direction he had set his face. He and his followers ascribed absolute significance to their achievement that October, during those 'ten days that shook the world'. Subsequently, that ascription was transmuted into the tyranny of Bolshevism, the system of control protective of the fact and memory of that achievement.

Soviet Communism has now collapsed, its illusory absolutism crumbling into the relativities of history. Yet, from its rise and fall, there are disturbing lessons to be learnt. 'Lenin knew where he was going. Are we to say less of Jesus?' However illusory the absoluteness of the October Revolution may have been, 'it is very hard to see how anything which we can continue significantly to call Christianity can survive the withdrawal of the predicate *final* from the work of Christ'.[31]

The challenge to Christianity – to its social practice and to its images and narratives of hope – is to sustain that recognition of absolute finality without the aid of those institutions and intellectual habits of authoritarian control to which the eschatological character of its belief has too often rendered it susceptible. In our own day, Teilhard de Chardin, whose voice

[30] Donald MacKinnon, 'Absolute and relative in history: a theological reflection on the centenary of Lenin's birth', *Explorations in Theology* 5 (London: SCM Press, 1979), p. 59.
[31] MacKinnon, pp. 64, 59 (his italics).

many found attractively prophetic of the 'Omega', serves as a chilling instance of such perversion. This was the man who welcomed the production of the atomic bomb as evidence of team-work; the man who said, in 1936: 'Fascism may possibly represent a fairly successful small-scale model of tomorrow's world. It may perhaps be a necessary stage in the course of which men have to learn, as though on a small training-ground, their human role.'[32]

In the cultures of modernity, Christian consideration of the future of the world has too often either been reactive – a matter of dancing to tunes composed by other people – or else, through dualistic dissociation of spirituality from politics, has supposed that it has nothing in particular to say (nothing, that is, more interesting than abstract disapproval).

It is, however, possible that 'the pathos of modern theology is its false humility'; that, with the supposed neutrality of secular reason decoded as ideology (an ideology, moreover, knowing no options other than either chaos or control), a Christianity converted towards trust in God might find the tranquillity and confidence in which to offer to the world the promise, and the practice, and the poetry of given peace, 'the discourse of non-mastery'.[33]

Now, as in the time of the Gospel's first appearing, it is always and only along the *via dolorosa* that this offer is enacted, this peace outpoured. None of us, however – no individual and no social form, especially the form we call 'the Church' – knows the extent to which, along that road, we are companions of the Crucified or collaborators in his crucifixion. The history of Christianity is a history of people passing to and fro beneath the image, on the doorway's tympanum, of final judgement: 'In the midst of history, the judgment of God has already happened. And either the Church enacts the vision of paradisal community which this judgment opens out', or else it becomes an 'anti-Church', confining Christianity, 'like

---

[32] Pierre Teilhard de Chardin, 'The salvation of mankind' in *Science and Christ* (London: Sage, 1968), p. 141.
[33] Milbank, *Theology and Social Theory*, pp. 1, 6.

everything else, within the cycle of the ceaseless exhaustion and return of violence'.[34] God's peacefulness, which is the end of history, is gift and promise, but it is also absolute command.

[34] Milbank, p. 433; see Hans Urs von Balthasar, *The Glory of the Lord*, I, *Seeing the Form* (Edinburgh: T. & T. Clark, 1982), pp. 680–1; Lash, *Believing Three Ways*, p. 63.

List of works cited

Allott, Philip *Eunomia. New Order for a New World*, Oxford: Oxford University Press, 1990.

Alston, William P. 'God's action in the world' in Ernan McMullin (ed.), *Evolution and Creation*, Notre Dame: University of Notre Dame Press, 1985, pp. 197–220.

Anselm *S. Anselmi cantuariensis archiepiscopi opera omnia*, 1, (ed.) F. S. Schmitt, Stuttgart: Friedrich Fromann Verlag, 1968.

  St Anselm's Proslogion. With a Reply on Behalf of the Fool by Gaunilo and the Author's Reply to Gaunilo, (trans. and ed.) M. J. Charlesworth, Oxford: Clarendon Press, 1965.

Apel, Karl-Otto *Towards a Transformation of Philosophy*, London: Routledge and Kegan Paul, 1980.

Aquinas, Thomas *Summa theologiae*, (trans.) Fathers of the English Dominican Province, London: Eyre and Spottiswoode, 1964.

Atkins, Peter *The Creation*, Oxford: Freeman, 1986.

Augustine *The City of God*, (trans.) G. G. Walsh and D. J. Honan, Washington: Catholic University of America Press, 1964.

  De civitate Dei, Corpus Christianorum Series Latina, XLVIII, Turnhous: Brepols, 1955.

Balthasar, Hans Urs von *The Glory of the Lord*, 1, *Seeing the Form*, Edinburgh: T. & T. Clark, 1982.

Barrett, Lee C. 'Theology as grammar: regulative principles or paradigms and practices', *Modern Theology*, 4 (1988), 155–72.

Barrow, John D. and Tipler, Frank J. *The Anthropic Cosmological Principle*, Oxford: Clarendon Press, 1986.

Barth, Karl *Anselm: Fides Quarens Intellectum. Anselm's Proof of the Existence of God in the Context of his Theological Scheme*, (trans.) I. W. Robertson, London: SCM Press, 1960.

  Karl Barth. Letters 1961–1968, (ed.) Geoffrey W. Bromiley, Edinburgh: T. & T. Clark, 1981.

  Protestant Theology in the Nineteenth Century. Its Background and History, (trans.) Brian Cozens, John Bowden, et al., London: SCM Press, 1972.

Baum, Gregory 'Modernity: a sociological perspective' in Claude Geffré and Jean-Pierre Jossua (eds.), *The Debate on Modernity. Concilium*, 1992/6, 3–9.

Bayart, J. 'Le triple visage du divin dans l'hindouisme', *Nouvelle revue théologique*, 60, 3 (1933), 227–48.

Beck, Ulrich *Risk Society. Towards a New Modernity*, London: Sage, 1992.

Berger, Peter *The Sacred Canopy: Elements of a Sociological Theory of Religion*, Garden City, NY: Doubleday, 1967.

Bernal, J. D. *The World, the Flesh and the Devil*, London, 1929.

Bernstein, Richard 'New issues born from communism's death knell', *New York Times*, 31 August 1991, 1.

Bernstein, Richard J. (ed.) *Beyond Objectivism and Relativism. Science, Hermeneutics and Praxis*, Oxford: Basil Blackwell, 1983.

Bhagavad Gita, (ed.) Juan Mascaro, London: Penguin Books, 1962.
    (trans.) Antonio de Nicolas, York Beach, ME: Nicolas-Hays, 1990.
    (trans.) Winthrop Sargeant, (revised ed.) Christopher Chapple, New York: State University of New York Press, 1994.
    (trans.) R. C. Zaehner, Oxford: Clarendon Press, 1969.

Blake, William *Blake. Complete Writings*, (ed.) Geoffrey Keynes, Oxford: Oxford University Press, 1972.

Braaten, Carl E. 'The kingdom of God and the life everlasting' in Peter C. Hodgson and Robert H. King (eds.), *Christian Theology. An Introduction to its Traditions and Tasks*, Philadelphia: Fortress, 1982.

Brück, Michael von *The Unity of Reality: God, God-Experience, and Meditation in the Hindu–Christian Dialogue*, (trans.) James V. Zeitz, New York: Paulist, 1991.

Buckley, Michael J. *At the Origins of Modern Atheism*, New Haven: Yale University Press, 1987.
    Motion and Motion's God: Thematic Variations in Aristotle, Cicero, Newton and Hegel, Princeton, NJ: Princeton University Press, 1971.
    'Religion and science: Paul Davies and John Paul II', *Theological Studies*, 51 (1990), 310–24.

Burnet, John *Essays and Addresses*, London: Chatto and Windus, 1929.

Burns, Robert I. *Muslims, Christians and Jews in the Crusader Kingdom of Valencia*, Cambridge: Cambridge University Press, 1984.
    '*Stupor Mundi*: Alfonso X of Castile, the Learned' in R. I. Burns (ed.), *Emperor of Culture: Alfonso X the Learned of Castile and his*

Thirteenth Century Renaissance, Philadelphia: University of Pennsylvania Press, 1990, 1–13.

Burrell, David B. *Aquinas: God and Action*, London: Routledge and Kegan Paul, 1979.

    Freedom and Creation in the Three Traditions, Notre Dame: University of Notre Dame Press, 1993.

    Knowing the Unknowable God: Ibn-Sina, Maimonides, Aquinas, Notre Dame: University of Notre Dame Press, 1986.

Butler, Christopher *The Theology of Vatican II*, London: Darton, Longman and Todd, 1967.

Butterfield, Herbert *The Origins of Modern Science, 1300–1800*, London: G. Bell, 1968.

Campbell, Richard *From Belief to Understanding*, Canberra: Australian National University, 1976.

Carroll, Lewis *Alice in Wonderland*, London: New Orchard Editions, 1990.

Cavanagh, William T. ' "A fire strong enough to consume the house": the Wars of Religion and the rise of the State', *Modern Theology* (October 1995), 397–420.

Cavell, Stanley *The Claim of Reason*, Oxford: Clarendon Press, 1979.

Chaturvedi, Benarsidas and Sykes, Marjorie *Charles Freer Andrews*, London: George Allen and Unwin, 1949.

Chenu, M.-D. *Toward Understanding St Thomas*, (trans.) A. M. Landry and D. Hughes, Chicago: Henry Regnery, 1963.

    'Une théologie de la vie mystique', *La vie spirituelle*, 50 (1937), 46–50.

Chopp, Rebecca S. *The Power to Speak: Feminism, Language, God*, New York: Crossroad, 1989.

Clayton, John 'Thomas Jefferson and the Study of Religion', an inaugural lecture at the University of Lancaster, 18 November 1992.

Clifford, Richard J. 'The Hebrew scriptures and the theology of creation', *Theological Studies*, 46 (1985), 507–23.

Clooney, Francis X. *Theology after Vedanta. An Experiment in Comparative Theology*, New York: State University of New York Press, 1993.

Coulson, John *Religion and Imagination*, Oxford: Clarendon Press, 1981.

Cox, Harvey *The Secular City. Secularization and Urbanization in Theological Perspective*, London: SCM Press, 1965.

Craig, Edward *The Mind of God and the Works of Man*, Oxford: Clarendon Press, 1987.

Crick, Francis and Koch, Christof 'The problems of consciousness', *Scientific American*, 267 (September 1992), 110–17.

Dante Alighieri *La divina commedia*, I, *Inferno*, and *La divina commedia*, III, *Paradiso*, (eds.) U. Bosco and G. Reggio, Firenze: Le Monnier, 1979.

Davies, Paul *God and the New Physics*, London: Dent, 1983.

Day, William *Genesis on Planet Earth: The Search for Life's Beginning*, East Lansing: House of Talos, 1979.

De Certeau, Michel *The Mystic Fable*, I, *The Sixteenth and Seventeenth Centuries*, (trans.) Michael B. Smith, Chicago: University of Chicago Press, 1992.

Descartes, René 'Principles of philosophy' in (trans.) John Cottingham, Robert Stoothof and Dugald Murdoch, *The Philosophical Writings of Descartes*, I, Cambridge: Cambridge University Press, 1985.

Devey, Joseph *The Physical and Metaphysical Works of Lord Bacon*, London: Henry G. Bohn, 1864.

Dockrill, D. W. and Mortley, Raoul (eds.) *The Via Negativa*, supplementary number of *Prudentia*, Auckland: University of Auckland, 1981.

Dryden, John *John Dryden*, (ed.) Keith Walker, Oxford: Oxford University Press, 1987.

Dulles, Avery 'Paths to doctrinal agreement: ten theses', *Theological Studies*, 47 (1986), 32–47.

Duquoc, Christian 'Postscript: the institution and diversion' in Christian Duquoc and Gustavo Gutiérrez (eds.), *Mysticism and the Institutional Crisis. Concilium*, 1994/4, 101–6.

Durkheim, Emile *Suicide: A Study in Sociology*, (trans.) John A. Spaulding and George Simpson, London: Routledge and Kegan Paul, 1970.

Dyson, Freeman 'Time without end: physics and biology in an open universe', *Review of Modern Physics*, 51 (1979).

Edelman, Gerald M. *Bright Air, Brilliant Fire: On the Matter of the Mind*, London: Allen Lane, Penguin Press, 1992.

Eliot, T. S. 'Little Gidding' in *The Complete Poems and Plays of T. S. Eliot*, London: Faber, 1969.

Ernst, Cornelius 'Metaphor and ontology in *Sacra Doctrina*' in *Multiple Echo*, (eds.) Fergus Kerr and Timothy Radcliffe, London: Darton, Longman and Todd, 1979.

Evans, G. R. *Anselm and a New Generation*, Oxford: Clarendon Press, 1980.

Ferrier, James F. *Institutes of Metaphysic: The Theory of Knowing and Being*, Edinburgh: William Blackwood, 1854.

Feuerbach, Ludwig *The Essence of Christianity*, (trans.) George Eliot, New York: Harper and Row, 1957.

Fischbach, Gerald 'Mind and brain', *Scientific American*, 267 (September 1992), 24–33.

Frei, Hans W. *The Eclipse of Biblical Narrative: A Study in Eighteenth and Nineteenth Century Hermeneutics*, New Haven: Yale University Press, 1974.

Fukuyama, Francis *The End of History and the Last Man*, London: Hamish Hamilton, 1992.

'The end of history?', *The National Interest*, 16 (1989), 3–18.

'A reply to my critics', *The National Interest*, 18 (1989–90), 21–8.

Funkenstein, Amos *Theology and the Scientific Imagination from the Middle Ages to the Seventeenth Century*, Princeton: Princeton University Press, 1986.

Furbank, P. N. *Diderot. A Critical Biography*, London: Secker and Warburg, 1992.

Gadamer, Hans-Georg *Truth and Method*, (trans.) Garrett Barden and John Cumming, London: Sheed and Ward, 1975.

Gibbs, M. E. *The Anglican Church in India, 1600–1970*, Delhi: SPCK, 1972.

Grant, Sr Sara *Towards an Alternative Theology. Confessions of a Non-dualist Christian*, Bangalore: Asian Trading Corporation, 1991.

Griffiths, Bede *Universal Wisdom*, London: Fount, 1994.

Habermas, Jürgen 'A reply to my critics' in John B. Thompson and David Held (eds.), *Habermas: Critical Debates*, London: Macmillan, 1982.

Halbfass, Wilhelm *India and Europe: An Essay in Understanding*, Albany, NY: State University of New York Press, 1988.

Hamlyn, D. W. 'Epistemology, history of' in Paul Edwards (ed.), *The Encyclopaedia of Philosophy*, III, New York: Macmillan, 1967, p. 9.

Hankey, W. M. *God in Himself: Aquinas' Doctrine of God as Expounded in the Summa Theologiae*, Oxford: Oxford University Press, 1987.

Harrison, Peter *'Religion' and the Religions in the English Enlightenment*, Cambridge: Cambridge University Press, 1990.

Haskins, C. H. *Studies in the History of Medieval Science*, Cambridge, MA: Harvard University Press, 1984.

Hawking, Stephen *A Brief History of Time*, London: Bantam Press, 1988.

Hay, David *Religious Experience Today: Studying the Facts*, London: Mowbray, 1990.

Review of N. Lash, *Easter in Ordinary, Numinis*, 7 (1990), 10–11.

Heaney, Seamus 'The peninsula', 'Bogland' in *Door into Dark*, London: Faber and Faber, 1969.

Hegel, G. W. F. *Lectures on the Philosophy of Religion*, 1, *Introduction and Concept of Religion*, Peter C. Hodgson (ed.), Berkeley: University of California Press, 1984.

Hesse, Mary 'In defence of objectivity' in *Revolutions and Reconstructions in the Philosophy of Science*, Brighton: Harvester, 1980.

Holloway, Julia Bolton 'The road through Roncesvalles: Alfonsine formation of Brunetto Latini and Dante — diplomacy and literature' in Robert I. Burns (ed.), *Emperor of Culture: Alfonso X the Learned of Castile and his Thirteenth Century Renaissance*, Philadelphia: University of Pennsylvania Press, 1990, 109–23.

Hooker, Edward N. 'Dryden and the atoms of Epicurus' in Bernard N. Schilling (ed.), *Dryden. A Collection of Critical Essays*, Englewood Cliffs: Prentice Hall, 1963.

Horkheimer, Max 'Thoughts on religion' in *Critical Theory*, (trans.) M. O'Connell et al., New York: Continuum, 1972.

Hügel, Friedrich von *The Mystical Element of Religion as Studied in Saint Catherine of Genoa and her Friends*, II, 2nd edn, London: Dent, 1923.

James, P. D. *Devices and Desires*, London: Faber, 1989.

James, William *Pragmatism and the Meaning of Truth*, Friedrich Burkhardt, Fredson Bowers, and Ignas K. Skrupskelis (eds.), Cambridge: Cambridge University Press, 1978.

Jay, Martin *The Dialectical Imagination: A History of the Frankfurt School and the Institute of Social Research 1923–1950*, London: Heinemann, 1973.

Jordan, Mark D. 'The names of God and the being of names' in Alfred J. Freddoso (ed.), *The Existence and Nature of God*, Notre Dame: University of Notre Dame Press, 1983, 161–90.

Julian of Norwich *Showings*, (trans. and intro.) Edmund Colledge and James Walsh, New York: Paulist Press, 1978.

Jüngel, Eberhard *God as the Mystery of the World: On the Foundation of the Theology of the Crucified One in the Dispute between Theism and Atheism*, (trans.) Darrell L. Guder, Edinburgh: T. & T. Clark, 1983.

Kant, Immanuel 'An answer to the question: what is enlightenment?' in Hans Reiss (ed.), H. B. Nisbett (trans.), *Kant's Political Writings*, Cambridge: Cambridge University Press, 1970.

Kasper, Walter *The God of Jesus Christ*, London: SCM Press, 1984.

Kermode, Frank *The Genesis of Secrecy*, Cambridge, MA: Harvard University Press, 1979.

Kerr, Fergus *Theology after Wittgenstein*, Oxford: Basil Blackwell, 1986.

'Idealism and realism: an old controversy dissolved' in Kenneth Surin (ed.), *Christ, Ethics and Tragedy: Essays in Honour of Donald*

MacKinnon, Cambridge: Cambridge University Press, 1989, pp. 15–33.

'Rescuing Girard's argument?', *Modern Theology*, 8 (1992), 385–99.

Lash, Nicholas *Believing Three Ways in One God. A Reading of the Apostles' Creed*, London: SCM Press, 1992.

Easter In Ordinary. Reflections on Human Experience and the Knowledge of God, Charlottesville: University Press of Virginia, 1988.

A Matter of Hope: A Theologian's Reflections on the Thought of Karl Marx, London: Darton, Longman and Todd, 1981.

Theology on the Way to Emmaus, London: SCM Press, 1986.

'The broken mirror', *America* (16 May 1992), 432–34.

'Considering the Trinity', *Modern Theology*, 2, 3 (1986), 183–96.

'Conversation in Gethsemane' in Werner G. Jeanrond and Jennifer L. Rike (eds.), *Radical Pluralism and Truth: David Tracy and the Hermeneutics of Religion*, New York: Crossroad, 1991, pp. 51–61.

'Friday, Saturday, Sunday', *New Blackfriars*, 71 (1990), 109–19.

'In search of the prodigal', *America* (6–13 June 1992), 506–8.

'Production and prospect: reflections on Christian hope and original sin' in Ernan McMullin (ed.), *Evolution and Creation*, Notre Dame: University of Notre Dame Press, 1985, pp. 273–89.

'Reason, fools and Rameau's nephew', *New Blackfriars*, 76 (1995), 368–77.

Review of Lindbeck, *The Nature of Doctrine. Religion and Theology in a Postliberal Age*, *New Blackfriars*, 66 (1985), 609–10.

'Theology on the way to Stuttgart', *America* (4 April 1992), 266–8.

Lash, N. A. *Elephanta. Written mostly for and dedicated entirely to, The Rovers under the Red Duster*, Bombay, 1923.

Lindbeck, George A. *The Nature of Doctrine. Religion and Theology in a Postliberal Age*, London: SPCK, 1984.

Lipner, Julius *Hindus. Their Religious Beliefs and Practices,* London: Routledge, 1994.

'On women and salvation in Hinduism: paradoxes of ambivalence' in Ninian Smart and Shivesh Thakur (eds.), *Ethical and Political Dilemmas of Modern India*, London: Macmillan, 1993, pp. 160–80.

and Gispert-Sauch, George (eds.) *The Writings of Brahmabandhab Upadhyay*, I, Bangalore: United Theological College, 1992.

Lonergan, Bernard J. F. *Verbum, Word and Idea in Aquinas*, (ed.) David B. Burrell, London: Darton, Longman and Todd, 1968.

'Theology in its new context' in William J. F. Ryan and Bernard J. Tyrrell (eds.), *A Second Collection*, London: Darton, Longman and Todd, 1974, pp. 55–67.

Lyotard, Jean-François *The Postmodern Condition: A Report on Knowledge*, (trans.) Geoff Bennington and Brian Masumi, Manchester: Manchester University Press, 1984.

McGinn, Bernard *The Presence of God: A History of Western Christian Mysticism*, I, *The Foundations of Mysticism*, London: SCM Press, 1992.

MacIntyre, Alasdair *After Virtue. A Study in Moral Virtue*, Notre Dame: University of Notre Dame Press, 1981.

Three Rival Versions of Moral Enquiry, London: Duckworth, 1990.

Review of J. Sacks, *The Persistence of Faith*, *The Tablet*, 245 (23 February 1991), 242.

MacKinnon, Donald M. *God the Living and the True*, London: Dacre Press, 1940.

Themes in Theology. The Three-fold Cord: Essays in Philosophy, Politics and Theology, Edinburgh: T. & T. Clark, 1987.

'Absolute and relative in history: a theological reflection on the centenary of Lenin's birth', *Explorations in Theology 5*, London: SCM Press, 1979.

Maclean, Alasdair *Night Falls on Ardnamurchan. The Twilight of a Crofting Family*, London: Penguin, 1986.

McLellan, David *Marxism and Religion*, London: Macmillan, 1987.

Mandelstam, Nadezhda *Hope against Hope. A Memoir*, (trans.) Max Hayward, London: London Collins Harvill, 1989.

Mandelstam, Osip 'Fourth prose' in *The Noise of Time and other Prose Pieces*, (trans.) Clarence Brown, London: Quartet Books, 1988, p. 186.

'Poem 117' in *Selected Poems*, (trans.) Clarence Brown and W. S. Mervin, London: Penguin, 1977.

Manuel, Frank E. *The Religion of Isaac Newton*, Oxford: Clarendon Press, 1974.

Margulis, Lynn and Sagan, Dorion *Microcosmos. Four Billion Years of Evolution from our Microbial Ancestors*, New York: Allen and Unwin, 1987.

Martin, David *A General Theory of Secularization*, Oxford: Basil Blackwell, 1978.

Marx, Karl 'Economic and philosophical manuscripts' in *Early Writings*, (trans.) Rodney Livingstone and Gregor Benton, Harmondsworth: Penguin Books, 1975.

Mascarenhas, H. O. *The Quintessence of Hinduism. The Key to Indian Culture and Philosophy*, Bombay: St Sebastian Goan High School, 1951.

Metz, Johann-Baptist *Faith in History and Society*, London: Burns and Oates, 1980.

Midgley, Mary *Science as Salvation. A Modern Myth and its Meaning*, London: Routledge and Kegan Paul, 1992.
'Fancies about human immortality', *The Month*, 251 (1990), 458–66.
Milbank, John *Theology and Social Theory: Beyond Secular Reason*, Oxford: Basil Blackwell, 1990.
'The end of dialogue' in Gavin D'Costa (ed.), *Christian Uniqueness Reconsidered. The Myth of a Pluralistic Theology of Religions*, New York: Orbis Books, 1990, pp. 174–91.
'The end of enlightenment: post-modern or post-secular?' in Claude Geffré and Jean-Pierre Jossua (eds.), *The Debate on Modernity. Concilium*, 1992/6, 39–48.
Review of Michael J. Buckley, *At the Origins of Modern Atheism*, *Modern Theology*, 8 (1992), 89–92.
'The second difference: for a trinitarianism without reserve', *Modern Theology*, 2 (1986), 213–34.
Moltmann, Jürgen 'Political theology and liberation theology', *Union Theological Seminary Quarterly Review*, 45 (1991), 205–17.
Mooney, Christopher F. 'Theology and science: a new commitment to dialogue', *Theological Studies*, 52 (1991), 289–329.
Mueller-Vollmer, Kurt *The Hermeneutics Reader. Texts of the German Tradition from the Enlightenment to the Present*, New York: Continuum, 1985.
Neuhaus, Richard John *The Naked Public Square. Religion and Democracy in America*, Grand Rapids: Eerdmans, 1984.
Newman, John Henry *The Letters and Diaries of John Henry Newman*, xxx, (eds.) C. S. Dessain and Thomas Gornall, Oxford: Clarendon Press, 1976.
The Theological Papers of John Henry Newman. On Faith and Certainty, (eds.) Hugo M. de Achaval and J. Derek Holmes, Oxford: Clarendon Press, 1976.
Nicholas Cusanus *De pace fidei*, (ed.) Raymund Klibansky, London: Warburg Institute, 1956.
Nichols, Aidan *The Theology of Joseph Ratzinger*, Edinburgh: T. & T. Clark, 1988.
Niebuhr, Richard R. *Schleiermacher on Christ and Religion*, London: SCM Press, 1965.
Nielsen, Kai 'God and coherence: on epistemological foundations of religious belief' in Leroy S. Rouner (ed.), *Knowing Religiously*, Notre Dame: University of Notre Dame Press, 1985, pp. 89–102.
Nietzsche, Friedrich *On the Genealogy of Morals*, (trans.) Walter Kaufman and R. J. Hollingdale, (ed.) Kaufman, New York: Vintage Books, 1989.

Novak, Michael *The Spirit of Democratic Capitalism*, 2nd edn, London: IEA Health and Welfare Unit, 1991.

Oatley, Keith *Brain Mechanisms and Mind*, London: Thames and Hudson, 1972.

O'Brien, David J. 'The historical context of North American theology: the US story' in George Kilcourse (ed.), *Catholic Theology in the North American Context, Current Issues in Theology*, 1, CTSA, 1987, pp.1–15.

Origen *Contra Celsum*, (trans.) H. Chadwick, Cambridge: Cambridge University Press, 1953.

Pagels, Heinz R. *The Dreams of Reason*, New York: Bantam, 1989.
  Perfect Symmetry. The Search for the Beginning of Time, London: Michael Joseph, 1985.

Painadath, Sebastian 'Ashrams: a movement of spiritual integration' in Christian Duquoc and Gustavo Gutiérrez (eds.), *Mysticism and the Institutional Crisis. Concilium*, 4 1994/4, 36–46.

Panikkar, Raimundo *The Trinity and the Religious Experience of Man: Icon–Person–Mystery*, New York and London: Orbis Books and Darton, Longman and Todd, 1973.
  The Vedic Experience. Mantramanjari. An Anthology of the Vedas for Modern Man and Contemporary Celebration, London: Darton, Longman and Todd, 1977.
  'The Jordan, the Tiber and the Ganges. Three kairological moments of christic self-consciousness' in John Hick and Paul F. Knitter (eds.), *The Myth of Christian Uniqueness*, London: SCM Press, 1988, pp. 89–116.

Pascal, Blaise *Pensées*, (ed.) Francis Kaplan, Paris: Editions du Cerf, 1992.

Peacocke, Arthur R. *Creation and the World of Science*, Oxford: Clarendon Press, 1979.

Pickering, W. S. F. (ed.) *Durkheim on Religion. A Selection of Readings and Bibliographies*, London: Routledge and Kegan Paul, 1975.

Pieris, Aloysius *An Asian Theology of Liberation*, Edinburgh: T. & T. Clark, 1988.

Pippard, Brian 'The invincible ignorance of science', *Contemporary Physics*, 29 (1988), 393–405.

Placher, William C. 'Paul Ricoeur and postliberal theology: a conflict of interpretations?', *Modern Theology*, 4 (1987), 35–52.

Popper, Karl *The Open Society and its Enemies*, II, *The High Tide of Prophecy: Hegel, Marx, and the Aftermath*, 5th edn, London: Routledge and Kegan Paul, 1966.

Purchas, Samuel *Purchas His Pilgrimage, Or: Relations of the World and the*

Religions Observed in all Ages and Places Discovered, from the Creation unto this Present, London, 1613.

Quinlan [Lash], Will *To High Kailas,* Hind Kitabs, 1947.

Rahner, Karl *Foundations of Christian Faith. An Introduction to the Idea of Christianity,* (trans.) William V. Dych, London: Darton, Longman and Todd, 1978.

'Concerning the relationship between nature and grace' in *Theological Investigations,* I, *God, Christ, Mary and Grace,* (trans.) Cornelius Ernst, London: Darton, Longman and Todd, 1961, pp. 297–317.

'The hermeneutics of eschatological assertions' in *Theological Investigations,* IV, *More Recent Writings,* (trans.) Kevin Smyth, London: Darton Longman and Todd, 1966, pp. 323–46.

'The inexhaustible transcendence of God and our concern for the future' in *Theological Investigations,* XX, *Concern for the Church,* (trans.) Edward Quinn, London: Darton, Longman and Todd, 1988, pp. 173–86.

'Natural science and reasonable faith' in *Theological Investigations,* XXI, *Science and Christian Faith,* (trans.) Hugh M. Riley, London, Darton Longman and Todd, 1988, pp. 16–55.

'On the relationship between natural science and theology' in *Theological Investigations,* XIX, *Faith and Ministry,* (trans.) Edward Quinn, London: Darton, Longman and Todd, 1984, pp. 16–23.

'Philosophy and philosophising in theology' in *Theological Investigations,* IX, *Writings of 1965–7 (1),* (trans.) Graham Harrison, London: Darton, Longman and Todd, 1972, pp. 46–63.

'Possible courses for the theology of the future' in *Theological Investigations,* XIII, *Theology, Anthropology, Christology,* (trans.) David Bourke, London: Darton, Longman and Todd, 1975, pp. 32–60.

'The question of the future' in *Theological Investigations,* XII, *Confrontations (2),* (trans.) David Bourke, London: Darton, Longman and Todd, 1974, pp. 181–201.

'Remarks on the dogmatic treatise *De Trinitate*' in *Theological Investigations,* IV, *More Recent Writings,* (trans.) Kevin Smyth, London: Darton, Longman and Todd, 1966, pp. 77–102.

'Science as a "confession"?' in *Theological Investigations,* III, *The Theology of the Spiritual Life,* (trans.) Karl-H. and Boniface Kruger, London: Darton, Longman and Todd, 1967, pp. 385–400.

'Theology as engaged in an interdisciplinary dialogue with the sciences' in *Theological Investigations,* XIII, *Theology, Anthropology, Christology,* (trans.) David Bourke, London: Darton, Longman and Todd, 1974, pp. 80–93.

'Wissenschaft als "Konfession"?' *Schriften zur Theologie*, III, *Zur Theologie des Geistlichen Lebens*, Einsiedeln: Benziger, 1962, pp. 455–72.

and Vorgrimler, Herbert (eds.) *Concise Theological Dictionary*, London: Burns and Oates, 1965.

Ratzinger, Joseph *Eschatologie. Tod und Ewiges Leben*, Regensburg: Pustet, 1977.

Rayan, Samuel 'Hindu perceptions of Christ in the nineteenth century' in Leonardo Boff and Virgil Elizondo (eds.), *Any Room for Christ in Asia? Concilium*, 1993/2, 13–23.

Ricks, Christopher *Tennyson*, 2nd edn, London: Macmillan, 1989.

Ricoeur, Paul 'Toward a hermeneutic of the idea of revelation' in Lewis S. Mudge (ed.), *Essays on Biblical Interpretation*, London: SPCK, 1981, pp. 73–118.

Rig Veda. An Anthology, (ed.) Wendy Doniger O'Flaherty, London: Penguin Books, 1981.

Rorty, Richard *Consequences of Pragmatism*, Minneapolis: University of Minnesota Press, 1982.

Philosophy and the Mirror of Nature, Oxford: Basil Blackwell, 1980.

Roth, Norman 'Jewish collaboration in Alfonso's scientific work' in Robert I. Burns (ed.), *Emperor of Culture: Alfonso X the Learned of Castile and his Thirteenth Century Renaissance*, Philadelphia: University of Pennsylvania Press, 1990, pp. 59–71.

Sacks, Jonathan *The Persistence of Faith*, London: Weidenfeld and Nicolson, 1991.

Sartre, Jean-Paul *Being and Nothingness*, (trans.) Hazel E. Barnes, London: Methuen, 1958.

Schillebeeckx, Edward *God Among Us: The Gospel Proclaimed*, London: SCM Press, 1983.

Schlegel, Jean-Louis 'The strategies of reconquest in the new Europe and the impossibility of getting past secularization' in Claude Geffré and Jean-Pierre Jossua (eds.), *The Debate on Modernity. Concilium*, 1992/6, 97–106.

Schleiermacher, Friedrich *The Christian Faith*, Edinburgh: T. & T. Clark, 1928.

Schüssler-Fiorenza, Elisabeth *But She Said: Feminist Practices of Biblical Interpretation*, Boston: Beacon Press, 1992.

Smith, Wilfred Cantwell *The Meaning and End of Religion*, New York: Macmillan, 1962.

Soares-Prabhu, George M. 'Class in the Bible: the biblical poor, a social class?' *Vidyajyoti*, 49 (1985), 320–46.

Southern, R. W. *Saint Anselm. A Portrait in a Landscape*, Cambridge: Cambridge University Press, 1990.

Staal, Frits *Exploring Mysticism*, Harmondsworth: Penguin, 1975.

Steiner, George *Real Presences. Is There Anything IN What We Say?*, London: Faber and Faber, 1989.

Strange, Thomas Lumisden *How I Became and Ceased to be a Christian*, London: Trübner and Co, 1881.

The Supreme Power in the Universe, London: Thomas Scott, 1877.

What is Christianity? An Historical Sketch; Illustrated with a Chart, London: Trübner and Co, 1880.

Taylor, Charles *Hegel*, Cambridge: Cambridge University Press, 1975.

Teilhard de Chardin, Pierre 'The salvation of mankind' in *Science and Christ*, London: Sage, 1968.

Tennyson, Alfred Lord 'Ulysses' in *Tennyson's Poetry*, (ed.) Robert W. Hill Jr, New York: W. W. Norton and Company, 1971, pp. 18–21.

Toulmin, Stephen 'The genealogy of "consciousness"' in Paul Secord (ed.), *Explaining Human Behavior: Consciousness, Human Action, and Social Structure*, London: Sage, 1982, pp. 53–70.

Turner, Denys *The Darkness of God. Negativity in Christian Mysticism*, Cambridge: Cambridge University Press, 1995.

Upadhyay, Brahmabandhab 'Christianity in India', *The Tablet*, 3 January 1903, 8.

The Upanishads, (ed.) Juan Mascaro, London: Penguin Books, 1965.

The Principal Upanisads, (ed.) S. Radhakrishnan, London: George Allen and Unwin, 1953.

Updike, John *Assorted Prose*, London: André Deutsch, 1965.

Wakefield, Gordon 'The future programme of the Centre', *Numinis*, 7 (1990).

Ward, Barbara and Dubos, René *Only One Earth. The Care and Maintenance of a Small Planet*, New York: Penguin, 1972.

Weisheipl, James A. *Friar Thomas D'Aquino. His Life, Thought and Works*, Oxford: Basil Blackwell, 1975.

White, Victor *Holy Teaching: The Idea of Theology according to St Thomas Aquinas*, London: Blackfriars, 1958.

Whitehead, Alfred North *Religion in the Making*, Cambridge: Cambridge University Press, 1927.

Wilfred, Felix *From the Dusty Soil*, Madras: University of Madras, 1995.

Williams, Rowan 'Butler's *Western Mysticism*: towards an assessment', *Downside Review*, 102 (1984), 197–215.

'Trinity and pluralism' in Gavin D'Costa (ed.), *Christian Uniqueness Reconsidered. The Myth of a Pluralistic Theology of Religions*, New York: Orbis Books, 1990, pp. 3–15.

'Trinity and revelation', *Modern Theology*, 2 (1986), 197–212.

Williams, Stephen 'Lindbeck's regulative christology', *Modern Theology*, 4 (1988), 173–86.

Wippel, John F. 'Metaphysics' in Norman Kretzmann and Eleonore Stump (eds.), *Cambridge Companion to Aquinas*, Cambridge: Cambridge University Press, 1993, pp. 85–127.

Zaehner, R. C. *The Bhagavad-Gita, With a Commentary based on the Original Sources*, Oxford: Oxford University Press, 1969.

Index

Abel, 235–6
Abraham, 204, 209–10, 216–18
  Abrahamic history, 28
  Abrahamic traditions, 64
Abulafia, David, 27
adoration, 61, 64, 160, 208
  see worship
advaita 55, 61
Advaitic Vedanta, 9, 66
  see Hinduism
  see Vedantic Hinduism
agnosticism, 92, 247
Alfonso X of Castile, 217–18
Allott, Philip 256–7
Alston, William P., 129
Amos, 45
ananda, 68
Andrews, C. F., 72
Anselm, 5–6, 57, 150–63, 176–7
Apel, Karl-Otto, 82
apocatastasis, 259
Aquinas, Thomas, 45, 60, 62, 83, 97, 104,
    129–30, 133, 135, 139–49, 150, 169–70,
    203–4, 254
Aristotle, 97, 104, 117, 158
  Aristotelians, 54
Arjuna, 3, 35, 41, 44, 46–7
Arnold, Matthew, 198
atheism, 13, 53, 75, 131–2, 137–8, 242–3
Atkins, Peter, 261
atman, 39–40, 56
Augustine, 68, 144, 162, 167, 169, 220, 228,
    233, 235

Bacon, Francis, 12, 17, 79
von Balthasar, Hans Urs, 264
Barrett, Lee C., 133

Barrow, John D. and Tipler, Frank,
    259–60
Barth, Karl, 152–5, 157, 161, 163, 175
Baum, Gregory, 186–7
Baur, F. C., 175
Bayart, J., 67–9
Beck, Ulrich, 252, 256
Berger, Peter, 191–2
Bernal, J. D., 261
Bernstein, Richard, 228–9
Bernstein, Richard J., 82, 98
Bethlehem, 197
Bhagavad Gita, 3, 6, 23, 28–9, 33–6, 38–41,
    44–8, 59
bhakti movement, 57
  bhaktimarga, 61
Blake, William, 35
Blount, Charles, 14
Bolle, Kees W., 39, 41, 45
Bonhoeffer, Dietrich, 243
Boot, Keith, 199
Braaten, Carl E., 254–5
Brahe, Tycho, 140
Brahman, 26, 31, 33, 59–60, 68
Brerewood, Edward, 10
Bromiley, Geoffrey, 152
Brown, Clarence, 204, 215
von Brück, Michael, 69
Buber, Martin, 89
Buckley, Michael J., 16, 76–7, 79, 97, 117,
    124, 132–3, 136–43, 147–9, 243
Buddhism, 15, 21, 30, 35–6, 55, 65, 108,
    171, 211, 222
Burnet, John, 113–14
Burns, Robert I., 217–18
Burrell, David, 50, 55, 60, 64, 66, 83
Butler, Bishop Christopher, 30–1